Women and Poetry, 1660–1750

Women and Poetry, 1660–1750

Edited by

Sarah Prescott

and

David E. Shuttleton

First published 2003 by
PALGRAVE MACMILLAN
Houndmills, Basingstoke, Hampshire RG21 6XS and
175 Fifth Avenue, New York, N. Y. 10010
Companies and representatives throughout the world

PALGRAVE MACMILLAN is the global academic imprint of the Palgrave Macmillan division of St. Martin's Press, LLC and of Palgrave Macmillan Ltd. Macmillan® is a registered trademark in the United States, United Kingdom and other countries. Palgrave is a registered trademark in the European Union and other countries.

ISBN-13 978-1–4039–0654–0 hardback
ISBN-10 1–4039–0654–8 hardback

ISBN-13 978-1–4039–0655–7 paperback
ISBN-10 1–4039–0655–6 paperback

This book is printed on paper suitable for recycling and made from fully managed and sustained forest sources. Logging, pulping and manufacturing processes are expected to conform to the environmental regulations of the country of origin.

A catalogue record for this book is available from the British Library.

Library of Congress Cataloging-in-Publication Data
Women and poetry, 1660-1750 / edited by Sarah Prescott and David E. Shuttleton.
     p. cm.
    Includes bibliographical references and index.
    ISBN 1-4039-0654-8 – ISBN 1-4039-0655-6 (pbk.)
    1. English poetry–Women authors–History and criticism. 2. Women and literature–Great Britain–History–18th century. 3. Women and literature– Great Britain–History–17th century. 4. English poetry–Early modern, 1500-1700–History and criticism. 5. English poetry–18th century–History and criticism. I. Prescott, Sarah, 1968- II. Shuttleton, David.

PR555.W6W65 2003
821'.4099287–dc21   2003048271

10   9   8   7   6   5   4   3   2   1
12 11 10 09 08 07 06 05 04 03

Contents

Notes on the Contributors

Margaret J. M. Ezell is the John Paul Abbott Professor of Liberal Arts at Texas A&M University. Her publications include *The Patriarch's Wife: Literary Evidence and the History of the Family, Writing Women's Literary History* and *Social Authorship and the Advent of Print*. Presently she is at work on Volume V of the new Oxford English Literary History Series, *1645–1714: Authors, Readers, and Literary Life*.

Germaine Greer has an international reputation as a writer, broadcaster and feminist intellectual. She teaches literature at the University of Warwick. In 1979 she co-edited the ground-breaking *Kissing the Rod: an Anthology of Seventeenth Century Women's Verse*. Her many other publications include *The Obstacle Race: the Fortunes of Women Painters and Their Work* (1979), *Slip-Shod Sibyls: Recognition, Rejection and the Woman Poet* (1995) and *The Whole Woman* (2000). Professor Greer also runs and owns Stump Cross Press, publishing neglected early women poets.

Claudia Thomas Kairoff is Professor of English and Associate Dean of the College at Wake Forest University in North Carolina. She is author of *Alexander Pope and His Eighteenth-Century Women Readers* (1994) and co-editor of *'More Solid Learning': New Perspectives on Alexander Pope's* Dunciad (2000). She has written a number of articles on Pope and on women writers. She is currently researching a study of Elizabeth Tollet and also plans a book on Anna Seward.

Jennifer Keith has written several articles on eighteenth- and nineteenth-century poets, including Anne Finch, Alexander Pope, James Thomson and William Blake. She contributed the chapter on 'Preromanticism and the Ends of Eighteenth-Century Poetry', in John Sitter (ed.), *The Cambridge Companion to Eighteenth-Century Poetry*. Her book-length study of poetic representation from Aphra Behn to William Cowper is forthcoming. She teaches at the University of North Carolina at Greensboro.

Kathryn R. King teaches English at the University of Montevallo in Alabama. She is the author of *Jane Barker, Exile: a Literary Career 1675–1725* (2000), co-editor with Alex Pettit of Eliza Haywood's *The Female*

Spectator and *Selected Works of Eliza Haywood* (2001), and has written many essays on early modern women writers. She is currently at work on a cultural history of war in the long eighteenth century.

Donna Landry is Professor of English at Wayne State University in Detroit and an Honorary Research Fellow and Visiting Professor at the University of Exeter in Britain. The history of the English countryside, women's writing, labouring-class writing, early modern British horsemanship and travellers to the Middle East are her current research interests. Her most recent book is *The Invention of the Countryside: Hunting, Walking and Ecology in English Literature, 1671–1831* (2001). Other books include *The Muses of Resistance: Laboring-Class Women's Poetry in Britain, 1739–1796* (1990) and, co-edited with Gerald MacLean and Joseph P. Ward, *The Country and the City Revisted: England and the Politics of Culture, 1550–1850* (1999).

Rebecca M. Mills completed her D.Phil. on polemical prose and poetry by women in the early eighteenth century at the University of Oxford in the summer of 2000. She has written on the politics of Custom in the works of Augustan women writers and is currently working on an edition of Elizabeth Thomas's (1675–1731) poems and letters. She is an English teacher for Durant Senior High School and an adjunct instructor at Hillsborough Community College in Tampa, Florida.

Sarah Prescott is Lecturer in English Literature at the University of Wales, Aberystwyth, where she teaches women's writing, eighteenth-century literature, detective fiction and feminist theory. She is author of *Women, Authorship and Literary Culture, 1690–1740* (2003), and has published widely on women writers of the early eighteenth century, particularly Penelope Aubin, Jane Brereton, Eliza Haywood and Elizabeth Singer Rowe. She has edited a special issue of the journal *Women's Writing* on Augustan women writers (2000) and is currently working on a study of Welsh writing in English in the eighteenth century.

Valerie Rumbold is Senior Lecturer in English at the University of Birmingham. She is author of *Women's Place in Pope's World* (1989) and of a range of articles on Pope and on women writers of the eighteenth century. She is editor of the Longman Annotated Texts Alexander Pope: *The Dunciad in Four Books (1743)* (1999), and is currently working as one of the editors of the Longman Annotated Pope.

David E. Shuttleton teaches literature, theory and film in the English Department at the University of Wales, Aberystwyth. He has published widely in journals and anthologies on eighteenth-century literature, with a specialist interest in medical and philosophical contexts. His interest in women's poetry took off from curiosity over the use of somatic metaphors in the poetry of Mary Chandler who reputedly died of self-starvation as the over-zealous follower of the famously obese dietician Dr George Cheyne. His first essay on Chandler appeared in *Women's Poetry of the Enlightenment: Essays on the Making of a Canon, 1730–1820*, edited by Isobel Armstrong and Virginia Blaine (1998). He is currently editing Cheyne's letters for *The Cambridge Edition of the Works and Correspondence of Samuel Richardson* and writing a monograph on smallpox and the literary imagination.

Jane Spencer is Reader in English Literature at the University of Exeter, where she works on writing from the seventeenth to the nineteenth centuries, specializing in feminist literary history. She has edited Aphra Behn's drama and written widely on women's fiction, poetry and periodical writing. Her books include *The Rise of the Woman Novelist* (1986), *Elizabeth Gaskell* (1993) and *Aphra Behn's Afterlife* (2000). She is currently writing a book on kinship metaphors, family relationships and the construction of the English literary tradition. She is one of the General Editors of the *Oxford Encyclopaedia of Fiction in English, 1500–1800*.

Carol Shiner Wilson is Dean of the College for Academic Life and Assistant Professor of Humanities at Muhlenberg College. Her books include *The Galesia Trilogy and Selected Manuscript Poems of Jane Barker* (1997) and *Re-Visioning Romanticism: British Women Writers, 1776–1837* (1994). Her research interests include women and needlework in imaginative literature and social history, and microlending and social justice for women in developing nations. She is committed as dean to working collaboratively with faculty, students and staff to develop the most engaged learning and teaching environment possible. She has received support for her research from the National Endowment of the Humanities and the American Philosophical Society. She is deeply appreciative of NEH seminar leaders Stuart Curran and Paula Backscheider, colleagues of those seminars and her home institution, family and members of her Feminist Research Group for their support of her administrative and scholarly pursuits.

S. J. Wiseman teaches in the School of English and Humanities, Birkbeck College, University of London.

Chronology

b.   = birth of
d.   = death of
pub. = first publication of (unless otherwise stated)
ed.   = editor
c.   = *circa* (conjectural date)

1660	**Restoration of Charles II**
1661	b. Anne Kingsmill (later Finch)
1664	d. Katherine Philips, 'The Matchless Orinda' (b. 1632); pub. of her *Collected Poems* (unauthorized)
1666	b. Mary Astell
1667	pub. Katherine Philips, *Collected Poems* (2nd, authorized edition; reprinted 1669, 1678, 1710)
1670	b. Sarah Fyge (later Egerton); b. Delarivière Manley
1674	b. Elizabeth Singer (later Rowe)
1675	b. Elizabeth Thomas
1679	b. Catherine Trotter (later Cockburn)
1679	pub. [unidentified] *Female Poems On several Occasions. Written by Ephelia*
1683	pub. [Anon] *Triumphs of Female Wit, Or the Emulation . . . by a Young Lady*
1684	pub. Aphra Behn, *Poems upon Several Occasions : with a Voyage to the Island of Love*
1685	**d. Charles II; accession of James II (VII)**
1685	d. Anne Killigrew (b. 1660); d. Anne Wharton (b. 1659)
1685	(December) pub. *Poems by Mrs. Anne Killigrew* (with John Dryden's 'To the Pious Memory of the Accomplisht Young Lady Mrs Anne Killigrew . . . ')
1686	pub. Sarah Fyge (Egerton), *The Female Advocate* (reprinted 1706)
1688	pub. Jane Barker, *Poetical Recreations*
1688	b. Alexander Pope
1688/89	**(winter) Abdication of James II and accession of William and Mary (The Glorious Revolution)**
1689	d. Aphra Behn (b.c.1640); b. Mary Pierrepont (later Wortley Montagu)
1694	pub. Mary Astell, *A Serious Proposal to the Ladies* (Part II pub. 1697)
1694	**(December) d. Queen Mary II**
1696	pub. Elizabeth Singer (Rowe), *Poems on Several Ocassions by Philomela* ('The Pindarick Lady')
1700	d. John Dryden (b. 1631)
1700	pub. Delarivière Manley (ed.), *The Nine Muses or, Poems on the Death of the Late Famous John Dryden Esq.* (contributions from Sarah Fyge and playwrights Catherine Trotter, Susanna Centlivre and Mary Pix)

1700	pub. Mary Astell, *Some Reflections on Marriage*
1701	pub. Mary, Lady Chudleigh (née Lee), *The Ladies Defence*
1701	pub. Charles Gildon (ed.), *New Collection of Poems on Several Occasions* (includes Anne Finch, 'The Spleen')
1702	**d. William III; accession of Queen Anne**
1703	pub. Mary, Lady Chudleigh, *Poems on Several Occasions* (revised 1709, reprinted 1713, 1722, 1750)
1703	pub. Sarah Fyge (Egerton), *Poems on Several Occasions* (reissued as *A Collection of Poems on Several Occasions . . . by Mrs Sarah Fyge Egerton* (1706)
1710	d. Mary, Lady Chudleigh (b. 1656)
1712	pub. Alexander Pope, *The Rape of the Lock* (enlarged 1714)
1713	pub. Anne Finch, *Miscellany Poems, on Several Occasions*
1714	**d. Queen Anne; accession of George I (Elector of Hanover)**
1716	pub. Lady Mary Wortley Montagu (with John Gay), *Court Poems* (unauthorized)
1716	pub. (posthumous) Mary Monck (née Molesworth, *c*.1678–1715), *Poems* (edited by her father)
1717	b. Elizabeth Carter (d. 1806)
1717	Alexander Pope (ed.), *Poems on Several Occasions* (includes poems by Anne Finch)
1720	d. Anne Finch, Countess of Winchilsea
1722	pub. Elizabeth Thomas, *Miscellany Poems on Several Subjects* (reissued as *Poems on Several Ocassions. By a Lady* 1726, 1727)
1722	b. Mary Leapor
1723	d. Sarah Fyge-Egerton ('Clarinda')
1724	d. Delarivière Manley
1724	pub. (anonymously) Elizabeth Tollet (1694–1754), *Poems on Several Occasions*
1726	pub. Martha Sansom (née Fowke) ('Clio', 1690–1736), *Miscellaneous Poems* (subscription, ed. Richard Savage)
1727	**d. George I; accession of George II**
1728	pub. Elizabeth Singer Rowe, *Friendship in Death, in Letters from the Dead to the Living* (prose)
1730	pub. Elizabeth Thomas, *The Metamorphosis of the Town; Or, a View of the Present Fashions*
1731	d. Mary Astell
1731	d. (in poverty) Elizabeth Thomas ('Corinna')
1733	pub. Alexander Pope, *The First Satire of the Second Book of Horace* (with attack on Lady Mary Wortley Montagu as 'Sappho')
1733	pub. Lady Mary Wortley Montagu (anonymously with Lord Hervey), *Verses Addressed to the Imitator of . . . Horace*
1733	Mary Chandler (1687–1745), *A Description of Bath* (eight editions by 1767)
1734	Mary Barber (*c*.1690–1757), *Poems on Several Occasions* (subscription, printed by Samuel Richardson)
1736	pub. Elizabeth Singer Rowe, *History of Joseph* (expanded edition 1737)
1737	d. Elizabeth Singer Rowe
1737	pub. *Philomela* (Curll's pirated reprint of Rowe's 1696 *Poems*)

1738	pub. Elizabeth Carter (1717–1806), *Poems Upon Particular Occasions*
1739	pub. *The Miscellaneous Works In Prose and Verse of Mrs Elizabeth Singer Rowe* (2 vols)
1739	pub. Mary Collier (1690?–*c*.1762), *The Woman's Labour: An Epistle to Stephen Duck*
1744	d. Alexander Pope
1744	pub. Jane Brereton (1685–1740), *Poems on Several Occasions* (posthumous subscription)
1746	d. Mary Leapor
1747	pub. Lady Mary Wortley Montagu (ed. Horace Walpole), *Six Town Eclogues. With Some Poems*
1748	pub. Mary Leapor, *Poems Upon Several Subjects* (posthumous subscription)
1749	d. Catherine Trotter (Cockburn) (playwright, philosopher and poet)
1750	pub. Mary Jones (d. 1778), *Miscellanies in Prose and Verse* (Oxford)
1752	pub. George Ballard, *Memoirs of Several Ladies of Great Britian Who have Been Celebrated for their Writings* (Oxford)
1753	pub. Rober Shiells (Shiels) (ed. but attributed to Theophilus Cibber on titlepage), *The Lives of the Poets of Great Britain and Ireland*
1754	pub. John Duncombe, *The Feminiad*
1755	pub. George Colman and Bonnell Thornton (eds), *Poems by Eminent Ladies*
1762	d. Lady Mary Wortley Montagu

1
Introduction: From Punk to Poetess

Sarah Prescott and David E. Shuttleton

For *Punk* and *Poetess* agree so pat,
You cannot well be This and not be That. (from Robert Gould, *The
Poetess: A Satyr*, 1707)

This volume of scholarly critical essays is concerned with female poetic
practice in an important transitional period of women's literary history. From the post-Restoration to mid-eighteenth century we witness
a major shift in that practice from having been predominantly coterie,
to the emergence of the professional woman poet within an expansive
print culture. Such a transition required women poets to indulge in
complex acts of self-fashioning as they embraced, negotiated or contested a range of stereotypes from the antifeminist label of immoral
'punk' to the domesticated ideal of virtuous 'poetess'. Women's poetic
practice in the early modern period has until very recently remained
largely invisible to literary historians and the critical establishment. A
now mature academic feminist literary historiographical project is actively engaged in recovering and evaluating a vast body of hitherto
neglected women's poetry. Groundbreaking anthologies like *Kissing the
Rod* (1988), edited by Germaine Greer et al., and Roger Lonsdale's pi-
oneering *Eighteenth-Century Women Poets* (1989) alerted many of us to
long-suspected riches and importantly served to make a selection of
this material available for undergraduate and post-graduate teaching
purposes. A glaring lack of scholarly editions of specific women poets
has begun to be rectified, notably by the Women Writers Project based
at Brown University, Providence. This is currently employing innovative data-base technology to make available a sizeable body of pre-1830
material, much of it poetry, through 'on-demand' publishing and,
more traditionally, through a projected 30-volume series in association

1

with Oxford University Press. New student-anthologies, notably *Eighteenth-Century Poetry* (1999) edited by David Fairer and Christine Gerard, finally give substantial representation to women's poetry. Such editorial activity is starting to have an immediate practical impact upon teaching curricula, and prompting new research interests. As academic teachers who, like many, have begun to include these newly available, often lively texts on undergraduate courses, we have come up against the frustrating fact that much of the new critical material on women's poetry 1660–1750 is scattered throughout scholarly journals. The present volume of essays was designed and specially commissioned from leading scholars in this field to make these new historical and critical approaches more accessible to students and general readers alike.

A veritable flurry of journal articles and a major monograph by Carol Barash, *English Women's Poetry, 1649–1714: Politics, Community, and Linguistic Authority* (1996), reveals that critical work on women's poetic practice, stylistics, canon formation and publishing history has reached a stage of maturity. The important international academic conference 'Rethinking Women's Poetry 1730–1930', held at Birkbeck College, London, in July 1996, generated two companion volumes of papers, published by Macmillan now Palgrave Macmillan in 1999. But as participants in the Birkbeck Conference, we have been aware that the earlier of these volumes, *Women's Poetry in the Enlightenment: the Making of a Canon, 1730–1820*, edited by Isobel Armstrong and Virginia Blaine, starts effectively around 1740. Therefore the period from 1660 to 1750, only partly covered in Barash's groundbreaking monograph, remains under-represented in accessible general studies. In particular Barash, by identifying an important Royalist, High-Church, Tory and frequently pro-Stuart women's poetic tradition, has set an important framework against which we can now place other cultural strands: Whig, dissenting, pietist, mercantile, labouring-class, etc. The new essays in this current volume reflect a growing awareness that we need to examine more closely the precise political, social and personal contexts within which women poets both wrote and circulated their work, be it in manuscript or print (or both). Although modern feminist agendas fuelled historical recovery, it is becoming increasingly apparent that the work of individual poets cannot always easily be defined as conservative or progressive at a time when affiliations to respective, but sometimes non-commensurate ideologies concerning the fixity or otherwise of class and gender structures do not necessarily conform to modern expectations.

The essays in *Women and Poetry, 1660–1750* concern themselves with the multiplicity of female poetic practice and with the public image of the woman poet between the Restoration and the mid-eighteenth century. In this period, a variety of women from a range of contexts and circumstances became important producers of poetry. Alongside aristocratic figures like Mary Lady Chudleigh, Lady Mary Wortley Montagu and Anne Finch, Countess of Winchilsea, often writing under the influence of the proto-feminist writings of Mary Astell (1666–1731), there is the important emergence of female working-class voices such as that of the Washer-Woman poet, Mary Collier, and the gardener's daughter, Mary Leapor. Between these two groupings there is a large body of verse published by women from the educated 'middling-ranks', who form an important emergent social formation as both producers and critical consumers of the poetry being published in the burgeoning journals and miscellanies. Such figures as Elizabeth Thomas, Elizabeth Rowe, Mary Barber and Mary Chandler who found a wide readership in their day, and helped to forge the public perception of women as professional poets, have hitherto remained in the margins of our literary history, overshadowed, if not blatantly maligned by an insecure male literary establishment. By the 1750s literary luminaries like Johnson and Richardson are starting to display anxieties about the emergence of professional women poets, and attempts were already being made to describe a canon of post-Restoration female poets. This important, transitional and varied tradition of women's post-Restoration poetic practice is the concern of the contributors to this volume.

The earliest attempts of a first generation of female literary historians to map this territory in the late 1970s and early 1980s tended to speak of isolated, individual voices crying in a hostile literary wilderness. Certainly, as our title suggests, for a woman of the late seventeenth century to publish her poetry was to run the risk of being deemed at best improper, if not wholly immoral. However, attention to the dedications and addressees of much of this material reveals that it was not produced in social isolation. We know about the exclusively male homosocial contexts of eighteenth-century literature – the Kit-Kat Club, the Scriblerians, etc. – but we are only now starting to uncover the contexts of female poetic production and patronage. Attention is now being drawn to the complex female, homosocial networks of patronage and influence within which much of this verse was produced. Such attention also re-illuminates established canonical figures such as John Dryden, Alexander Pope, Jonathan Swift, Samuel

Richardson and Dr Johnson, who wrote in reaction to or, more positively, served as patrons or models for a number of women poets previously ignored.

The present volume is organized into three sections. Part I contains relatively short accounts of eight important women poets of the period. Each account provides a brief biographical summary, an overview of poetic range and critical responses and pointers to the direction for further research. Each concludes with a bibliography including available modern editions and specific secondary reading. All of the writers featured here are discussed in different contexts in the essays that follow, allowing the reader to add to the initial portraits presented in this opening section and to view these writers in relation to the social and literary contexts in which they were writing, including the work of other women poets of the time. The four essays in Part II are concerned specifically with the historical, social, commercial and critical contexts within which women poets worked. The essays in Part III address poetic practice, including questions of poetic genre, form and language.

While we have elected not to include any internal cross-referencing, this three-part arrangement will, we hope, allow the reader to navigate the volume in a number of ways depending upon their concerns. For anyone interested in a specific poet, the general index will enable you to locate further discussions. We feel that the limited, if inevitable degree of overlap that emerged across and between the more discursive essays usefully serves to highlight certain key themes as they emerge within differing critical perspectives.

The eight poets represented in Part I range from court-based writers such as Anne Killigrew and Anne Finch through to the middling-class poet Elizabeth Singer Rowe and the labouring-class Mary Leapor. The list of names included here is not, of course, exhaustive. By singling out these eight writers we are not engaged in any form of 'canon formation'. Rather, our aim was to provide in succinct form a useful introduction to a range of women poets writing in a variety of styles from multiple contexts and social backgrounds. We are aware, however, of some prominent omissions. Among these Katherine Philips is perhaps the most notable poet not to be included here due to her influence on women poets writing immediately after her death in 1664 and her continued high standing throughout the eighteenth century. The main reason for omitting Philips from this first section was a simple one of dates. Philips wrote much of her work in the 1650s and died only four years into our date span, even though her poetry was published in a pirated edition in 1664 and posthumously in 1667. Nevertheless, it is indisputable that her significance for her female predecessors was high. Known as 'the matchless Orinda', Philips was often pitted against Aphra Behn as a model of chastity and modesty which women writers often found easier to emulate than the scandalous and professional image of Behn. Therefore, even though she does not feature as one of our 'individual poets', Philips is still an important presence in this volume. For example Jane Spencer, in her essay, 'Imagining the Woman Poet' (Part II), provides a detailed and provocative analysis of Abraham Cowley's commendatory ode 'Upon Mrs. K. *Philips* her Poems' (1664, rept. 1667), which did much to further Philips's fame as well as to set a precedent for commendatory verses on women's poetry. In addition, Kathryn King (Part III) begins her assessment of women's political poetry with Philips, suggesting that she is 'arguably Britain's first female poet of state'. In contrast to Philips's image of private modesty, then, King emphasizes the overtly political nature of Philips's verse and places her at the forefront of a tradition of women's defence of monarchy and authorization of female political agency.

Among other poets with no dedicated account are, in the early period, 'Ephelia', the pseudonymous, and still elusive author of *Female Poems On Several Occasions* (London, 1679), Lucy Hutchinson (1620–81), memoirist and translator of Lucretius, and the coterie poet Anne Wharton (1659–85), of whose work relatively little survives. For biographical information on these and later less-canonical poets such as Sarah Fyge Egerton (1670–1723), the teenage author of *The Female Advocate* (1686), and largely one-volume poets such as 'Corinna', Elizabeth Thomas (1675–1731), we point the reader to the diligent biographical notes in *Kissing the Rod* and Lonsdale's Oxford anthology.

Part II opens with an essay by Jane Spencer on 'Imagining the Woman Poet' in which she illustrates and addresses the range of poetic personas either imposed upon or deliberately adopted by women poets. For the increasing numbers of women publishing verse in our period, the persistence of traditional conceptions of the poet as male, and his muse or source of inspiration, as female, posed a problem. As Spencer illustrates, for some misogynist male critics, the very notion of a female poet was a contradiction in terms leaving the defenders of women poets having radically to reimagine the relationship between sexuality and poetry. Spencer considers how women poets sought to negotiate the fact that Apollo as the god of poetry was, according to the myth of his pursuit of Daphne, also a potential rapist: the bays of poetry being the reward for male sexual sublimation. As one of the more radical reimaginings of this relationship, Spencer discusses a poem by the pseudonymous 'Philo-Philippa' who figures male poetry as the result of sexual violence, whereas that of Katherine Philips enjoys 'the freedom of her consensual relationship with inspiration' (the same commendatory poem is the likely source for Anne Killigrew's related invocation of the same myth in her key poem 'Upon, the saying . . . ').

In the heart of her essay Spencer considers how the woman poet 'was imagined not only as muse but as angel, Amazon, nightingale, whore, mother, amorous woman, domestic matron, virgin, hermaphrodite'. But as Spencer emphasizes from the outset, whether being positively or negatively invoked, as 'hyperbolic praise, anxious self-justification, or satiric detraction, these images dealt in their various ways with one all-pervasive problem, recently theorized as the mismatch within patriarchal society between female embodiment and full human subjectivity'. Spencer's ensuing analysis of each of these poetic personas in turn benefits from her attention to this problem of embodiment; a problem amplified by the fact that while the rhetoric of poetic 'birth' was readily if incongruously applied to male poets, for women themselves their actual generative power was traditionally associated with gross materiality, a wayward imagination and the monstrous.

This misogynist discourse (often active in Scriblerian satire) informed Augustan images of the female poet as a hysterical victim of fashionable, purportedly female 'nervous disorders' such as the vapours or spleen, and provides the context for reading Anne Finch's autobiographical riposte, 'The Spleen, a Pindaric Poem'. For others, like the dissenter Elizabeth Rowe, the answer lay in exploiting the image of the Nightingale or 'Philomela' (her given pen-name), a bird that provided a suitably disembodied metaphor for the religious poet's 'rising soul'. But as Spencer notes, somewhat ironically Rowe's often ecstatic religious verses brought charges of 'Enthusiasm', being deemed by some as overly passionate. Although the derogatory image of the female poet as 'slattern' was still being activated at the close of our period, Spencer shows how a commonly invoked late-seventeenth century dichotomy between the female poet as either virgin (Philips) or whore (Behn) was gradually replaced in the early Georgian period by less extreme models; most notably the perhaps more accommodating, if still limiting image of the female poet as genteel 'matron' in whom practical maternal duties, benevolent charity-work and public poetic practice were allowed respectable coexistence. Spencer observes how, in this 'Augustan compromise', exemplified in the motherly persona of Anglo-Irish poet Mary Barber, we find that a 'good woman's poetry came from a tamed, domesticated body, and could involve, indeed, a distinctive sensual response to animal and everyday life'.

Valerie Rumbold opens her essay 'Rank Community and Audience: the Social Range of Women's Poetry' with a warning that we should avoid imposing anachronistic social categories onto the lives of early modern women poets. In the wake of the first phase of feminist-fuelled historical recovery, Rumbold observes how we are starting 'to read these women poets not only in relation to modern agendas, but also in relation to specific social and economic issues and assumptions of their times'. Emphasizing how individual women were caught up in complex processes of social and economic change, Rumbold traces how, after the Glorious Revolution, '[r]ank was increasingly re-negotiated around polite sociability that required property to sustain it'. She observes how the resulting social tensions were rarely articulated in terms of 'class': indeed, the term only came into usage late in our period, and then almost exclusively in relation to the 'lower class'. In the core of her essay Rumbold categorizes some key women poets according to the meanings attached at the time to a whole range of contemporary terms for social positioning. Moving downwards from the top of the social hierarchy these included the nobility, the gentry, members of the professions (physicians, clerics, lawyers), the 'Middling Sort' (mainly urban traders) and yeomen (their rural equivalents), down to the 'Low' or 'Mean Sorts' (servants and manual labourers).

Early in her essay Rumbold also confronts a key question often raised in relation to the first post-Restoration generation of women poets: if women's writing practice was inherently transgressive, why were so many of them political conservatives, being High-Anglican Tories, if not Catholic-Jacobites? This question takes on resonance in the light of Barash's account of the enabling use made of monarchist imagery by largely upper-class women poets prior to Queen's Anne's death in 1714. Drawing on the work of Paula McDowell, Rumbold suggest that since many poets, like Philips, Chudleigh and Finch, benefited from their high social rank in terms of affording to publish without any need for financial remuneration, it was in their interests to uphold conservative notions of a fixed social structure. Chudleigh in particular presents modern readers with the apparent contradiction of a woman poet wedded to a strongly conservative sense of hierarchy, who nonetheless found common cause with other 'Ladies', if not her gender as a whole. This raises the wider question of the extent to which women poets of all social groups found common ground with other women poets in terms of gender. In this context, and anticipating some concerns of the next essay, Rumbold closes by considering what was at stake when middle-ranking and labouring-class women sought publication through patronage and subscription publishing.

In the following essay 'From Manuscript to Print: a Volume of Their Own?', Margaret Ezell urges us to historicize the relationship between gender, authorship and audience as we consider how women poets of this period sought to circulate their work in manuscript or print, and how and why they decided to move from one into the other. As Ezell notes, some women such as Elizabeth Bury did not require print to find an audience, but may have publicly suppressed her poetry more than prose. Certainly much seventeenth-century women's poetry and other writing was devotional and domestic in nature, confined to private commonplace books, diaries and letters. Poets such as Anne Wharton and Anne Killigrew, both active in the 1680s, typically circulated their manuscript poetry among semi-private coterie readers, but made no obvious efforts to publish in print. It was not uncommon for such poetry to appear posthumously, either – as with Killigrew – in a carefully edited memorial volume overseen by the father or other family members, or as in Wharton's case sporadically in miscellanies. Wharton was just one of many women poets whose work was 'pirated' by commercially minded booksellers eager to trade on the fashionable novelty of poetry by 'Ladies'.

For those women who actively sought an audience through print and thus primarily saw themselves as poets, Ezell considers the range of opportunities and contexts within which this might be achieved: from single poems of public commemoration as broadsides and pamphlets, to periodicals such as *The Athenian Mercury*, to miscellanies and songbooks (an under-researched field for locating previously 'lost' women's poetry). As Ezell remarks

> songbooks and verse miscellanies . . . can be seen as a type of publishing middle-ground, where circulated manuscripts of women poets could be posthumously preserved in print, where living social poets could contribute a small piece or two with little expense or effort, and where commercial writers such as Aphra Behn, Mary Pix, Susanna Centlivre, and Delarivière Manley could reprint songs from their plays, poetic dedications and miscellaneous occasional verse.

Miscellanies also served as 'the initial print venue' of women poets who later publish single-author volumes, including Rowe, Finch and Montagu. Of these individual 'Works', Ezell distinguishes between those women such as Rowe, Chudleigh, Finch and Montagu who could afford to ignore the profit motive and those other, would-be more professional writers, such as Behn, Thomas and Barber, who published their poetry in the hope of often much-needed financial gain. As Ezell concludes, increased commercial commodification of women's poetry brought with it its own problems: by the 1740s several writers were complaining in verse that potential readers, both men and women, were rapidly growing sick of being pestered for subscriptions.

In drawing attention to the material conditions of publication and print Ezell's study also alerts us to the fact that as modern editors and readers we risk making a false separation between poetry and prose that was simply not present in contemporary publishing contexts. Poetry, for example, is often to be found printed amid prose in the more under-examined body of devotional and prophetic literature of the period. Among more canonical writers, Delarivière Manley, Eliza Haywood and in particular Jane Barker all published works in which their own poetry and that of others was interspersed within, and in the latter case tellingly framed by, their own prose narratives. More commonly, women's poetry was often printed willy-nilly alongside prose essays, translations and letters, within the far less controllable context of pirated miscellanies.

In the closing essay in Part II, Germaine Greer presents a detailed account of one such publishing 'pirate', the London-based bookseller Charles Gildon who, as perhaps the most active hack-editor of women's writing working at the close of the seventeenth and start of the eighteenth century, sought to exploit a fashionable interest in work purportedly by 'Ladies'. In what is effectively a historical case study of the circumstances in which some women's poetry and other writing found its way into commercial print, Greer meticulously scrutinizes a number of Gildon's publishing ventures, including his exploitative printing of salacious women writer's private letters and his gradual claims on the posthumous oeuvre of Behn, to reveal how such mercenary, unscrupulous activities present modern scholars with glaring problems of attribution. Greer calls for editorial vigilance for, while several poems attributed to canonical women writers are only known from unreliable printings initiated by Gildon, he seems to have been prepared to pass off the work of men as being by women. Greer's essay reminds us of the need for continued scholarly spadework in research libraries and archives to recover the precise circumstances within which early modern women's poetry was created, circulated and increasingly found its way into print.

The complementary essays in Part III investigate women's actual poetic practice in a number of key areas: the use of classical and biblical models, political verse and poetry of the labouring class. Claudia Thomas Kairoff's essay, 'Classical and Biblical Models: the Female Poetic Tradition', explores women's relation to a classical tradition which had historically excluded women. Women's lack of access to a classical education had, as Kairoff argues, direct implications for their standing as poets. For men, a familiar knowledge of the classics was one of the prerequisites for membership of the republic of letters and lack of classical learning could be used to undermine a writer's status and pretensions to literary excellence. For women writers, therefore, classical models represented a difficult literary legacy that often marked their exclusion from the male literary establishment.

As Kairoff demonstrates, despite such obstacles, 'by the Restoration, most women with pretensions to literature had to overcome insufficient, often nonexistent, classical training to pay their respects to the Parnassian Muses'. Aphra Behn circumnavigated her lack of classical education by 'updating and revising others' translations or by writing original poems in classical genres'. Many other women poets writing into the eighteenth century found 'Horatian satire in the Popeian vein' an inspiring model for their poetic voices. Later examples include Mary Leapor and Mary Jones (1707–78), and in her early poems Lady Mary Wortley Montagu, self-taught in Latin, was one of the few women poets to adopt the pose of the Augustan classical satirist, skilled in the art of Horatian imitation. Kairoff also introduces us to a much lesser-known poet – Elizabeth Tollet (1694–1754) – whose career anticipates that of Elizabeth Carter (1717–1806), and whose work provides an interesting testing ground for charting the development of a female poetic tradition in the years immediately following the period covered by Barash's important study (1649–1714). In contrast to many of her female contemporaries, Tollet was well-educated in Latin and used her classical knowledge to produce original translations of, for example, the Apollo and Daphne myth of Ovid's *Metamorphoses* as well as several Horatian translations. Tollet is an excellent example of how the work of an individual, and relatively obscure, poet can help to revise, or qualify, our broader assumptions about female poetic practice in the early eighteenth century.

In comparison to classical precedent, the Bible was a much more accessible and enabling model for women's poetic practice. In fact, devotional poetry was often the staple of women's poetic production. Elizabeth Singer Rowe was perhaps the most high-profile of the many women known for their devotional poetry and prose, but many others found a rich source of poetic inspiration in biblical imagery and biblical stories. As Kairoff demonstrates, one of Mary Lady Chudleigh's most interesting poems is 'The Song of the Three Children Paraphras'd', and many of Anne Finch's most well-known work is replete with scriptural resonance and biblical imagery. Tollet also drew extensively on the Scriptures and translations of the psalms in order to 'demonstrate that classical philosophy and modern science supported, rather than undermined, biblical truths'. Although early eighteenth-century women's use of the Bible does not have the political edge of women's religious verse of the seventeenth century, biblical models continued to provide women poets with a framework for expressing their views and asserting their authority.

Kathryn R. King's essay, 'Political Verse and Satire: Monarchy, Party and Female Political Agency', challenges the traditional view of women's poetry as being mainly confined to private themes executed on a small and unambitious scale. With reference to a range of poets from a variety of political backgrounds, King demonstrates that women poets from the Restoration to the mid-eighteenth century, participated at every level in the politics of their time. As King argues,

> They stated opinion on affairs of state, smeared political enemies, displayed loyalty, entered into religious controversy, shaped public opinion, and explored the questions of allegiance, integrity and national memory that troubled nearly all thoughtful members of the political nation during this uncertain time.

King's focus is on 'high literary forms' – state poems, panegyrics on the monarchy, odes and royal elegies – but the variety of poets discussed here range from pro-Stuart and Jacobite poets to the Whiggish poets emerging in the 1690s, and the political writing in the reigns of Queen Anne and George I. King's survey begins with the political verse of Katherine Philips whose work includes 'one of the first of many instances of a woman poet stepping forward to defend, champion or counsel a beloved monarch'; a stance taken up by the royal odes of Aphra Behn. Immediately following Philips we find the beginnings of what King terms 'The Jacobite Tradition', which includes the later work of Behn and the Jacobite poetry of Jane Barker and Anne Finch. Although all three poets are writing from similar political perspectives, the way in which they do so differs dramatically. Whereas Behn's royal verse addresses a print audience and deals in 'baroque splendour' Barker's poetry, mainly circulated in manuscript, 'employs unheroic, homely, even rough effects'. By contrast again, Finch includes alongside her Jacobite sympathies a complex exploration of the 'relations among poetry, female utterance and the public realm'.

The link between High Tory and pro-Stuart politics and female poetics has often been seen as representative of early modern women's writing. For women writing from this tradition, as the poetry of Barker and Finch clearly shows, the Revolution of 1688–89 was a time of national mourning, personal regret and grief. The Whiggish women writers who viewed the Revolution as indeed 'Glorious' have been less well documented in accounts of women's poetry. King's essay offers a welcome counter-balance to our rapidly growing knowledge of a Jacobite and/or High Tory female poetic tradition. A study of the poetry of women such as Elizabeth Singer Rowe and Sarah Fyge Egerton reveals a very different side to women's political verse. As King argues, when compared with the work of Behn, Barker and Finch,

> Nothing could be more different than the verse of the next generation of women poets, a self-consciously forward-looking lot who eagerly attached themselves to the new Whig order and advanced a cultural and political agenda that was Protestant, militaristic, triumphalist and intensely nationalistic.

Such a stance was continued into the age of Anne, as shown by the Whiggish verse of the popular playwright Susannah Centlivre (1669?–1723). As King suggests, 'the assumption that the female political sensibility in the early modern period was predisposed toward royalist or Tory positions is not borne out by the evidence'. Furthermore, what distinguishes much women's poetry in the Hanoverian age is a move away from partisan politics towards a 'search for a unified national voice – one suitable for a Britain that increasingly identified itself with empire, international trade and naval supremacy'. The role women poets played in the creation of such a voice and therefore in the shaping of notions of Britishness in the early eighteenth century – a theme recently explored by Harriet Guest for the post-1750 period in *Small Change: Women, Learning, Patriotism, 1750–1810* (2000) – is an exciting area of study as yet under-represented in current scholarship on the earlier part of the century.

In the final essay of the volume, 'The Labouring-Class Women Poets: "Hard labour we most chearfully pursue" ', Donna Landry discusses the work of the two most prominent labouring-class women poets of the period: Mary Collier and Mary Leapor. Both women suffered from prejudiced views about the capacity of the lower classes to be educated and to write. However, their poetry clearly demonstrates their literary skill and intelligence, not just 'potential unfulfilled'. As Landry suggests, it is not enough simply to read the work of labouring-class poets in terms of 'autobiographical testimony or statements of lived experience'; that is, just in relation to their social positions. Rather, 'The artistry of both poets is at least as significant as their testimony of labouring-class experience.' Landry's detailed reading of Collier's most well-known poem, *The Woman's Labour*, clearly demonstrates the poet's intricate response not only to Stephen Duck's poem *The Thresher's Labour* (to which Collier is directly responding) and her own experience as a working woman, but also her complex, and often comic, reworking of classical precedent. Mary Leapor, a poet whose reputation is currently rising swiftly, was also well-versed in literary precedent, and, like Collier, was 'nothing if not fearlessly witty in her engagement with the traditions of English poetry'. Both women were also viewed by the critical establishment as having the ability to be part of a British literary heritage. Leapor 'was perceived as something of a national treasure' in the years after her death, for, as Landry notes, she held a special place, for example, in George Colman and Bonnell Thornton's *Poems by Eminent Ladies* (1755), '118 pages of which are devoted to Leapor, more pages than are occupied by any other poet, including Aphra Behn and Anne Finch'. Mary Collier too, in her poem on George III, makes a claim for national importance through her patriotic support of the Hanoverian succession and her celebration of 'the civilizing force of Britishness'. The participation of women such as Collier and Leapor in the creation of a national poetic tradition and a unified sense of Britishness adds yet another dimension to our understanding of the significance of women's poetry in the period. As Landry states: 'If even a washerwoman could write so eloquently about the new king's imperial mission, then Britain must be the finest nation in the world.'

In conclusion, throughout the planning and compilation of this volume, we have remained aware of the practical need for accessible and reliable editions of the poets discussed. For while Lonsdale's

Oxford anthology remains essential, and small selections of key poems by women poets are increasingly included in 'student anthologies', there are still very few representative editions available for anyone wishing to study or simply read and enjoy a range of work by any given poet. As noted above, this problem is in part being remedied by an increase in on-line access and downloadable hyper-texts. Academically rigorous databases such as the aforementioned Brown University Women Writers Project and other related collaborative ventures such as The Orlando Project based in Canada at the University of Alberta, with an international team of scholars working towards 'An Integrated History of Women's Writing in the British Isles' and The Perdita Project, designed to compile a database of women's literary manuscripts of the sixteenth and seventeenth centuries, currently based at Nottingham Trent University, have already had both on-line and conventional publication outcomes. This use of the new electronic media clearly suggests an important forward direction, but we feel that there is still a glaring need for some reasonably priced, critical editions designed to allow both students and a general readership the opportunity to explore and appreciate the distinctiveness of women's poetry from this crucial period.

Part I
Individual Poets

2
Aphra Behn (1640?–89): Virginia Woolf and the 'Little Gods of Love'

Susan Wiseman

Aphra Behn, perhaps now most famous for her short fiction *Oroonoko* (1688) and the play *The Rover* (1677) was a prolific playwright, a writer of fiction, translation and poetry. She was a spy for Charles II, she may have gone to Surinam, she was involved in Tory political campaigns and writing. In the last year of her life she seems to have rejected invitations to assist the new government of William of Orange. The lawyer John Hoyle was probably her lover: we know of her connection with him and with some others. But, as Janet Todd notes, 'Aphra Behn refuses to reveal a single plausible life' – we have clues, hints, possibilities but beyond her evident political commitment to the Stuarts, her spying and the more enigmatic information offered by her writing little about her life is absolutely clear.[1] Behn might have been born in Kent in the early 1640s: we do know that she died in April 1689 and was buried in Westminster Abbey.

When, in 1928, Virginia Woolf suggested that Behn's interment in Westminster Abbey was both scandalous and 'rather' appropriate she expressed the two central issues in the critical interpretation of her work; much of her writing, as Jane Spencer's research shows, was consistently performed and read in the generations after her death, but it (and she) were also understood as scandalous.[2] Behn's very reputation for scandal – whether understood as biographical, personal, 'real' or literary and discursive – has played an important part in her writing's critical reception and her reputation.[3] From the eighteenth-century pairing of Behn as the looser and more forward 'Astrea' with Katherine Philips's chaste 'Orinda' to more recent assessments of her as politically powerful and innovative in her writing on sexuality, Behn – at times problematically fused by critics with the speakers of her poems – has been understood as a sexual and poetic adventurer.[4] However, as the subjects which preoccupy her poetry – power, desire, ambiguity, what would now be thought of as sexuality – have come to be more critically central, so has that adventurousness been valued more highly. Where the eighteenth-century poet Jane Brereton saw her as 'Politely lewd and wittily prophane', the critic Harriette Andreadis sees a willingness to 'write knowingly and transgressively' so that her poems signal a shift in the way in which desire – including same-sex desire – was represented at the Restoration.[5]

Although critical reception of the poetry of Aphra Behn did not begin with Virginia Woolf, the very dramatic, even tragic, way in which Woolf poses the task and life of the early modern women writers, and her characterization of these writers as lost to history, has been influential. In *A Room of One's Own* (1928), Woolf wrote that Behn:

> had to work on equal terms with men. She made, by working very hard, enough to live on. The importance of that fact outweighs anything she actually wrote, even the splendid 'A Thousand Martyrs I have made', or 'Love in Fantastic Triumph Sat', for here begins the freedom of the mind.[6]

Woolf uses Behn to make her key point: 'freedom of the mind' begins with money. Though we do not know that Behn actually did make a living by her pen, for Woolf the 'important fact' of Behn's place in the market is much more important than her aesthetic achievements.[7] Indeed, it seems that, for Woolf, Behn's achievement as a poet is actually compromised by the very conditions that make her 'free' – her market success. Woolf seems to be ambivalent about Behn's sexual reputation, too, writing that 'It is she – shady and amorous as she was – who makes it not quite fantastic for me to say to you tonight: Earn five hundred a year by your wits.'[8] Woolf's emphasis on Behn's importance as a commercial writer for some time threw into the shadows other – aesthetic, collaborative, generic, thematic – aspects of Behn's work.[9] Woolf's judgement also singles Behn out as a 'first', while her poetry, much of which is published in collaborative miscellanies, makes it clear that she inhabited a vivid social and political milieu with other writers.

But what kind of writer did Woolf present through the two poems that she praised? How did the selection of these two 'splendid' poems from the one hundred or so that we now have by Behn (Woolf did not have quite so many to select from) characterize her achievement?[10] 'Love in

Fantastique Triumph satt' is the first line of the 16-line poem 'Love Arm'd, a 'Song'.[11] This song opens Behn's tragedy *Abdelazar* (performed 1676).[12] Between them the lovers have armed the god of Love, but it is the speaker's heart 'alone is harm'd,/Whilst thine the Victor is, and free' (15–16). The speaker, suffering from the 'Tyranick power' (4) the god of Love shows his victim, in being conquered by Love's deployment of her own effects ('desire' (7), 'sighs and tears' (9)) is simultaneously conquered by her beloved and Love. The speaker is not explicitly sexed, nor is the beloved. The God of Love is abstract, emblematized by the 'Bleeding Hearts' (2) the poem visualizes around him. The description of Cupid situates the poem as part of the body of English poetry which reworks the Petrarchan tradition in which lovers burn with icy fire. The poem uses the Petrarchan triad of lover, beloved and Cupid (or maybe, rather, Eros) to suggest a particular experience from which the poem is abstracted. It was, though, also a 'song', inviting a reader to think about the poem in terms of a pattern of sound rather than formally.

Woolf does not say *why* she chose this poem to represent the height of Behn's achievement, but it is a choice which, in reminding the reader of Behn's use of formal antecedents and particularly Behn's use of Petrarchan convention, steers them to think formally. Rather than think about the poem in relation to the preoccupations of Behn's other poetry the reader is reminded to see her poems in relation to a literary canon – such a poem can readily be seen beside Donne's *Songs and Sonets* or the poems of Behn's highly valued contemporary, Katherine Philips. That this text is not especially important in debates about Behn suggests, perhaps, that this particular poem might not address what seem to be Behn's central concerns.

The second lyric Woolf selects, though, suggests Behn as a more complex writer. 'A thousand Martyrs' makes a pair with 'Love in Fantastique Triumph satt' in being, as the first line suggests, written from the point of view of the male lover, Lycidus (who shares his names with that sometimes indicating Behn's lover Hoyle in her poems), in the context of an only partly justified boast:

> Alone the Glory and the Spoil
>   I always Laughing bore away;
> The Triumphs, without Pain or Toil,
>   Without the Hell, the Heav'n of Joy.
> And while I thus at random rove
> Despise the Fools that whine for Love[13]

In this choice Woolf registers Behn's agile assumption of voice and position – her ability to use the first person (or apparently autobiographical enunciation) to stage experiences. Woolf also implicitly acknowledges the power with which Behn writes about love and desire. If a contemporary reader of *A Room of One's Own* had looked up 'A thousand Martyrs' in the edition Woolf was using – Montague Summers's 1915 edition of Behn – they would have found it in the midst of one of Behn's more libertine texts, a narrative mixing poetry and prose to canvass the rakish sexual politics of a man's voyage to – and from – the Isle of Love.[14] *Lycidus; or, the Lover in Fashion* (1688) is an adaptation of Tallement's continuation of *A Voyage to the Island of Love*, translated by Behn in 1663.[15] Described by the male narrator as 'the History of my Heart, which I assure you, boasts itself of the Conquests it has made', the narrative ends with him bidding goodbye to Love's 'Gilting tricks and quillets'.[16] From being a 'managed' coxcomb the narrator comes to abandon love altogether and so the Petrarchan aspects of this poem are linked to the libertine genres which Behn wrote in, and ambiguously to the world of desire, rejection and sexual competition which Behn often used pastoral vocabulary to stage.

The selection of this poem, with its use of male and female personae, focuses the reader's attention on an erotics of power relations, and its location in the 'odyssey' of a libertine lover with its focus on betrayal and desire indicates an implicit acknowledgement on Woolf's part that the power of Behn's poetry has an adventurousness which as well as formal is simultaneously thematic – Behn writes 'about' female desire, same-sex desire, sexual disappointment and uses pastoral, dialogue, lament and libertine genres. In choosing to pair these two lyrics Woolf perhaps implies something more than, or slightly different from, what she actually says about the power of Behn's poetry: one enunciates in a possibly, but not definitively, feminine voice the position of the victim of eros, desiring and triumphed over; the other, assuming the position of explicitly masculine triumph, is situated in a narrative in which desire overrides attachment in sexual relations. Taken out of context both poems offer Behn as a poet writing about love and power. Returned to its context the second poem suggests that Behn's writing is important not despite her being 'shady and amorous', but precisely because of the power with which she writes about the betrayals of love.

It is true, though, that Woolf's selection of short lyrics represents only a narrow strand of Behn's writing. In 'A Paraphrase on Oenone *to* Paris', for instance, paraphrased from Ovid's *Heroides* (in which abandoned heroines lament the loss of their lovers), it is evident that Behn saw the potential of first-person narration and, in this instance, female complaint to use the extreme situations of love and abandonment, and to describe – and eroticize – differences in power. Behn also threads pastoral – a sexual and political discourse in seventeenth-century poetry – into her translations and poems. Doubling the length of the original, Behn's 'paraphrase' claims a place in the tradition of translation and interpretation. It dramatizes the fixed state of the river nymph Oenone as opposed to Paris's physical and social mobility by building up a very full identity for an explicitly *pastoral* world they shared:

> Till Swains had learn'd the Vice of Perjury,
> No yielding Maids were charg'd with Infamy.
> 'Tis false and broken Vows make Love a Sin,
> Hadst thou been true, We innocent had been. (279–82)

Voicing as fully as possible Oenone's understanding of her position, Behn paraphrases Ovid to present Oenone as inhabiting a pastoral world preserved by non-institutional faith and vows as opposed to the hierarchies, perjuries and titles of the world of power which invades it. Thus, Paris 'Lord of my Desires' (1) from having 'no Title, but *The Lovely* Swain' (28) becomes a 'Prince' (4). The poem sets a free pastoral fullness, a golden age, against the language of 'Empire' (112), 'Renown' and 'Glory' (154). Paris's vows that she, Oenone, was 'design'd' 'for a Queen!' (295) enable her to ask:

> Why then for *Helen* dost thou me forsake?
> Can a poor empty name such a difference make? (296–7)

Helen, from Oenone's point of view, is an empty name, for the substance of queenliness resides in behaviour. Behn's massive extension of Ovid's poem and its location in a pastoral world suggest that, besides her ready assumption of voices and positions, her poems share an imagistic vocabulary, in many ways a vocabulary of staging (shepherds, swains, trees, nymphs, glades), which she uses to maintain the tension between disclosure of specific situations and the rendering of them into an already sexualized, yet distanced, vocabulary. Thus pastoral tropes and names both invite and distance a reader to 'frame' the visualization of shifting scenes.[17]

While the two poems that Woolf recommends certainly do show Behn dramatizing the power relations of love with one conquered and one victor, 'Oenone' hints more clearly at the preoccupations of Behn's poetry where the way the vocabulary of sexual power, often appearing itself to have been imported from the worlds of tournament or empire, can describe actions and failings with political implications. In this way, Behn's use of a world of pastoral power politics at times maps on to the active political world in which she was involved. Thus 'Song. *To a New Scotch Tune*' (1681) circulated as a broadside ballad responding to Whig propaganda about James, Duke of Monmouth, Charles II's illegitimate son, uses a quasi-pastoral vocabulary to describe the beauties – and illegitimacy – of the Duke.[18] In Behn's song 'Jemmy', appropriately 'The Glory of the Groves,/The Joy of ev'ry tender Lass' (23–4) is undone by 'Ambition' (26) and 'Busie Fopps of State' (27).

If 'Song. *To a New Scotch Tune*' is currently at the margins of the critical debate on Behn, arguably because of issues of attribution and its participation in political discourse, pastoral is also tellingly used in a more often discussed example, 'The Disappointment'. This poem, using the sub-genre called the 'imperfect enjoyment' poem, though often characterized as a poem 'about' premature ejaculation, might be more precisely described as a poem tracing the emotional dynamic of a virgin's sexual consent and a man's sexual failure: the 'disappointment' is both sexual and, significantly, emotional. This poem is another of Behn's poems that could loosely be called an adaptation, based on a French poem published in Amsterdam.[19] In its presentation of the interplay of virgin desire and (rakish?) failure the failed sex is described as provoking embarrassment, shame and a sense of the subject as called upon to admit desire without experiencing fulfilment. The encounter is set up as a 'surprise' – a word with connotations of rape and abduction – of 'Cloris' by Lysander. 'In a Thicket made for Love,/Silent as yielding Maids consent' (11–12) she both draws her lover to her and breathes in his ear:

> She cry'd-*Cease, Cease – your vain Desire,*
> *Or I'll call out-What would you do?*
> *My Dearer Honour ev'n to You,*
> *I cannot, must not give – Retire,*
> *Or take this Life, whose chiefest part*
> *I gave you with the Conquest of my Heart.* (25–30)

Ultimately

> Abandon'd by her Pride and Shame,
> She does her softest Joys dispence

Off'ring her Virgin Innocence (64–6)

It is at this point that:

Ready to taste a thousand Joys,
The too transported hapless Swain
Found the vast Pleasure turn'd to Pain; (71–3)

Cloris, who began as a maid 'surprised' (albeit by her lover) in a thicket, ends the poem blushing with 'Disdain and Shame', in flight. Her 're-sentments' combine the making explicit of her (virgin) desire and its failed fulfilment. The psyche of Lysander, left in the shadowy and darkened pastoral, on the thicket's now 'Gloomy' bed (120) ends the poem. However, unlike the treatments of this genre by her contempo-raries such as Rochester, Behn uses it centrally to explore feminine desire. Through staging and pastoral it investigates particularly the complexity of Cloris's sexual refusal, agreement, and finally her *dis-avowal* of desire as it is precipitately exposed by Lysander's failure. In some ways like Rochester's treatment of this genre in 'The Imperfect Enjoyment' Behn's poem offers the reader a libertine version of *serio ludens* (serious play); the kind of encounter she very fully imagines is both comic and used to explore the problem of unspoken desire and consent suddenly exposed as unfulfilled contract.

Behn brings something of the same libertine energy to her elegy on the death of Rochester. As Kate Lilley has argued, rather than following the lead of elegists who were memorializing the famous rake's death-bed conversion, Behn laments him as poet and lover. Rochester, she writes, 'was but lent this duller World t'improve/In all the charms of Poetry, and Love;'.[20] As Lilley comments, 'a heroic figure of interde-pendent intellectual, verbal and sexual energy' Rochester is to be mourned by poets, beauties and 'all ye little Gods of Love' (52).[21] The complex dynamic of subjectivities at play in this poem, as well as its focus on desire and loss make Behn's elegy for Rochester in some ways a limit case for the way in which she can use genre to, apparently, articulate a world and milieu while writing poems which strongly invite the reader to identify with them.

If desire, explored in the two poems Woolf chose, is crucial to Behn's poetry so are the subjects of seduction. The question of Behn's relation-ship to her poetry is complicated. Some critics see her poems as bio-graphical, and this is tempting. However, Ros Ballaster's understanding of the author as a *figure* in Behn's texts, used consistently to keep in play the idea of the poem as staging an experience grounded in a world, though developed primarily as a way of reading Behn's seductive fictions, is suggestive for the poetry.[22] Thus, in 'The Disappointment', as in some others of Behn's poetry, the drama of desire involves the interplay of the beloved – perhaps unavailable, unresponsive – and the lover. Yet these positions both blur and switch. The subjects of Behn's poems are sometimes fixed in the polarities of 'Love in Fantastique Triumph satt' – locked into postures of supplication and rejection – but in the longer poems and fictions (including 'On Desire', *Lycidus*, 'The Disappointment') the reader is drawn on by a seductive interplay and shift in the relations between subject and object. They are also drawn in by the way in which, as Janet Todd puts it, Behn is 'a sort of ventriloquist' provoking the reader to imagine various psychic states and scenes.[23]

    Though what she said about Behn is still influential, the two poems which Woolf chose to represent her are not likely to be among the first readers encounter. As Harriette Andreadis points out, current anthologies and interpretations of Behn mean that readers are likely to first meet poems of sexual drama, such as the elegy for Rochester, 'The Disappointment' and 'To the fair Clarinda, who made love to me, imagin'd more than Woman'. Among the poems appended to *Lycidus*, 'To the Fair Clarinda' explores same-sex desire. The poem deliberately canvasses precisely the meaning or meanings of the title. Is Clarinda 'Fair lovely Maid' (1) or 'Lovely Charming Youth' (4)? Is the speaker's desire justified to 'without Blushes' 'the youth pursue', or is it truer to say that with the *maid* 'no Crime . . . we can commit/Or if we shou'd – thy Form excuses it' (14–15). The complications are already deeply layered: is it impossible for women to sin with other women? Is it Clarinda's form as a maid or as a youth that would excuse such a transgression? The second stanza describes Clarinda as a 'beauteous Wonder of a different kind' (18), but this still leaves the question of what Clarinda is different *from* – boys or girls? Playing on anatomy and Clarinda's being equipped with a (prosthetic?) penis, the poem explores the change made or not made to the speaker, by the change (or not) of Clarinda. Rather than classify Clarinda and desire as being of and for one or other sex, up to the final line the poem offers different ways of understanding Clarinda and desire for her – ways which are double, yes, but more importantly hold in tension male and female, masculine and feminine rather than requiring a choice. Ending the poem with a collective 'we' extending 'noblest Passions' – 'The Love to *Hermes*, *Aphrodite* the Friend' (22–3), Behn both refuses to solve the paradox and invokes the ambiguous force of classical discourse. Harriet Andreadis sees this poem as part of the evidence for a shift in the articulation of same-sex desire in the late seventeenth century and her analysis, linking formal and other poetic concerns, situates Behn's poetry not as an isolated 'first' but as a text linked to others in its strategies for articulating desire.[24]

Readers whose first encounter with Behn is through the pastoral poems, poems on desire, even the elegy on Rochester, might come to the central concerns of Behn's poetry more readily than those following up either of the lyrics recommended by Woolf. Yet where Woolf's selection of a poem from *Lycidus* might make an oblique allusion to some of the central concerns of Behn's texts, both the poems Woolf chose do focus the reader's attention on the formal aspects of Behn's texts. Other critics, by a strategy almost the opposite of Woolf's use of implication, ground their discussions of the poems in biography. However, while 'Clarinda' does invite interpretation as biography (even as it actually refuses to answer biographical questions), it also locates its drama in classical discourses and pastoral. Furthermore, even this late in her career, the poem is published in a text where Behn's poetic voice interlocks not only with that of the text she translates but also with the poems of a range of her contemporaries, albeit with her poems singled out.[25]

Notes

1. Janet Todd, *The Works of Aphra Behn*, 7 vols (London: William Pickering, 1992–96), Vol. 1, p. ix.
2. Jane Spencer, *Aphra Behn's Afterlife* (Oxford: Oxford University Press, 2000), pp. 144–5 and *passim*, gives a comprehensive analysis of how those following Behn interpreted her legacy, and of twentieth-century critical interpretation.
3. For further discussion and a comparison with Katherine Philips, see Harriette Andreadis, *Sappho in Early Modern England: Female Same-Sex Literary Erotics 1550–1714* (Chicago: University of Chicago Press, 2001), p. 88.
4. Scandal is explicitly dealt with in the writings of three of the most incisive critics of her poetry: Andreadis, *Sappho*, p. 88; Ros Ballaster, *Seductive Forms: Women's Amatory Fiction from 1684 to 1740* (Oxford: Clarendon Press, 1992); and Kate Lilley, 'Blazing Worlds: Seventeenth-Century Women's Utopian Writing', in Clare Brant and Diane Purkiss (eds), *Women, Texts & Histories 1575–1760* (London: Routledge, 1992), pp. 102–33.
5. Jane Brereton, 'Epistle to Mrs Anne Griffiths. Written from London, in 1718', *Poems on Several Occasions* (London: Edward Cave, 1744), pp. 30–6; Andreadis, *Sappho*, pp. 144–5.
6. Virginia Woolf, *A Room of One's Own* (London: Hogarth Press, 1928; rpt Penguin, 1945), p. 64.
7. Germaine Greer, *Slip-Shod Sybils: Recognition, Rejection and the Woman Poet* (London: Viking, 1995), pp. 173–7.

8. Woolf, *Room*, p. 66.
9. A parallel point is made by Elizabeth Eger, that while the historical resources available to Woolf have been massively superseded, giving current
   scholars increasing access to sources of women's poetry, her 'assumptions'
   that there was a 'gaping absence of historical foremothers' 'retain an
   almost mythic currency'. See 'Fashioning a Female Canon: Eighteenth-
   Century Women Poets and the Politics of the Anthology', in Isobel Armstrong and Virginia Blain (eds), *Women's Poetry in the Enlightenment* (Basingstoke: Macmillan now Palgrave Macmillan, 1999), pp. 201–15 (205).
10. See Todd, *Works*, Vol. 1.
11. Ibid., Vol. 1, p. 53. Unless otherwise stated, all future references are to
    Todd's edition.
12. For discussion of this play, see Derek Hughes, *The Theatre of Aphra Behn*
    (Basingstoke: Palgrave now Palgrave Macmillan, 2001), pp. 56–70. *Abdela-
    zar, or The Moor's Revenge. A Tragedy* (London: 1677).
13. From *Lycidus; or, The Lover in Fashion* (1688). See Montague Sommers (ed.),
    The Works of Aphra Behn, 6 vols (London and Stratford-on-Avon: William
    Heinemann and A. H. Bulen, 1915), Vol. 6, p. 305, and Todd, *Works*, Vol. 4,
    p. 385.
14. Summers, *Works*, Vol. 6, pp. 299–342 (305).
15. See Todd, *Works*, Vol. 4, pp. 377–421.
16. Summers, *Works*, Vol. 6, p. 342.
17. On Behn's use of pastoral in her poetry as opposed to other writings, see
    Ann Messenger, *Pastoral Tradition and the Female Talent* (New York: AMS
    Press, 2001), pp. 15–38.
18. Todd, *Works*, vol. 1, pp. 97–8, 400.
19. Richard E. Quaintance, 'French Sources of the Restoration "Imperfect En-
    joyment" Poem', *Philological Quarterly* XLII, 2 (1963), pp. 190–9. The poem
    was first published in *Recueil de divers poesies choises non encore imprimés*
    (Amsterdam, 1661).
20. Aphra Behn, 'On the Death of the late Earl of Rochester', 7–8, Todd, *Works*,
    Vol. 1, p. 161.
21. Kate Lilley, 'True State within: Women's Elegy 1640–1740', in Isobel
    Grundy and Susan Wiseman (eds), *Women, Writing, History 1640–1740*
    (London: Batsford, 1992), pp. 72–92 (76–9).
22. Ros Ballaster writes of the fiction: 'Behn repeatedly inscribes herself into her
    tales of love, compulsively turning her reader's gaze from the amorous couple
    to the amatory narrator, who then uncannily retreats or withholds herself
    from view, in order to set the pursuit in train again' (*Seductive Forms*, p. 69).
23. Todd, 'Textual Introduction', *Works*, Vol. 1, p. xxxix.
24. Andreadis, *Sappho*, pp. 16, 88–90.
25. Ibid., pp. 88–90.

Bibliography

Biographical sources

Duffy, Maureen, *The Passionate Shepherdess, Aphra Behn 1640–89* (London:
    Methuen, 1989).

Goreau, Angeline, *Reconstructing Aphra: a Social Biography of Aphra Behn* (Oxford: Oxford University Press, 1980).
Todd, Janet, *The Secret Life of Aphra Behn* (London: André Deutsch, 1996).
Woodcock, George, *The Incomparable Aphra* (London: Boardman, 1948).

Manuscript sources

O'Donnell, Mary Ann, 'A Verse Miscellany of Aphra Behn: Bodleian Library MS Firth c. 16', in P. Beal and J. Griffiths (eds), *English Manuscript Studies, 1100–1700*, vol. 2 (Oxford: Blackwell, 1990).

Library and modern editions

Greer, Germaine (ed.), *The Uncollected Verse of Aphra Behn* (Stump Cross: Stump Cross Books, 1989).
Salzman, Paul (ed.), *Oroonoko and Other Writings* (Oxford: Oxford University Press, 1994).
Summers, Montague (ed.), *The Works of Aphra Behn*, 6 vols (London and Stratford-on-Avon: William Heinemann and A. H. Bulen, 1915).
Todd, Janet (ed.), *Oroonoko, The Rover and Other Works* (London: Penguin Books, 1992).
Todd, Janet (ed.), *The Works of Aphra Behn*, 7 vols (London: William Pickering, 1992–96).

Selected secondary sources

Andreadis, Harriette, *Sappho in Early Modern England: Female Same-Sex Literary Erotics 1550–1714* (Chicago: University of Chicago Press, 2001).
Ballaster, Ros, *Seductive Forms: Women's Amatory Fiction from 1684 to 1740* (Oxford: Clarendon Press, 1992).
Hughes, Derek, *The Theatre of Aphra Behn* (Basingstoke: Palgrave now Palgrave Macmillan, 2001).
Hutner, Heidi, *Rereading Aphra Behn: History, Theory, Criticism* (Charlottesville: University Press of Virginia, 1993).
Lilley, Kate, 'True State within: Women's Elegy 1640–1740', in Isobel Grundy and Susan Wiseman (eds), *Women, Writing, History 1640–1740* (London: Batsford, 1992), pp. 72–92.
Lilley, Kate, 'Blazing Worlds: Seventeenth Century Women's Utopian Writing', in Clare Brant and Diane Purkiss (eds), *Women, Texts & Histories 1575–1760* (London: Routledge, 1992), pp. 102–33.
Medoff, Jeslyn, 'The Daughters of Behn and the Problem of Reputation', in Grundy and Wiseman, *Women, Writing, History*, pp. 33–54.
Mermin, Dorothy, 'Women Becoming Poets: Katherine Philips, Aphra Behn, Anne Finch', *English Literary History* 57 (1990), pp. 335–55.
Munns, Jessica, 'But to the touch were soft': Pleasure, Power, and Impotence in "The Disappointment" and "The Golden Age" ', in Todd, *Aphra Behn Studies*, pp. 178–96.
O'Donnell, Marry Anne, Bernard Dhuicq and Guyon Leduc, *Aphra Behn (1640–1689), Identity, Alterity, Ambiguity* (Paris: Harmattan, 2000).
Quaintance, Richard E., 'French Sources of the Restoration "Imperfect Enjoyment" Poem', *Philological Quarterly* XLII, 2 (1963), pp. 190–9.

Spencer, Jane, *Aphra Behn's Afterlife* (Oxford: Oxford University Press, 2000).

Todd, Janet (ed.), *Aphra Behn Studies* (Cambridge: Cambridge University Press, 1996).

Todd, Janet, *The Critical Fortunes of Aphra Behn* (Columbia: Camden House, 1998).

Todd, Janet (ed.), *Aphra Behn*, New Casebooks (Basingstoke: Macmillan now Palgrave Macmillan, 1999).

Wiseman, S. J., *Aphra Behn*, Writers and Their Work (Plymouth: Northcote House, 1996).

3
Anne Killigrew (1660–85): ' . . . let 'em Rage, and 'gainst a Maide Conspire'

David E. Shuttleton

The poet and painter Anne Killigrew died prematurely of smallpox on 16 June 1685. She was only 25 and had spent her short adulthood as a personal attendant to Mary, Beatrice of Modena, the Duchess of York, who had become queen to her husband James II (VII) less than six months prior to Killigrew's death. There is no evidence that Killigrew made any efforts to have her poetry printed, but she left behind a small but significant collection of manuscript poems covering a range of conventional genres including pastoral dialogues, philosophical meditations, moral epigrams and the opening of an abandoned epic. Her work reveals a serious concern with the craft of poetry and has a consistently high moral tone. Alongside undoubtedly sincere gestures towards spiritual transcendence, we detect in Killigrew's poetry an obvious desire for poetic 'Fame', but also a self-conscious awareness that her gender complicated any claims to literary authority.

All her mere 30 known poems were printed as *Poems by Mrs Anne Killigrew* (London, 1686), swiftly compiled with her father's approval within months of her death.[1] Designed as her memorial, it carries an engraved frontispiece derived from one of the poet's self-portraits.[2] Killigrew's own poems are prefaced by some tributary verses 'from the Publisher to the Reader' and 'The Epitaph Engraved on Her TOMB'[3] (both possibly by her father), but more famously by John Dryden's Pindaric ode 'To the Pious Memory of the Accomplisht Young Lady, Mrs Anne Killigrew'.

Dryden, a family associate, obviously knew Killigrew's poetry and paintings. In his ode, the early death of that double prodigy, a *female* poet *and* painter symbolizes redemptive innocence in a 'lubrique and

29

adult'rate age' when the muse has been rendered 'prostitute and profligate'. She is offered up as a sacrificial 'Vestal' to 'attone' for communal transgression. From the opening address to Killigrew as 'Thou Youngest Virgin of the Skies' to its closing vision of her apotheosis as a 'Sweet Saint', Dryden's ode renders its subject, in Joanna Lipking's telling phrase, 'a disembodied figure'.[4] It is not Killigrew's artistic talent – she is portrayed as an enthusiastic amateur – but her unsullied, testable innocence that concerns Dryden; an emphasis upon Killigrew's sexual chastity expressed more crudely in the often quoted phrase that 'a Virgin bright this POEM writ/A Grace for Beauty and a Muse for Wit!' from 'the Publisher to the Reader'.

Dryden's ode has often been commended – Samuel Johnson thought it 'undoubtedly the noblest ode our language has produced' – but, as Ann Messenger illustrates, although Killigrew's 'earliest biographers said Dryden did not exaggerate her worth', Dryden's readers often felt obliged 'to explain or explain away' such hyperbolic praise.[5] As Messenger succinctly observes, 'Dryden's praise stands, both literally and figuratively, between the reader and Anne Killigrew's poems'. While generations of critics, invariably male, have disagreed over what Dryden is doing in his tribute they have always assumed that Killigrew's own poetry was of no significance.[6] It is only with the recent recovery work of feminist critics that modern scholars have troubled actually to read her poetry (or trace her paintings).

In her lifetime Killigrew's poetry was widely circulated in manuscript (though no authorial manuscripts are extant).[7] Undoubtedly Dryden's ode kept Anne's name alive throughout the following century.[8] George Ballard's brief account of Killigrew in his *Memoirs of Several Ladies of Great Britain* (1752) was largely copied in subsequent biographical notices such as that prefacing the nine Killigrew poems included in *Poems by Eminent Ladies* (1757). But in the nineteenth and early twentieth centuries Killigrew's poetry was largely ignored, though her work as a painter was recognized in Ellen C. Clayton's *English Female Artists* (1876). Modern interest in Killigrew begins in 1967 with the publication of the Gainesville Facsimile reprint of her 1686 *Poems* with a short introduction by Richard Morton. Five poems were later included in *Kissing the Rod: an Anthology of Seventeenth-Century Women's Verse* (1988). Messenger's groundbreaking reappraisal appeared in her 1986 essay collection *His and Hers*. This has been followed by what now amounts to a substantial, if hitherto scattered, body of detailed criticism, and Killigrew is currently well represented on websites devoted to historical women's writing.

In contrast, our knowledge of Killigrew's biography remains meagre. Little has changed since 1876 when art historian Ellen Clayton observed that while 'much was said of her wit . . . no one thought it worthwhile to make the most trifling memorandum of even a solitary repartee'.[9] The few biographical facts mostly derive from Anthony Wood's *Athenae Oxoniensis* (1721), who partly relied upon information elicited from the poet's father.[10] Wood recorded that Anne Killigrew was 'born in St. Martin's lane in London . . . a little before the restoration of King Charles II, and christened in a private Chamber, when the offices in the Common-Prayer were not publicly allowed'.[11] We know nothing of Anne's mother Judith, but for several generations the Killigrews had been close associates with the Stuart court. Anne's father Dr Henry Killigrew (1613–1700) was Anglican Chaplain to James, Duke of York. At the Restoration he was reinstated as a Prebendery of Westminster and made Master of the Savoy Hospital. He had a tragedy, *The Conspiracy*, performed in 1638 (published as *Pallantus and Eudora*, 1653) and published sermons and poems. Anne's two paternal uncles were more particularly engaged with the theatre. The eldest, Sir William Killigrew (1606–95), a gentleman-usher to Charles I, and later Vice-Chamberlain to Charles II's queen, published two collections of plays. The younger uncle, Thomas Killigrew (1612–83), a page to Charles I and Vice-Chamberlain to Queen Henrietta Maria, later became private groom to Charles II who tolerated his scandalous antics. He wrote numerous comedies and was granted a patent by Charles II to build the public theatre eventually known as Drury Lane.

Anne Killigrew's childhood intimacy with this theatrical culture provides a context for understanding her later poetic use of coterie codes and shifting voices. Wood records that she was 'tenderly educated', but in a backhanded compliment Dryden claimed that 'Art she had none, yet wanted, none./For Nature did that want supply' (Stanza V). In response, Messenger asks rhetorically: 'Does knowledge of the Bible, of classical mythology, and of contemporary philosophical debate come from "nature"?'[12] Dryden was probably prompted by Killigrew's own claim, at the opening of 'The Discontent', that lack of technical polish can more fully represent human truth:

> Here take no Care, take here no Care, my Muse,
> Nor ought of Art or Labour use:
> But let thy lines rude and unpolish't go,
> Nor Equal be their feet, nor Num'rous let them flow.

The ruggeder my measures run when read,
They'll livelier paint th'unequal Paths fond Mortals tread. (p. 51)

Dryden was happy to take Killigrew's rhetorical allusions to her 'dull muse' literally. In contrast, for Messenger these opening lines reveal Killigrew's sophisticated use of the varying line lengths and rhymes of the Pindaric form in a display of 'virtuosity most appropriate because prosody is itself the subject of the lines', a technique of matching 'sound' to 'sense' employed by Dryden himself and later by Alexander Pope.[13] In short, if Killigrew was not always the most technically sophisticated poet, she was not a naive primitive. Nor was Killigrew unaware of the impact her gender could have upon critical reception, as revealed in her best-known poem, 'Upon the saying that my verses were made by another'.

When reading early Augustan poetry we cannot always assume the personal authenticity of the poetic voice, but Killigrew's 'Upon the saying' is surely the nearest we get in her oeuvre to autobiography. It belongs within a recognizable sub-genre of poems in which women respond directly to hostile reactions to their assumption of literary authority.[14] 'Upon the saying' opens with an invocation recollecting her commitment to poetry – 'Next Heaven my Vows to thee (O Sacred Muse!)/I offer'd up, nor didst's thou them refuse' – and her promise to value the 'Muses laurel' more than 'a Crown of Gold'. This is addressed to her Royal patroness as the 'Queen of Verse' to whom the poet offers herself up as an 'undivided sacrifice', body and soul (p. 44). When 'the judicious praise'd my Pen', she was 'Emboldened' with ambition for 'Fame', but

By thee deceiv'd, methought, each Verdant Tree,
Apollos transform'd *Daphne* seem'd to be;
And ev'ry fresher Branch, and ev'ry Bow
Appear'd as garlands to empale my Brow . . . (p. 45)

When her poems are circulated in manuscript disbelieving readers attribute them to some other established poet: 'My Laurels thus an Others Brow adorn'd./My Numbers they admir'd, but Me they scorn'd.' Like Aesop's 'Painted Jay' who was 'Riffl'd' for parading in borrowed feathers, Killigrew bitterly records how 'What ought t'have brought me Honour, brought me shame!' She compares this humiliation with the high praise accorded 'The Matchless Orinda', the poet Katherine Philips, who 'Ow'd not her Glory to a Beauteous face', but to her inner worth, 'Nor did her Sex at all obstruct her Fame'.[15] Killigrew closes 'Upon the saying' by dismissing her critics – 'But let 'em Rage, and 'gainst a Maide Conspire' – and recommitting herself to poetry with the assertion that 'I willing accept Cassandra's Fate,/To Speak the truth, although believ'd too late'.

Cassandra, the prophetess who was punished for refusing Apollo's sexual advances by being never believed provides a perhaps fitting but fatalistic model of the female poet for Killigrew to adopt. Kristina Straub argues provocatively that although 'the word "rape" is never mentioned in the poem', Killigrew's allusive use of myth establishes 'a metaphorical paradigm in which she envisions herself as victimized by her audience and more finally and devastatingly by poetry itself in the person of Apollo'. For Straub, 'Upon the saying' is 'an attempt to force her readers to recognize their own complicity in her victimization'.[16] Taking issue, Carol Barash responds that

> Apollo has not metaphorically raped the speaker . . . rather her belief in her own writing has caused her to imagine the myth from the male poet's point of view: Daphne has not been raped but 'transform'd' into the laurel branch to crown the conceited female Petrachan poet.

Nonetheless Barash agrees that the phrase 'empale my Brow' implies that worldly 'Fame' is 'confining, if not violently dangerous to the woman poet'. Barash notes that this conflicted relationship is felt elsewhere in Killigrew's poetry where 'Fame' always serves to 'draw her back to the stakes of worldly success', when she would prefer a more distanced position from which to adopt a prophetic voice.[17]

More generally, Barash draws attention to Killigrew's place within the coterie surrounding Mary of Modena, where another maid of honour was the young poet Anne Finch, later Countess of Winchilsea. In keeping with a French tradition of *precieuses* (aristocratic women intellectuals), Mary of Modena 're-created . . . a sense of a female community associated with European convents' at an English court where, despite her devout image, she encouraged continental music, theatrics and literature. In its English post-Restoration version, this gynocentric subculture drew upon the image of the *femme forte* (heroic woman) to make claims for artistic and political authority.[18] It exalted complex relationships between mistress and servant as pertained in the pre-war court of Queen Henrietta Maria. Thus in Killigrew's 'On My Aunt Mrs A. K. Drown'd under London-bridge, in the QUEENS Bardge [*sic*], Anno

1641', the subject is recollected as being so noble that she 'seem'd a Friend, not servant to the Queen' (p. 76). As Barash observes, Killigrew frequently invokes such relationships 'ambiguously situated between the spiritual quality of friendship, which undermines the class differences . . . and royal allegory, in which the servants' individual lives cease to matter' (notably in 'On the Birth day of Queen Katherine' and 'To The Queen', both addressed to Charles II's wife, Catherine of Braganza).[19]

As placed in the 1686 sequence, 'To The Queen' forms a sequel to the opening unfinished epic fragment 'Alexandreis', celebrating Alexander the Great. This begins with a confident call for a muse fit to celebrate this 'King-Destroying King'. Although Killigrew trusts that her presumptive 'female Pen' will not 'his Conquests derogate', she soon loses faith: 'Ah, that some pitying Muse would now inspire/My frozen style with a Poetique fire'. The fragment ends just as the *femme forte* figure of Panthesilea, 'Th'Heroick' Queen of the Amazons, is set to challenge Alexander. Here an editorial endnote states that this 'was the first essay of this Young Lady in poetry, but finding the task she had undertaken hard, she laid it by till Practice and more time should make her equal the great Work' (p. 5). Killigrew explains her own failure to complete her 'first flight' in poetry in 'To the Queen', where a pivotal point is the speaker's realization that her 'Heav'n-born Queen' is a more worthy subject: 'And from that time I'gan to treat/With Pitty him the World call'd Great' (p. 7). Here Killigrew comes very close to a wholesale critique of the masculine values behind the 'ill deeds' of epic heroes who 'Whole Kingdoms do depopulate,/To raise a proud and short-liv'd State' (p. 7). Instead, Killigrew choses to rear 'Altars of Praises . . . /Like a Queen's Present, to a Queen' (p. 7), by comparing herself with the Old Testament figure Araunah the Jebusite, a humble man who becomes kinglike by gifting the materials needed for a sacrifice to King David (2 Samuel 24.16–25). However, as Barash notes, once the queen's virtue is allegorized she disappears from the poem leaving the speaker likening herself to a dove that flies 'Between the Deluge and the Skie'. Killigrew often employs this redemptive biblical image of the dove released from Noah's Ark but also evocative of the Holy Ghost, to present a spiritualized image of herself as a poet who shuns earthly ambitions for a higher spiritual calling.[20]

Killigrew's pastoral dialogues address more worldly romantic concerns. In the 1686 frontispiece Killigrew is dressed as a fashionable court beauty; Wood left a note that she was 'of so curious, so pleasing a feature & exact symmetry of body, yt some men esteemed her generally a Goddess & the Venus of the earth'.[21] In her pastoral lyric 'Love, the Soul of Poetry', Killigrew upholds a courtly cult of Venus, but in a resolutely Platonic strain reminiscent of the Society of Friendship encouraged by Philips.[22] Killigrew remained Anglican, but her emphasis upon 'Virgin Love' (p. 12) is in keeping with the court values of Mary of Modena, a devout Catholic who opposed the licentiousness associated with her brother-in-law, Charles II. In this context, Killigrew's 'On a Picture Painted by her self, representing two Nimphs [*sic*] of DIANA's, in a posture to Hunt, the other batheing', implies a deliberate counter-allegory representing Mary of Modena's coterie for whom mythological poetry could subtly encode political criticism:

> We are *Diana's* Virgin-Train,
> Descended of no Mortal Strain; [. . .]
> We *Fawns* and Shaggy *Satyrs* awe;
> To *Sylvan* Pow'rs we give the Law:
> Whatever does provoke our Hate,
> Our Javelins strike, as sure as *Fate*;
> Though *Venus* we transcend in Form,
> No wanton Flames our Bosomes warm! (pp. 28–9)

This prompted Dryden to insist that when Killigrew's muse spoke of love it 'Was but a *lambent-flame* which play'd about her Brest':

> So cold herself, which she such Warmth exprest,
> 'Twas *Cupid* bathing in *Diana's* Stream. (Stanza V)

To modern readers 'cold' has negative connotations but, as Messenger notes, in the late seventeenth century it could simply mean chaste, adding that Dryden nonetheless acknowledges the 'warmth' of passion in Killigrew's love poetry.[23] More crucially, Dryden's insistence on essentially *passive* female virtues downplays the assertive, implicitly political claim for female empowerment felt when Killigrew boldly speaks as one of Diana's attendants.

Killigrew's 1686 *Poems* close with three striking, interrelated odes headed by an editorial note stating that 'being found among Mrs Killigrew's papers, I was willing to print though none of hers' (p. 84). It has been argued on stylistic evidence alone that they *are* the work of Killigrew, and unconvincingly conjectured that her father denied his daughter's authorship because of their sensational contents.[24] For Messenger they 'appear to be concerned with a tragic love for a woman and the poet's rescue from despair by another woman, who in turn practised flagellation on yet another woman'.[25] Without endorsing Messenger's explicitly homo-erotic reading, Barash nonetheless agrees that

> if we shift our emphasis from the question of who wrote them to the question of what culture produced them . . . it becomes clear that they are filled with stories and allusions that grow out of the myth and ritual at the court of Mary of Modena.[26]

There where rumours of lesbianism at Mary's court, but while Killigrew was obviously aware of the homosocial cult of female friendship surrounding Philips, the extent to which such contemporary expressions of intense female same-sex love and desire can be interpreted as fully sexual remains a matter for debate.[27] Killigrew's poems certainly contain unexplored clues that could lead to further biographical information, but while it seems unlikely that any unknown poems will emerge from the archive, there is every chance that eventually more Killigrew paintings will be either traced or, after cleaning, rightfully identified as hers. An extant self-portrait, in which Killigrew stands in front of a framed canvas amid fragments of classical sculpture and looks straight at the viewer while pointing to an unfurled manuscript held up in her other hand, suggests her own sense of an inextricable connection between her work as both poet and painter.[28]

A note on Anne Killigrew's paintings

A portrait of Mary of Modena mentioned by Dryden is untraced, but a full-length portrait of James, Duke of York, once attributed to the 'school of Lely' but revealed on cleaning to bear Killigrew's signature, is in the Royal collection. Two other extant paintings, *Venus Attired by the Graces* and a self-portrait in a symbolic landscape, are both in private collections.[29] In addition we have I. Beckett's frontispiece engraving of an untraced self-portrait, and an engraving by Lens (Yale Center for British Art) of a lost *Venus and Adonis*. Three of her poems describe untraced paintings: *Herodias' Daughter Presenting her Mother St John the Baptist's Head on a Charger, St John the Baptist in the Wilderness* and *Two Nimphs [sic] of DIANA's, in a posture to Hunt, the other batheing*. The notebooks of George Vertue (British Library, Add Mss 23,070), record several of Killigrew's paintings being auctioned with her brother's effects in 1727, including a *Satyr Playing a Pipe*, a *Judith and Holofernes* and a *Woman's Head* (all untraced).[30] Barash in particular has made links between her dark, brooding landscapes littered with narrative classical sculptural fragments and the atmosphere of some poems. Other paintings imply the female appropriation of biblical and Classical themes and may reflect Killigrew's knowledge of the works of Artemisia Gentileschi.[31] Horace Walpole (II, 106) reprinted a portrait of Anne Killigrew engraved by J. Thomson drawn 'from an original by Sir Peter Lely' (this latter privately owned, but photograph with the National Portrait Gallery, London). Lely may have been Killigrew's teacher.

Notes

1. Anne Killigrew, *Poems by Anne Killigrew* [1686] *A Facsimile Reproduction with an Introduction by Richard Morton* (Gainesville, Florida: Scholars' Facsimiles & Reprints, 1967), prelim. [a]. Subsequent references, in parentheses, are to this edition. Hugh Macdonald, *John Dryden: a Bibliography of Early Editions and Drydeniana* (Oxford: Clarendon Press, 1939), pp. 42–3.
2. Engraved from Killigrew's original in two versions, by I. Beckett's engraving: see Macdonald, *John Dryden*, p. 43.
3. From a marble memorial erected in the Savoy Chapel but entirely destroyed by fire in the 1870s.
4. Joanna Lipking, 'Fair Originals: Women Poets in Male Commendatory Poems', *Eighteenth-Century Life* 12 (1988), pp. 58–72 (62).
5. Ann Messenger, 'A Problem of Praise: John Dryden and Anne Killigrew', *His and Hers: Essays in Restoration and Eighteenth-Century Literature* (Lexington: University Press of Kentucky, 1986), pp. 14–40 (15); and Dryden's possible motives, pp. 36–40. See also David M. Vieth, 'Irony in Dryden's Ode to Anne Killigrew', *Studies in Philology* 62 (1965), pp. 91–100.
6. Messenger, 'Problem of Praise', p. 15.
7. Carol Barash, *English Women's Poetry, 1649–1714: Politics, Community, and Linguistic Authority* (Oxford: Clarendon Press, 1996), traces unpublished examples of Killigrew imitations and elegies: see p. 163, footnote 38; example by Chatwin (Bod. MSS Rawlinson. Poet, 94, fos. 149–52) printed as Appendix D; Stuart Gillespie, 'Another Pindaric Ode "To the Pious Memory of Mrs Ann Killigrew" ', *Restoration: Studies in English Literary Culture, 1660–1700* 20, I (Spring 1996), pp. 31–5.
8. In 1691 the poet's father referred Wood 'to her Book' which 'you say is in many hands at Oxon [Oxford]', but had a copy to send. Allan Pritchard, 'According to Wood: Sources of Anthony Wood's Lives of the Poets and Dramatists', *Review of English Studies*, New Series, 28 (August 1977), pp. 268–89.
9. Ellen Creathorne Clayton, *English Female Artists*, 2 vols (London: 1876), Vol. I, p. 66. Clayton relates Killigrew's obscurity to a wider problem of women's history, English female artists in particular, where we 'feel as if in the presence of a circle of wax models'.
10. Pritchard, 'According to Wood', pp. 272–90.
11. Anthony Wood, *Athenae Oxoniensis: An Exact History of all the Writers and Bishops who have had their Education at the University of Oxford* (Oxford: 1721), Vol. 2, Columns 1,035–6.

12. Messenger, 'Problem of Praise', p. 19.
13. Ibid., p. 26.
14. Examples cited in the notes on 'Upon the saying', in Germaine Greer, Susan Hastings, Jeslyn Medoff and Melinda Sansone (eds), *Kissing the Rod: an Anthology of Seventeenth-Century Women's Verse* (London: Virago Press, 1988), pp. 299–308 (306).
15. As a Maid of Honour Killigrew may have attended a performance of Philips's translations of Corneille's *Pompey* and *Horace.*
16. Kristina Straub, 'Indecent Liberties with a Poet: Audience and the Metaphor of Rape in Killigrew's "Upon the Saying" and Pope's "Arbuthnot" ', *Tulsa Studies in Woman's Literature* 6, I (1987), pp. 27–45 (30).
17. Barash, *English Women's Poetry,* p. 166.
18. Quotation Barash, *English Women's Poetry,* pp. 150 and 32–40 (*precieuse* tradition).
19. Ibid., p. 162.
20. Ibid. and Messenger, 'Problem of Praise', p. 18.
21. Pritchard, 'According to Wood', p. 289, quoting Bod. Tanner MSS, 454, f. 55.
22. Messenger ('Problem of Praise', p. 30) suggests that in referring to 'Dorinda's matchless Laies' in 'A Pastoral Dialogue' (p. 11) Killigrew may be alluding to Philips as 'The Matchless Orinda'.
23. Messenger, 'Problem of Praise', p. 24.
24. Ibid., p. 29 (but why not simply suppress them?).
25. Ibid.
26. Barash, *English Women's Poetry,* p. 154 (and footnote 19).
27. Ibid.; Harriette Andreadis, 'The Sapphic-Platonics of Katherine Philips, 1632–1664', *Signs: Journal of Women in Culture and Society* 15, i (1989), pp. 34–60.
28. Reproduced in Barash, *English Women's Poetry,* p. 158.
29. Ibid., pp. 158–61.
30. Vertue, BL Add. MS, 23,070. A portrait of Thomas Killigrew at Lumley Castle, 'painted by another Killigrew', may be Anne's.
31. Barash, *English Women's Poetry,* pp. 157–8.

Bibliography

Biographical sources

Ballard, George, *Memoirs of Several Ladies of Great Britain, who have been celebrated for their writing or skill in the learned languages, arts and sciences* (Oxford: printed for the author by W. Jackson, 1752), pp. 337–45.

Loftis, William John, *Memorials of the Savoy* (London: 1878), pp. 199–200.

Pritchard, Allan, 'According to Wood: Sources of Anthony Wood's Lives of the Poets and Dramatists', *Review of English Studies,* New Series, 28 (August 1977), pp. 268–89.

Reynolds, Myra, *The Learned Lady in England 1650–1760* (Boston, New York and Cambridge: Houghton Miflin Company; Cambridge University Press, 1920), pp. 85–86, 139–41.

Wood, Anthony, *Athenae Oxoniensis: An Exact History of all the Writers and Bishops who have had their Education at the University of Oxford* (Oxford: 1721), Vol. 2, Columns 1,035–6.

Library and modern editions

Greer, Germaine, Susan Hastings, Jeslyn Medoff and Melinda Sansone (eds), *Kissing the Rod: an Anthology of Seventeenth-Century Women's Verse* (London: Virago Press, 1988), pp. 299–308.

Killigrew, Anne, *Poems by Mrs Anne Killigrew* [1686] *A Facsimile Reproduction with an Introduction by Richard Morton* (Gainesville, Florida: Scholars' Facsimiles & Reprints, 1967).

Selected secondary sources

Andreadis, Harriette, 'The Sapphic-Platonics of Katherine Philips, 1632–1664', *Signs: Journal of Women in Culture and Society* 15, i (1989), pp. 34–60.

Barash, Carol, *English Women's Poetry, 1649–1714: Politics, Community, and Linguistic Authority* (Oxford: Clarendon Press, 1996), pp. 149–174 (and reproduces extant paintings).

Gillespie, Stuart, 'Another Pindaric Ode "To the Pious Memory of Mrs Ann Killigrew"', *Restoration: Studies in English Literary Culture, 1660–1700* 20, I (Spring 1996), pp. 31–5.

Greer, Germaine, *Slip-Shod Sibyls: Recognition, Rejection and the Woman Poet* (London: Viking-Penguin, 1995), pp. 24–5.

Hobby, Elaine, *Virtue of Necessity: English Women's Writing, 1649–1688* (Anne Arbour: The University of Michigan Press, 1989).

Lipking, Joanna, 'Fair Originals: Women Poets in Male Commendatory Poems', *Eighteenth-Century Life* 12 (1988), pp. 58–72 (esp. 62–4).

Macdonald, Hugh, *John Dryden: a Bibliography of Early Editions and Drydeniana* (Oxford: Clarendon Press, 1939), pp. 42–3.

Messenger, Ann, 'A Problem of Praise: John Dryden and Anne Killigrew', *His and Hers: Essays in Restoration and Eighteenth-Century Literature* (Lexington: University Press of Kentucky, 1986), pp. 14–40; reprints 'The Discontent' and 'Cloris Charmes Dissolved by Eudora', pp. 226–34.

Straub, Kristina, 'Indecent Liberties with a Poet: Audience and the Metaphor of Rape in Killigrew's "Upon the Saying" and Pope's "Arbuthnot"', *Tulsa Studies in Woman's Literature* 6, I (1987), pp. 27–45.

Killigrew as painter

Barash, Carol, *English Women's Poetry, 1649–1714* (as above), reproduces extant paintings 158; pp. 160–1.

Clayton, Ellen C., *English Female Artists*, 2 vols (London: 1876), Vol. 1, pp. 56–70.

Reynolds, Myra, *The Learned Lady* (as above under Biography), pp. 85–6.

Walpole, Horace, *Anecdotes of Painting in England, with some account of the principal artists* [1762–71]; revised with additions by James Dalloway [etc.] four volumes (London: n.d.), Vol. 2, pp. 106–7.

4
Jane Barker (1652–1732): From Galesia to Mrs Goodwife

Carol Shiner Wilson

The literary oeuvre of Jane Barker, from her earliest days as composer of coterie poetry to her last publications of fiction for pay, is a chorus of richly varied voices, shifting tones and topics, always felt and alive: witty, playful, erudite, melancholic, vigorous. Her literature and life are testimony to resilience, female agency and the skilful negotiation of turbulent political times and a dynamically transforming literary landscape. Several times marginalized – unmarried by choice, often financially distressed, Jacobite, convert to Roman Catholicism, and woman writer – Barker strove to make virtue of necessity, including publishing for pay and promoting a mythology of a saintly James II. Little known by critics before Jane Spencer's 1983 article,[1] Barker now figures prominently in scholarship examining female authorship, the shift from manuscript to print publication, the emergence of the novel, and Jacobite poetry. Barker suggests her own intellectual and economic odyssey by her ongoing (re)constructions of Galesia, her semi-autobiographical literary persona, and the later construction of Mrs Goodwife, a Jacobite who transforms hardship into independence and cash.[2]

Barker was baptized on 17 May 1652 in Blatherwycke, Northamptonshire.[3] She died in 1732 in St Germain-en-Laye, France, once the court-in-exile of James II and her own residence in exile from 1689 to 1704. Barker's family had lost position, property and lives in battle in the Stuart cause. Her father Thomas Barker was secretary to the Lord Chancellor under Charles I.[4] Anne Connock, her mother, was of a Cornish family that fought in the Stuart armies. Although archival records fill in knowledge of Barker's life, much of our understanding remains shaped by her construction of Galesia, speaker in many of her poems and the semi-autobiographical narrator/protagonist/heroine of her fiction.[5] A learned country gentlewoman, Barker acquired some of her education through her brother, Edward, who studied medicine at Oxford University. Her 'faithfull'st *Lover*',[6] he died in 1675.[7] By her twenties, Barker vowed never to marry. Her studies included medicine, both academic and herbal, and Latin classics. She knew the medical theories of ancients Aristotle and Galen and contemporaries Harvey, Willis and Lower. Familiar with Ovid and Horace, she followed the latter's dictum in *Ars Poetica* of pleasing and instructing. In her early work, she alludes to Sidney, Philips, Behn, Cowley, Rochester and Dryden. In her later fiction, she incorporates popular tales, stock characters of romance, and even a market-place challenge to Defoe.

Barker's earliest literary compositions were poetical works, circulated among family and friends, including students at Cambridge University and a London publisher, Benjamin Crayle.[8] Barker's pen name was 'Galesia', the feminized form of 'Galaesus', son of Apollo, god of poetry and medicine. Barker's poems were published as Part I of *Poetical Recreations* (1688)[9] under her name, although 'without her consent', she later claimed.[10] Numbering over fifty, the poems range from charming occasional verse to sober poems on the death of her brother. 'A Virgin Life' celebrates the possibilities of female agency in singlehood (*PR*, pp. 12–13; *PWS*, pp. 139–40), and 'On the *Apothecary's* Filing my Bills amongst the *Doctor's*' (*PR*, pp. 31–4; *PWS*, pp. 116–19) celebrates Barker's creation of a medical plaster. Kathryn King discovered a 1685 advertisement for '*Dr. Barkers* Famous *Gout Plaister*' for sale at Crayle's bookshop.[11] Several poems examine the speaker's poetic vocation, including '*Necessity of Fate*' (*PR*, pp. 38–9; *PWS*, pp. 141–3), 'To My *Friends*, Against *Poetry*' (*PR*, pp. 95–6; *PWS*, pp. 127–8) and 'A Farewell to *Poetry*, with a long Digression on *Anatomy*' (*PR*, pp. 99–106; *PWS*, pp. 85–90). Commendatory verse by her associates places Barker among Spenser, Jonson and Shakespeare and designates her the successor to Katherine Philips, the 'Matchless Orinda'.

Part II of *Poetical Recreations* is a miscellany of verse, much of it by her male associates. A few poems are addressed to Galesia, and Crayle suggests that he would publish a royalist prose allegory by Barker. However, that work – *Exilius, or the Banish'd Roman* – did not appear until August 1714.[12] The Galesia of *Exilius* is a commanding Numidian princess and huntress of panthers, 'a Lady of Masculine Spirit' (*Exilius*, p. 32). Early on, then, Barker was writing verse and prose and was experimenting with different 'Galesia' figures.

After her father's death in 1681, Barker and her mother relocated to London. Presumably at this period, Barker converted to Roman Catholicism and met Poet Laureate John Dryden. When James II fled

London in 1688 following William of Orange's invasion of England, Barker was one of almost 40,000 supporters – soon to be called Jacobites – to follow James into exile. She lived with her cousin William Connock who later served as Barker's amanuensis.[13] Before fleeing London, Barker witnessed terrifying anti-Catholic riots (*MM*, p. 31). Her years in St Germain witnessed war, plague, famine and crushed hopes for a Stuart restoration. In France, Barker wrote and circulated her poetry privately.

Today Magdalen College, Oxford University, holds a three-part manuscript volume with 79 Barker poems. Part I, 'Refering to the Times', also exists as a 1700 New Year's gift volume for the 12-year-old Prince of Wales.[14] The 20 poems of Part I powerfully combine personal and public events, including 'Fidelia alone lamenting her parents lately dead, and her relations gone to the west against Monmoth' (*MM*, pp. 28–30). Fidelia, Barker's religious, poetic voice, also reflects upon her adopted Catholic faith. Poems in Part II, most written after Barker's relocation to France, celebrate the Stuarts, reflect upon religion, and describe the suffering of noncombatants. Barker also reveals that, because her 'eys [were] bound doun' after cataract surgery, she was unable to bid farewell to the king and his troops at Calais in 1696.[15] Parts I and II of the Magdalen MS manifest an urgency, political advocacy and solemnity unlike the poems of *Poetical Recreations*.

Part III includes 32 of the over fifty poems from the original *Poetical Recreations*, 'now corrected by [Barker's] own hand' (*MM*, p. 43) and accompanied by revealing glosses, marginalia and prefatory material. She interpolated several revised poems in her fiction, thereby significantly expanding the readership of her poetry. Scholars have begun to examine the three versions of the poems in order to chart Barker's revisioning of the woman artist and politics.

Barker returned to England in 1704. As a Catholic, she suffered many indignities, including double taxation on an inherited farm where she could barely scrape out a living.[16] She turned to publishing fiction in order to survive financially. *Love Intrigues* was published in 1713, its author designated 'A Young Lady'. Galesia its heroine, this extraordinary piece of psychological realism is an anti-romance, suspicious of idealized love and terrified of erotic love.[17]

Exilius appeared under Barker's name in 1715, and in 1718 Edmund Curll published her *Christian Pilgrimage*, a translation of Catholic Bishop Fenelon's Lenten meditations, dedicated to Anne, Countess of Nottingham, a devout Anglican.[18] *Love Intrigues* and *Exilius* were published together as *The Entertaining Novels of Mrs. Jane Barker* in

1719 and dedicated to Elizabeth Brownlow, Countess of Exeter.[19] A German version of the *Entertaining Novels* appeared in 1721. Other editions appeared in English after Barker's death: 1733, 1736 and 1743.

Barker claimed that the popularity of *Entertaining Novels* encouraged her to write a sequel to Galesia's story. *A Patch-Work Screen for the Ladies* (1723) is a 'lively hybrid genre – romance, bourgeois fiction, poems, hymns, odes, recipes, philosophical reflections, and more – woven together by multiple narrators, pulled together by principal narrator Galesia, with the whole introduced by the self-conscious narrator as author, Jane Barker'.[20] Reconfiguring Chaucer and Boccaccio, the work continues the sociability of coterie poetry through Barker's interpolated poems.

Central to the work is the celebration of women's quotidian, a sewn patchwork screen, as artistic and political vehicle worthy to explore the complexities of human nature. Galesia apologizes to her hostess for having no actual fabric to provide for a collaboratively worked screen. Rather, she has only her literary works: 'Pieces of *Romances*, *Poems*, Love-*Letters*, and the like' (*PWS*, p. 74). The lady validates Galesia as artist and woman when she asks her to place her literary creations alongside fabric contributed by the other women (*PWS*, p. 74). Her last work, *The Lining of the Patch Work Screen* (1726), mythologizes noble Jacobites whose St Germain epitomizes humility, piety, compassion, honour and esteem (*Lining*, p. 222).

Ill and virtually blind, Barker returned to France in 1727 to live with William Connock. Parish records note that 'Jeanne Barker' died in St Germain on 29 March 1732 (*Archives*).

Scholars emphasize female agency in Barker, beginning with the unmarried speaker in 'A Virgin Life' (1688). A poem of rural retreat, it participates in the 'female literary convention . . . [of] antimarriage poems' examined by Margaret Ezell.[21] The speaker celebrates her freedom to help her 'Neighb'ring Poor . . . serve her God, enjoy her Books and Friends' (*PR*, p. 13). Yet fear of male dominance complicates her claim: baby goats are devoured in the '*Lyon's Den*' of men's power (*PR*, p. 12; *PWS*, p. 140).

The most complete portrait of female agency is Mrs Goodwife in *Lining* (1726). Married to an ineffectual husband, she functions as might Barker's ideal single woman. Setting aside her genteel habits while keeping her genteel sensibilities, Mrs Goodwife uses ingenuity, hard work and small funds to build a thriving business in London (*Lining*, pp. 218–21).

Barker further complicates the agency of 'A Virgin Life' in later works concerning Galesia as intellectual. Destined by Fate to devote her life to learning and poetry, Galesia comments on her alienation: 'A Learned Woman [is] . . . at best but like a Forc'd Plant' (*PWS*, p. 83), doomed never fully to enjoy the fruits of 'the [Edenic] *Tree of Knowledge*' more readily tasted by men (*PWS*, p. 94). Initially an enthusiastic young woman, ostensibly seduced by the Muses into believing she would achieve the greatness of Katherine Philips, Galesia becomes a wise woman bemused by her young self's belief that she was '*Apollo's* darling Daughter, and Maid of Honour to the Muses' (*LI*, p. 15). Flattery and youthful ambition, not the Muses, were to blame.

Railing against the Muses in the collective, Galesia values her own muse as a friend who helps her 'discharge [her] Griefs' at her brother's death (*PWS*, p. 92) and who is to her mind 'so very good,/Its Consolation, Physick, Food' (*PWS*, pp. 123–4). Descendant of the Horatian pedestrian Muse, this friend also strides beside Galesia, who sings her own praise as a 'fam'd Physician' whose 'soft Female Hands' conquer 'the *Sturdy Gout*' (*PWS*, p. 117).

Barker relinquishes the anxiety and ambivalence regarding the poetic task in the dream sequence in *Lining*. Galesia's 'good Genius' tucks her unseen in a corner where she can observe the elaborate Annual Coronation of Orinda. The Faery Queen spots Galesia, hands some gold to a servant to take to the uninvited guest, and dismisses the mortal from the scene (*Lining*, pp. 275–7). As scholars note, Galesia is expelled into the new world of literary production for pay.[22] Unlike Spencer and King, I believe that while Barker may regret the passing of the world of genteel literary production, she is more liberated than discarded. After all, Mrs Goodwife does not dwell on regret for a world of genteel privilege but embraces the new world of commerce. She is a realistic reincarnation of the energy and independence of the Numidian princess of *Exilius*. Liberated by the production of prose for pay, Barker writes this jaunty address to her new readership: '*be sure to buy these* Patches *up quickly*' (*PWS*, p. 54). She knows that her work will, in the Horatian fashion, please and instruct. She also hopes to earn some cash.

Barker's literary Jacobitism also stimulates current scholarly interest. Carol Barash's *English Women's Poetry, 1649–1714* portrays Barker as a prominent political voice for whom Jacobitism and Roman Catholicism were inextricably bound together.[23] In her dedication to the 1700 'Refering to the Times', Barker addresses the Prince of Wales with the 'zeal and affection of a votary', claiming that she feels a 'secret satisfaction to have suffered something for such a cause' (*MM*, p. 25). Barker gave meaning to the suffering of all Jacobites and herself by constructing what King calls 'a mythology of banished righteousness . . . [intended to] turn the bleakness of exile into an affirmation of Jacobite ideals'.[24] Powerful biblical images link the royal family to that mythology. The Prince of Wales, for example, is compared to a tender and loving Christ whose 'royal life' is sought by 'Hell and Herods'.[25] After seeing the body of James II lying in state, Barker calls him a 'Hero, King, and glorious saint'.[26] She desired sainthood for James II, believing that the touch of cloth dipped in his blood had cured her niece's diseased eye and what she called 'a deaths head' on her own breast.[27]

Personal religious faith is linked to public events in the seven 'Fidelia' poems in the Magdalen MS. In her preface, Barker indicated that Fidelia was 'to speak the common dialect of Catholicks' (*MM*, p. 27). The speaker recounts the loss of her parents, her conversion to Roman Catholicism and her anguish and alienation in a world gone mad with war. Virulent images of the Jacobites' suffering and the perfidy of England's traitors appear in the powerful 'Miseries of St. Germains' where people cry for bread and mothers die unable to feed their children.[28] William, 'that monster Orange' in league with Lucifer, is responsible for the suffering of all caught in the conflict over succession.[29] As Barash notes, Barker's linking of William to Lucifer and the Ill Genius conveys 'the pain and sterility of loss rather than the closure of victory'.[30]

Barker circulated the manuscript exile poems among Jacobites in order to articulate a common vision, to assure its survival and probably to gain preferment at court. Although Barker's manuscript poems were known among some Jacobites, the largest number of readers would have known the Jacobite myth through *Lining*. In those narratives, set in England, Captain Manly, Lady Allgood and Mrs Goodwife claim that 'Vertue and Honour' were 'inseparable Companions' at St Germain (*Lining*, p. 222). From the poem 'Lovers Elesium', Toni Bowers argues that Barker was bitterly disappointed by the failure both of the Jacobite cause and the poetic calling, leaving her 'at once wholly committed and deeply equivocal'.[31]

Barker's readership over time has been significant if not large. Barash notes that Anne Finch and John Dryden read Barker.[32] *Poetical Recreations* was read well after its publication, as we learn from sources including the commonplace book of Poet Laureate, Robert Southey.[33] Certainly, many Barker poems were known through different editions of her fiction. Three Barker poems appeared in *British Anthologies* (1899–1901), containing poems 'with which every one ought to be acquainted'.[34] Garland reprinted *Exilius, Love Intrigues* and *Patch-Work Screen* in the 1970s. In 1985, two Barker poems appeared in *First Feminists*,[35] and three poems, including 'A Virgin Life' and the 'anatomy' poem, appeared in *Kissing the Rod* in 1989.[36] Barker's clever advertisement to the reader of *Patch-Work Screen* has been reproduced in several anthologies. In the early 1990s, the Women Writers Project, Brown University, made her works available through their electronic database. My Oxford edition of *The Galesia Trilogy and Selected Manuscript Poems of Jane Barker*, published in 1997, contains 17 poems from Part II of the Magdalen MS. In 1998 King published *The Poems of Jane Barker: the Magdalen Manuscript*, including 16 full-text poems and an index of first lines of all poems.

Although the poetry of Jane Barker is the focus of this volume, we must acknowledge the significance of her entire oeuvre, poetry and prose. Her richly varied tone and literary types, her participation in manuscript publication and publication for pay, and her voice as a single woman, committed political partisan and convert to Catholicism will continue to provide scholars with rich material for study and debate.[37]

Notes

1. Jane Spencer, 'Creating the Woman Writer: the Autobiographical Works of Jane Barker', *Tulsa Studies in Women's Literature* 2 (Fall 1983), pp. 165–81.
2. I introduced the Galesia to Goodwife theme in a 1996 Modern Language Association paper.
3. Northamptonshire Record Office, Blatherwycke Parish Register, 1621–89, 34, P/1.
4. Archives Municipales de Saint-Germain-en-Laye, Registre GG 99, 451. Cited as Archives.
5. See Kathryn R. King, with the assistance of Jeslyn Modoff, 'Jane Barker and Her Life (1652–1732): the Documentary Record', *Eighteenth-Century Life* 21, 3 (1997), pp. 16–38, and Carol Shiner Wilson (ed.), 'Introduction', *The Galesia Trilogy and Selected Manuscript Poems of Jane Barker* (New York and Oxford: Oxford University Press, 1997).
6. 'On the Death of My Brother', *Poetical Recreations: Consisting of Original Poems, Songs, Odes, &c. With Several New Translations. In Two Parts* (London: Benjamin Crayle, 1688), p. 47. Cited as *PR*. I cite the 1688 edition for Barker at this period and Wilson for revised and interpolated poems. The novels in Wilson are cited: *Love Intrigues* (*LI*); *A Patch-Work Screen for the Ladies* (*PWS*); *The Lining of the Patch Work Screen* (*Lining*).
7. Kathryn R. King, *Jane Barker, Exile: a Literary Career 1675–1725* (Oxford: Clarendon Press, 2000), p. 82 n. 31.
8. King, *Exile*, pp. 28–67.
9. The volume was available in December 1687: King, *Exile*, p. 31.

10. *The Poems of Jane Barker: the Magdalen Manuscript*, ed. Kathryn R. King, Magdalen College Occasional Paper 3 (Oxford: Magdalen College, 1998), p. 8. Cited as *MM*.
11. King, *Exile*, p. 75.
12. *Exilius; or, The Banish'd Roman: A New Romance: In Two Parts, Written after the Manner of Telemachus* (London: E. Curll, 1715); rpt Josephine Greider, ed. (New York: Garland, 1973). Cited as *Exilius*.
13. King, *Exile*, p. 123.
14. BL Add. MS 21,621.
15. Wilson, *Galesia Trilogy*, p. 295.
16. Lincolnshire Record Office, Kestevan Quarter Sessions: Papists' Estates Rolls, 1717.
17. Wilson, *Galesia Trilogy*, pp. 1, xxxv.
18. Ibid., p. xxx.
19. Ibid., pp. 2–4.
20. Ibid., p. xxxix.
21. Margaret J. M. Ezell, *The Patriarch's Wife: Literary Evidence and the History of the Family* (Chapel Hill: University of North Carolina Press, 1987), p. 108.
22. Spencer, 'Creating the Woman Writer', p. 178; King, *Exile*, p. 217.
23. Carol Barash, *English Women's Poetry, 1649–1714: Politics, Community, and Linguistic Authority* (Oxford: Clarendon Press, 1996), p. 175.
24. King, *Exile*, p. 102.
25. Wilson, *Galesia Trilogy*, p. 293.
26. Ibid., p. 310.
27. Royal Archives, Windsor Castle, Stuart Papers: 208/129.
28. Wilson, *Galesia Trilogy*, p. 303.
29. Magdalen MS 343, Pt 1, p. 40.
30. Barash, *English Women's Poetry*, p. 199.
31. Toni O'Shaughnessy Bowers, 'Jacobite Difference and the Poetry of Jane Barker', *ELH* 64.4 (Winter 1997), pp. 857–69 (868).
32. Barash, *English Women's Poetry*, p. 176.
33. John Warter Wood (ed.), *Southey's Common-Place Book*, 4 vols (London: Longman, Brown, Green, and Longmans, 1851), Vol. 4, p. 296.
34. Edward Arber (ed.), *British Anthologies*, 10 vols (London: Henry Frowde, 1899–1901), Vol. 7, p. 313.
35. Moira Ferguson (ed.), *First Feminists: British Women Writers 1578–1799* (Bloomington: Indiana University Press; Old Westbury, NY: The Feminist Press, 1985).
36. Germaine Greer, Susan Hastings, Jeslyn Medoff and Melinda Sansone (eds), *Kissing the Rod: an Anthology of Seventeenth-Century Women's Verse* (New York: Farrar Straus Giroux, 1989).
37. Warmest thanks to Jim Peck, Barri Gold and Daniel Wilson for their helpful responses to drafts of this essay.

Bibliography

Biographical sources

King, Kathryn R., *Jane Barker, Exile: a Literary Career, 1675–1725* (Oxford: Clarendon Press, 2000).

King, Kathryn R., with the assistance of Jeslyn Medoff, 'Jane Barker and Her Life (1652–1732): the Documentary Record', *Eighteenth-Century Life* 21, 3 (1997), pp. 16–38.

Wilson, Carol Shiner (ed.), 'Introduction', *The Galesia Triology and Selected Manuscript Poems of Jane Barker* (New York and Oxford: Oxford University Press, 1997).

Library and modern editions

Barker, Jane, *Poetical Recreations: Consisting of Original Poems, Songs, Odes, etc. With Several New Translations. In Two Parts* (London: Benjamin Crayle, 1688).

Barker, Jane, *Love Intrigues, or, the History of the Amours of Bosvil and Galesia; As Related to Lucasia, in St. Germains Garden. A Novel* (London: E. Curll and C. Crownfield, 1713); rpt ed. Josephine Greider New York (Garland Press, 1973).

Barker, Jane, *Exilius; or, The Banish'd Roman: A New Romance: In Two Parts, Written after the Manner of Telemachus* (London: E. Curll, 1715); rpt ed. Josephine Greider (New York: Garland Press, 1973).

Barker, Jane, *The Christian Pilgrimage; or, A Companion for the Holy Season of Lent* (London: Curll and C. Rivington, 1718).

Barker, Jane, *The Entertaining Novels of Mrs. Jane Barker. In Two Volumes* (London: A. Bettesworth and E. Curll, 1719).

Barker, Jane, *A Patch-Work Screen for the Ladies; or, Love and Virtue Recommended: In a Collection of Instructive Novels. Related After a Manner Intirely New, and Interspersed with Rural Poems, Describing the Innoocence of a Country-Life* (London: E. Curll and T. Payne, 1723); rpt ed. Josephine Greider (New York: Garland Press, 1973).

Barker, Jane, *The Lining of the Patch Work Screen: Design'd for the Farther Entertainment of the Ladies* (London: A. Bettesworth, 1726).

Barker, Jane, *The Entertaining Novels of Mrs. Jane Barker, of Wilsthorp in Northamptonshire*, 3rd edn (London: Bettesworth, Hitch, and E. Curll, 1736).

Barker, Jane, *The Galesia Triology and Selected Manuscript Poems of Jane Barker*, ed. Carol Shiner Wilson (New York and Oxford: Oxford University Press, 1997).

Barker, Jane, *The Poems of Jane Barker: the Magdalen Manuscript*, ed. Kathryn R. King, Magdalen College Occasional Paper 3 (Oxford: Magdalen College, 1998).

Selected secondary sources

Barash, Carol, *English Women's Poetry, 1649–1714: Politics, Community, and Linguistic Authority* (Oxford: Clarendon Press, 1996).

Bowers, Toni O'Shaughnessy, 'Jacobite Difference and the Poetry of Jane Barker', *ELH* 64.4 (Winter 1997), pp. 857–69.

Fitzmaurice, James, 'Jane Barker and the Tree of Knowledge, and Learning at Cambridge University', *Renaissance Forum* 3 (1998), URL: www.hull.ac.uk/ Hull/El Web/renforum.

King, Kathryn R., 'Galesia, Jane Barker, and a Coming to Authorship', in Carol J. Singley and Susan Elizabeth Sweeney (eds), *Anxious Power: Reading, Writing and Ambivalence in Narrative by Women* (New York: State University of New York Press, 1993), pp. 91–104.

King, Kathryn R., 'Jane Barker, *Poetical Recreations*, and the Sociable Text', *ELH* 61 (1994), pp. 551–70.

King, Kathryn R., 'Of Needles and Pens and Women's Work', *Tulsa Studies in Women's Literature* 14 (Spring 1995), pp. 77–93.

King, Kathryn, R., 'Jane Barker, Mary Leapor and a Chain of Very Odd Contingencies', *English Language Notes* 33 (1996), pp. 14–27.

Jane, Spencer, 'Creating the Woman Writer: the Autobiographical Works of Jane Barker', *Tulsa Studies in Women's Literature* 2 (Fall 1983), pp. 165–81.

5
Mary, Lady Chudleigh (1656–1710): Poet, Protofeminist and Patron

Rebecca M. Mills

'She was a lady of great virtue as well as great understanding', who, by 'her own love of books, her great industry in the reading of them and her great capacity to improve herself by them enabled her to make a very considerable figure among the literati of her time', wrote George Ballard in praise of Mary, Lady Chudleigh in *Memoirs of Several Ladies of Great Britain* (1752).[1] Ballard's adulation of Chudleigh, combined with the polemical nature of some of her poetry, was largely responsible for her lasting – albeit marginalized – standing in literary history. From the mid-eighteenth century to the present day, her reputation has endured through a handful of anthologies and biographical dictionaries under various appellations, including an 'Eminent Lady', a 'Female Worthy' and, ultimately, in the late twentieth century, a 'First Feminist'.[2] Whichever title one chooses, Chudleigh made a unique contribution to an early feminist movement that employed rational arguments on behalf of women's intellectual and spiritual autonomy.

Mary, Lady Chudleigh, was born Mary Lee to Richard and Mary (née Sydenham) Lee in the summer of 1656 and was baptized on 19 August of the same year.[3] Little is known about Chudleigh's early life, but according to one of her descendants she was well educated and encouraged in her intellectual pursuits from an early age by both her parents.[4] With 'her father's consent', on 25 March 1674, at Clyst St George, Devon, Mary Lee married George Chudleigh of Ashton, who became the third Baronet in 1691 upon his father's death.[5] Sir George and Mary, Lady Chudleigh, had several children, but only two of their sons, George (1683–1738) and Thomas (1687–1726), survived to adulthood. Chudleigh, herself, suffered from a severe rheumatic condition to which she succumbed on 15 December 1710.[6]

Chudleigh was a quintessential turn-of-the-eighteenth-century learned lady, since she participated in the two worlds of manuscript and print culture. The material evidence that survives also suggests that Chudleigh was involved in several epistolary networks. Letters offered Chudleigh, who was often resident in Devon, the chance to exchange poetry and to participate in the literary world from a distance. Chudleigh and her protégée, the poet Elizabeth Thomas (1675–1731), kept up a correspondence between 1701 and 1706, which was published primarily in *Whartoniana* (1727), *Pylades and Corinna* (1731) and *The Honourable Lovers* (1732). As well as exchanging letters and writings, Thomas also delivered letters on behalf of Chudleigh to her friends in London. In a letter dated 15 October 1703, Chudleigh says, 'I think my self infinitely obliged to Dr. [Samuel] *Garth*, to whom I desire you to do me the Favour to present the inclosed Letter';[7] and, in one dated 31 May 1706, Chudleigh thanks Thomas for passing on messages to their friends Mrs Bridgeman and Mrs Hemington.[8] Their letters provide an example of an epistolary network in action.

Chudleigh, however, was not only Thomas's friend – she was also her patron. At the turn of the eighteenth century women from a wide variety of backgrounds were often drawn together because of their mutual interests in women's role in society, specifically in relation to religion, education and marriage. As a result patron/protégée relationships often developed into friendships, despite discrepancies in social class. We do not know if Chudleigh ever gave Thomas gifts of money, but she certainly offered her other types of patronage, such as correspondence, conversation, introductions and ultimately friendship. The protofeminist inclinations of Thomas and Chudleigh drew them together and developed into a friendship, which in turn promoted further polemical and didactic writings.

The Ladies Defence: Or, The Bride-Woman's Counsellor Answer'd (1710)

John Sprint was a non-conformist minister who delivered an infamous sermon on 11 May 1699 at Sherborne in Dorsetshire which was published later that year as *The Bride-Womans Counseller*.[9] Aside from Chudleigh's, Sprint's sermon instigated one other response in print: *The Female Preacher* (*c.* 1699), later published as *The Female Advocate* (1700), by the pseudonymous writer Eugenia.

Sprint's stance on women was based on a conservative vein of 'domestic patriarchalism' which looked to Scripture as an authority to uphold the power of men. In his sermon, Sprint's demands for the complete submission of wives to their husbands are based on an interpretation of a verse from Corinthians: 'But she that is Married, careth for the things of the World, how she may please her Husband'.[10] He tells us that 'careth' means more than 'ordinary Care', and that it is *'a Duty incumbent on all Married Women, to be extraordinary Careful to content and please their HUSBANDS'*. Sprint uses examples from Scripture to prove that women have weaker capacities to learn, a subject that was hotly contested in the 1690s. He also claimed that a woman's motto should be *'LOVE, HONOUR, and OBEY'*;[11] and – his most infamous remark – that they should honour the *'Persian* Ladies' who wear an imprint of a foot on their coronets to show how they 'stoop to their Husbands Feet'.[12] For Chudleigh, who advocated spiritual and intellectual autonomy for women, his sermon must have seemed both offensive and ridiculous.

Chudleigh criticizes the major points of Sprint's sermon, especially those that deal with women's intellectual inferiority. In fact Chudleigh's defence of women is a combination of genres: she employs elements from formal rhetoric, particularly the tradition of *querelle des femmes*, satire and the Restoration stage.[13] Her use of a dialogue written in rhyming couplets is typical of Augustan satire, while her characters hearken back to those found in many Restoration plays.

Reason, embodied by the character Melissa, is the weapon Chudleigh employs to counter Sprint, whose views are represented by the three male characters: the Parson, Sir John Brute and Sir William Loveall. While the male characters espouse the unreasonable tenets of Custom and domestic patriarchalism, Melissa focuses on three main problems for women: their lack of education, the expectation of passive obedience and difficulties in the marriage market. All three problems are inter-related, and, according to Melissa, the solution is for women to be as proactive as they can about their education and spirituality and – if need be – to forego happiness in this life in order to reap rewards in heaven.

In relation to education, Melissa dismisses the Parson's assertions that women are 'Born Fools, and by resembling Idiots Nurst'.[14] Recalling Mary Astell's statement, 'So partial are Men as to expect Brick where they afford no Straw', from *A Serious Proposal to the Ladies* (1694), Melissa states:[15]

'Tis hard we should be by the Men despis'd,
Yet kept from knowing what wou'd make us priz'd:

Debarr'd from Knowledge, banish'd from the Schools,
And with the utmost Industry bred Fools.[16]

Melissa outlines the cycle in which women are caught: they are assumed to be less capable than men intellectually, but their potential is undeveloped because of inadequate education. Melissa argues that, given opportunity, women could make great improvements in themselves. The character, Sir William, then responds to Melissa with the argument that if women were educated, foolish men would never find wives. He asserts, 'While You are ignorant, We are secure,/A little Pain will your Esteem procure'.[17] In rebuttal Melissa espouses an instrumentally feminist belief about the utility of well-educated women;[18] she states that a proper education would 'Make us good Friends, good Neighbours, and good Wives'.[19] In regard to Sprint's assertions that 'Subjection and Obedience to their Husbands is required from Wives, as absolutely and peremtorily as unto Christ himself', Melissa reacts strongly.[20] In the preface to the reader, Chudleigh refers to passive obedience as 'ridiculous' and 'antiquated'.[21]

For all that's been said about *The Ladies Defence* and its invective satire, the religious undercurrent is what Chudleigh leaves with the reader at the close of the poem with an invocation to God:

Thus will we live, regardless of your hate,
Till re-admitted to our former State;
Where, free from the Confinement of our Clay
In glorious Bodies we shall bask in Day.[22]

This type of devotional ending, whereby the speaker of the poem looks to the afterlife for gratification and happiness, is typical of Chudleigh. The true source of Chudleigh's protofeminist beliefs, then, was intricately linked to her religious convictions.

Poems on Several Occasions (1703)

In the preface of *Poems on Several Occasions*, Chudleigh indicates a two-pronged motivation for printing her verses: to teach and delight her fellow women. The second part is evident when she opens her preface with the following statement:

The following Poems were written at several Times, and on several Subjects: If the Ladies, for whom they are chiefly design'd, and to whose Service they are intirely devoted, happen to meet with any thing in them that is entertaining, I have all I am at.[23]

Chudleigh, however, quickly switches to her didactic mode, and the first part of the Horatian tenet becomes apparent when she says that 'The way to be truly easie, to be always serene, [is] to have our Passions under a due Government'.[24] The publication of her poems, then, is part of her overall protofeminist inclination: to ameliorate the lives of her fellow women – especially gentlewomen whose 'Circumstances [do] not necessarily oblige them to lower Cares'.[25] Experienced as a spiritual quest by Marissa, who is the main speaker and Chudleigh's semi-autobiographical persona (similar to Jane Barker's poetic alter ego, Fidelia), Chudleigh encourages her readers to better themselves throughout the loosely strung narrative of her poems.[26]

Through rationalism and Christian devotion, women who applied Chudleigh's guidelines could achieve a type of spiritual autonomy while waiting for the ultimate freedom of the afterlife. For instance, in the poem 'Solitude', Reason is distinctly personified as a female monarch who does battle with Anarchy within the speaker's mind:

Reason her native Right may claim,
And strive to re-ascend the Throne,
But few, alas! her Pow'r will own.[27]

Again, in the poem 'The Resolve', Reason is a female monarch that rules 'within' the mind:

If Reason rules within, and keeps the Throne,
While the inferior Faculties obey,
And all her Laws without Reluctance own,
Accounting none more fit, more just than they.

The 'Resolve' in the poem is the female speaker's desire to let Reason rule in order to develop her mind to triumph 'over Vice and Fate'.[28]

Before a woman's ascension into heaven, however, Chudleigh espouses some of the benefits that Reason offers to the living. In 'The Offering', a short theodicy, Chudleigh argues that God's beauty can only be truly appreciated through rational thought. By describing the glory of the universe, the speaker begins the poem in prayer and proceeds to defend God's goodness ('Whose Kindness like himself is unconfin'd') and omnipotence ('He do's the Wants of all his Creatures know'):[29]

Accept, my God, the Praises which I bring,
The humble Tribute from a Creature due:
Permit me of thy Pow'r to sing,
That Pow'r which did stupendous Wonders do,
And whose Effects we still with awful Rev'rence view:
That mighty Pow'r which from thy boundless Store,
Out of thy self where all things lay,
This beauteous Universe did call,
This Great, this Glorious, this amazing All![30]

Next the speaker catalogues the wonders of God's creation, which can only be fully appreciated by those ruled by Reason: 'All those Delights I in my Reason find'.[31] The speaker also claims that to know God's 'unexhausted Bounty' is to thank Him: 'My Reason for him I'll employ,/ And in his Favour place my Joy'.[32] Chudleigh makes it clear that anyone can benefit from letting Reason rule their minds. Reminiscent of John Pomfret's (1667–1702) 'The Choice' (1700), Chudleigh's *beatus vir* poem, 'The Happy Man', reiterates that anyone can die happily who 'all his Passions absolutely sways,/And to his Reason cheerful Homage pays'.[33]

Although Chudleigh's poems are diverse in tone and style, she is remembered most for her poem, 'To the Ladies', which has often been interpreted autobiographically. It has been her most anthologized poem since the early eighteenth century, so much so, that it has become Chudleigh's signature poem. In miniature, it is a satirical, protofeminist comment on the more excessive elements of domestic patriarchalism. In the twentieth century, it has been interpreted as Chudleigh's personal mantra, especially the first two lines: 'Wife and Servant are the same,/ But only differ in the Name'. However, critics need to be wary of reading 'To the Ladies' only in a biographical framework. Evidence surrounding the state of Chudleigh's own marriage is contradictory and inconclusive; moreover, her ceaseless defence of women can be found throughout all her prose and poetry inasmuch as she consistently encourages women to improve themselves. While many readers respond strongly to this poem, it has other contexts in which it can be read. Polemical and satirical convention rather than personal anguish may be at work in 'To the Ladies'. Moreover, despite its reactive nature, the speaker still encourages women to pursue their goals at the close of the poem: 'Value your selves, and Men despise,/You must be proud, if you'll be wise'.[34] When the speaker tells women, they must be 'proud', she does not mean the vice deprecated in her *Essays*, but rather a type of self-respect.[35] In the preface to her poems, Chudleigh outlines this type of pride when she says,

> There is a noble Disdain, a becoming and allowable Pride; 'tis commendable to scorn to be below others in Things that are essentially Praise-worthy, and they may be permitted to put a true Value on themselves.[36]

Thus Chudleigh's prefatorial comments are echoed by the speaker of 'To the Ladies', in an attempt to continue the theme of self-empowerment.

An early feminist, Chudleigh was politically, religiously and philosophically literate. She was involved in manuscript circulation, correspondence networks, print culture and patronage. Her writings, republished in 1993, by Margaret J. M. Ezell, range in tone, form and genre from epistles, lyrics, pindaric odes, satires, pastoral dialogues, religious paraphrases to didactic and devotional essays. Throughout them all, she encouraged her women readers to strive for intellectual and spiritual freedom. Rationalism, then, is the key to understanding Chudleigh's protofeminism. ''Tis impossible to be happy without making Reason the Standard of all our Thoughts' is the mantra she repeats to inspire her women readers.[37]

Notes

1. George Ballard, *Memoirs of Several Ladies of Great Britain who have been Celebrated for their Writings or Skill in the Learned Languages, Arts and Sciences* (1752), ed. Ruth Perry (Detroit: Wayne State University Press, 1985).
2. Among others, Chudleigh is anthologized by George Colman and B. Thornton in *Poems by Eminent Ladies*, 2 vols (London: 1755); *Biographium Fœmineum. The Female Worthies*, 2 vols (London: 1766); and by Moira Ferguson, in *First Feminists: British Women Writers 1578–1799* (Bloomington: Indiana University Press, 1985).
3. *The Registers of Clyst St. George, co. Devon 1565–1812*, transcribed by Rev. John Lomax Gibbs (London: 1899), p. 41.
4. Bodleian Library, MS Ballard 74, fol. 301^r.
5. *The Registers*, p. 53.
6. Chudleigh was buried on 20 December 1710 in Ashton. Devon Record Office, Ashton Church Parish Register, MF 3.
7. *Whartonia: or, Miscellanies, in Verse and Prose*, 2 vols (London: 1727), Vol. 2, p. 115, and Elizabeth Thomas and Richard Gwinnett, *The Honourable Lovers: or, the Second and Last Volume of Pylades and Corinna* (London: 1732), p. 255.
8. Elizabeth Thomas and Richard Gwinnett, *Pylades and Corinna: or, Memoirs of the Lives, Amours, and Writings of Richard Gwinnett, Esq; Of Great Shurdington*

in Gloucestershire; and Mrs. Elizabeth Thomas Jun[r], Of Great Russel Street, Bloomsbury (London: 1731), p. 268.

9. John Sprint, *The Bride-Womans Counseller. Being a Sermon Preach'd at a Wedding, May the 11th, 1699, at Sherbourn, in Dorsetshire* (London: 1699), p. 2.
10. 1 Corinthians 7.34.
11. Sprint, *Bride-Womans Counseller*, pp. 3, 4 and 14.
12. Sprint, *Bride-Womans Counseller*, p. 11.
13. Joan Kelly, 'Early Feminist Theory and the *Querelle des Femmes*, 1400–1789', *Signs* 8 (1982), pp. 4–28 (17).
14. Lady Mary Chudleigh, *The Poems and Prose of Mary, Lady Chudleigh*, ed. Margaret J. M. Ezell (Oxford: Oxford University Press, 1993), p. 21.
15. Mary Astell, *A Serious Proposal to the Ladies, Parts I and II*, ed. Patricia Springborg (London: Pickering & Chatto, 1997), p. 10.
16. Chudleigh, *Poems and Prose*, p. 30.
17. Chudleigh, *Poems and Prose*, p. 32.
18. Alice Browne, *The Eighteenth-Century Feminist Mind* (Brighton: Harvester Press, 1987), p. 5.
19. Chudleigh, *Poems and Prose*, p. 35.
20. Sprint, *Bride-Womans Counseller*, p. 13.
21. Chudleigh, *Poems and Prose*, pp. 13–14.
22. Chudleigh, *Poems and Prose*, pp. 39–40.
23. Chudleigh, *Poems and Prose*, p. 44.
24. Chudleigh, *Poems and Prose*, p. 45.
25. Chudleigh, *Poems and Prose*, p. 251.
26. Jane Barker, *The Galesia Trilogy and Selected Manuscript Poems of Jane Barker*, ed. Carol Shiner Wilson (Oxford: Oxford University Press, 1997), p. xvi.
27. Chudleigh, *Poems and Prose*, p. 129.
28. Chudleigh, *Poems and Prose*, p. 144.
29. Chudleigh, *Poems and Prose*, p. 141.
30. Chudleigh, *Poems and Prose*, p. 140.
31. Chudleigh, *Poems and Prose*, p. 141.
32. Chudleigh, *Poems and Prose*, p. 141 and 143.
33. Chudleigh, *Poems and Prose*, p. 80.
34. Chudleigh, *Poems and Prose*, p. 83.
35. *Oxford English Dictionary.*
36. Chudleigh, *Poems and Prose*, p. 46.
37. Chudleigh, *Poems and Prose*, p. 44.

Bibliography

Biographical sources

Ballard, George, *Memoirs of Several Ladies of Great Britain who have been Celebrated for their Writings or Skill in the Learned Languages, Arts and Sciences* (1752), ed. Ruth Perry (Detroit: Wayne State University Press, 1985).
Biographium Fœmineum. The Female Worthies, 2 vols (London, 1766).
Bodleian Library, MS Ballard 74 fol. 301[1] and MS Rawlinson, Letters 90.
Devon Record Office, MF3.

The Registers of Clyst St. George, co. Devon 1565–1812, transcribed by Rev. John Lomax Gibbs (London: 1899).

Library and modern editions

Chudleigh, Mary, Lady, *The Poems and Prose of Mary, Lady Chudleigh*, ed. Margaret J. M. Ezell (Oxford: Oxford University Press, 1993).

Colman, George, and B. Thornton, *Poems by Eminent Ladies*, 2 vols (London: 1755).

Lonsdale, Roger (ed.), *Eighteenth-Century Women Poets: an Oxford Anthology* (Oxford: Oxford University Press, 1989).

Thomas, Elizabeth, and Richard Gwinnett, *Pylades and Corinna: or, Memoirs of the Lives, Amours, and Writings of Richard Gwinnett, Esq; Of Great Shurdington in Gloucestershire; and Mrs. Elizabeth Thomas Junr, Of Great Russel Street*, Bloomsbury (London: 1731).

Thomas, Elizabeth, and Richard Gwinnett, *The Honourable Lovers: or, the Second and Last Volume of Pylades and Corinna* (London: 1732).

Whartoniana: or, Miscellanies, in Verse and Prose, 2 vols (London: 1727).

Selected secondary sources

Astell, Mary, *Political Writings*, ed. Patricia Springborg (Cambridge: Cambridge University Press, 1996).

Astell, Mary, *A Serious Proposal to the Ladies, Parts I & II*, ed. Patricia Springborg (London: Pickering & Chatto, 1997).

Barash, Carol, *English Women's Poetry, 1649–1714: Politics, Community, and Linguistic Authority* (Oxford: Clarendon Press, 1996).

Barker, Jane, *The Galesia Trilogy and Selected Manuscript Poems of Jane Barker*, ed. Carol Shiner Wilson (Oxford: Oxford University Press, 1997).

Brown, Irene Q., 'Domesticity, Feminism, and Friendship: Female Aristocratic Culture and Marriage in England, 1660–1760', *Journal of Family History* 7 (1982), pp. 406–24.

Browne, Alice, *The Eighteenth-Century Feminist Mind* (Brighton: Harvester Press, 1987).

Coleman, Antony, 'The *Provok'd Wife* and *The Ladies Defence*', *N&Q* 17 (1970), pp. 88–91.

Ezell, Margaret J. M., *Social Authorship and the Advent of Print* (Baltimore: Johns Hopkins University Press, 1999).

Ferguson, Moira, *First Feminists: British Women Writers 1578–1799* (Bloomington: Indiana University Press, 1985).

Kelly, Joan, 'Early Feminist Theory and the *Querelle des Femmes*, 1400–1789', *Signs* 8 (1982), pp. 4–28.

Korshin, Paul J., 'Types of Eighteenth-Century Literary Patronage', *ECS* 7 (1973–74), pp. 453–73.

McDowell, Paula, *The Women of Grub Street: Press, Politics, and Gender in the London Literary Marketplace 1678–1730* (Oxford: Clarendon Press, 1998).

Reynolds, Myra, *The Learned Lady in England 1650–1760* (New York: Houghton Mifflin Co., 1920).

Smith, Hilda L., *Reason's Disciples: Seventeenth-Century English Feminists* (London: University of Illinois Press, 1982).

Sprint, John, *The Bride-Womans Counseller. Being a Sermon Preach'd at a Wedding, May the 11th, 1699, at Sherbourn, in Dorsetshire* (London: 1699).

Turner, Cheryl, *Living by the Pen: Women Writers in the Eighteenth Century* (London: Routledge, 1992).

Whyman, Susan E., *Sociability and Power in Late-Stuart England: the Cultural Worlds of the Verneys 1660–1720* (Oxford: Oxford University Press, 1999).

6
Anne Finch, Countess of Winchilsea (1661–1720): Sorrow into Song

Jane Spencer

The very first lines of a poem Finch called 'The Introduction' deny that she is introducing her work to the world: 'Did I, my lines intend for publick view,/How many censures, wou'd their faults persue'.[1] Included in manuscript volumes of her work compiled in the 1690s, the poem attempts to enforce a distinction between manuscript circulation intended for 'some few friends' (62, p. 6) and the public existence that would incur censure. The first section of the poem is an eloquent, much-quoted complaint about the opposition faced by 'a woman that attempts the pen' (9, p. 4), while the central section invokes biblical authority to argue that ''twas not ever thus': women's words once acted powerfully in public. Three illustrations of this are offered. In the first, 'holy Virgins' are said to have joined in the celebrations greeting the return of the Ark of the Covenant, their voices acting 'to soften, and refine' Israel's music (30–1, p. 5).[2] In the second, the young David's victory over the Philistines is greeted by a 'bright Chorus' of women, whose praise of him above Saul is an early indication that he will become king.[3] In the third and most striking example, 'A Woman here, leads fainting Israel on,/She fights, she wins, she triumphs with a song' (45–6, p. 6). This is the prophetess and Judge Deborah, who rouses the people of Israel to fight against their Canaanite oppressors, and sings a song of triumph on Israel's victory.[4] In seventeenth-century England, however, women, 'fal'n by mistaken rules', denied education, brought up to be dull, cannot sing, or, if they can, 'th' opposing faction' is too strong for them (51, 57, p. 6). There is a Jacobite undertone to this lament. The contrast between the public, poetic role taken by biblical women and the insignificant tasks allotted the contemporary English female implies a parallel contrast between the triumphs of Israel and the (unstated) sad situation of England after 1688, longing for the return of her rightful king. That 'faction' ostensibly refers simply to those who oppose women's writing; but it is surely also a political faction, the triumphant Williamites, who would oppose any attempt by Anne Finch to lead her nation with a song. The poem ends on a note of retreat:

> Be caution'd then my Muse, and still retir'd;
> Nor be dispis'd, aiming to be admir'd;
> Conscious of wants, still with contracted wing,
> To some few friends, and to thy sorrows sing;
> For groves of Lawrell, thou wert never meant;
> Be dark enough thy shades, and be thou there content. (59–64, p. 6)

Retreat, retirement, shade: these are Anne Finch's characteristic movement, state of being and preferred environment. Even Deborah, her model for a woman of virtuous public action, 'to the peacefull, shady Palm withdraws' after the battle, her rule sounding in Finch's formulation of it almost like a retreat (49, p. 6). Finch figures her muse as a bird in hiding, drawing in its wings, but still singing. This stance was shaped both by her situation as a woman and by political defeat; but gendered expectations and political pressures chimed with the personal temperament of a writer who suffered bouts of severe depression. The combination proved fruitful for her poetry: the shades were good for Anne Finch's muse.

Born Anne Kingsmill in 1661, from royalist landed families on both sides of her parentage, she was orphaned young and brought up by her grandmother and then in Northamptonshire by her uncle. Details of her education are not known, but she clearly had an unusually intellectual upbringing for a woman of her time. At 21 she became a maid of honour to Mary of Modena, second wife of James, Duke of York. Court life brought her into contact with prominent literary men, and like one of Mary's other maids of honour, Anne Killigrew, she was writing poetry, though she was careful not to become known for it. At court Kingsmill met Heneage Finch, a soldier and courtier also serving the House of York, and they married the year before James became king. Between 1684 and 1688 Anne Finch wrote a number of poems and songs and her first play, *The Triumphs of Love and Innocence*. At the 1688 Revolution the couple's fortunes changed dramatically. Arrested in 1690 as he tried to get to France to join James in exile, Heneage was tried for treason.

During this year Finch wrote her second play, the tragedy *Aristomenes: Or, The Royal Shepherd*, hoping to divert her 'melancholy thoughts' at this difficult time ('Preface', p. 12). On Heneage's acquittal late in 1690, the couple went to Eastwell in Kent as guests of the Earl of Winchilsea, Heneage Finch's nephew. Exiled from public life, Anne Finch adopted as pen name 'Ardelia', a name found in one of Katherine Philips's poems praising the joys of retirement.[5]

Finch represented Eastwell, full of 'objects naturally inspiring soft and Poetical immaginations', and owned by a man himself 'so indulgent to that Art', as the inspiration and encouragement for her return to 'the service of the Muses', a service she had been trying to resist, and would have 'wean'd' herself from had she remained in the public life of the court ('Preface', p. 8). Though we may not necessarily believe this last claim, it is true that life at Eastwell encouraged her writing. Her husband, his public career cut short, divided his time between antiquarianism and the service of her poetry. An octavo manuscript volume of her poems, apparently begun shortly before the move to Kent and continued there with Heneage Finch as amanuensis, was abandoned in favour of a more extensive, folio manuscript containing both plays and poems, which he began to compile around 1694/95.[6] A few of her songs appeared in print, and six religious poems were published in the collection *Miscellanea Sacra* in 1696. In 1701 more of her work reached print, with the publication of an elegy on the death of James II, and the anonymous appearance of some poems including 'The Spleen' in a miscellany by Charles Gildon. In the new century, too, the Finches returned to a more public life, and from 1708 divided their time between London and Eastwell. In 1709 three of her pastoral poems appeared in Jacob Tonson's *Poetical Miscellanies*, and 'The Spleen' in a pirated edition. Anne Finch became friendly with Swift, who encouraged her to publish, with Pope, and with Elizabeth Rowe. In 1713, a year after she had become Countess of Winchilsea on her husband's accession to his nephew's title, she published *Miscellany Poems, on Several Occasions*, containing 86 poems and the play *Aristomenes*. After a severe illness in 1715 the Countess continued to write, her later verse, much of it religious, being collected in another manuscript volume, probably begun on her behalf shortly before her death in 1720.

Finch's work includes short songs and hymns of various metres, some of them set to music, and ambitious Pindaric odes on public and religious themes: 'The Spleen', discussed below; 'A Pindarick Poem Upon the Hurricane in September 1703', with its commentary on a recent catastrophe; and 'All is Vanity', with its pointed refusal to exempt poetic fame from its dismissal of transient worldly goods. Like Katherine Philips, she celebrates female friendship, notably in the tetrameter dialogue 'Friendship Between Ephelia and Ardelia', in which Ardelia tries out a number of elevated definitions of friendship only to return at the close to her first simple formulation: *"tis to love, as I love you'* (20, p. 46). She also celebrates married love in her address to 'the Crown and blessing of my life,/The much-lov'd husband, of a happy wife' ('A Letter to Dafnis April: 2d 1685', 1–2, p. 19). She uses the heroic couplet extensively as an ordered yet flexible medium for her reflective poetry.

Satire, so favoured by Swift and Pope, is not her mode. In fact, much of her work embodies a resistance to this dominant Augustan genre. 'Who e'er of Satyre does my pen accuse/Knows not the stile of my well temper'd muse', she claims;[7] and even the heroic verse-epistle 'Ardelia's Answer to Ephelia', which has been called 'her most sustained effort at satire',[8] is more of an anti-satire: its main target, Almeria, is exposed not so much for the usual flaws of vanity and coquetry but for her love of 'finding fault' (106, p. 42). Ardelia refuses Ephelia's invitation to London because 'Satir' and 'sharpe detraction' are now the 'only conversation of the Town' (22, p. 39), and illustrates this with an extended description of her previous visit, which Almeria made miserable. As Ardelia reluctantly tours the streets with her acquaintance, Almeria points out an 'awk'ard creature' who Ardelia can only see as 'a lovely face', and when Ardelia praises the young woman's skin, Almeria informs her it is sickly, and her pink cheeks only a reflection from crimson material (108, 114, 120–3, p. 42); Almeria claims Alinda to be her 'best of friends', and then spreads malicious gossip about her passion for Damon (165, 182–92, pp. 43–4); yet ironically, this incessant carper attacks Piso for his fair criticisms of art (133–62, pp. 42–3). When Ardelia escapes Almeria and visits a church, Almeria spends the time criticizing her to a foppish beau of her acquaintance. While she is, of course, satirizing Almeria, Ardelia remains throughout conscious of her own vulnerability to fashionable satire – for being dull, for going to church, for writing poetry. She ends her epistle hoping that she will escape detraction herself, as long as she forbears to attack others.

Ardelia's longing for the harmony of the country, where 'Trees blast not trees, nor flow'rs envenom flow'rs' (131, p. 42), reveals her refusal of London as a return from satire to the kinder pastoral tradition, which Finch explores and develops in many of her other poems. Some of these, including 'A Nocturnal Reverie', express a sensitivity to the feelings and experiences of animals and birds which has been explained as characteristic of women poets' sense of their affinity with the Nature so often understood as feminine. When Finch notes with fellow-feeling that 'Their shortliv'd Jubilee the Creatures keep,/Which but endures, whilst Tyrant-*Man* do's sleep' (37–8, p. 269), the tyrant's masculinity seems to be as relevant as his humanity.[9] At the same time the poem maintains a sense of inevitable separation from the natural world, based on Christian conviction: the mind, while contemplating nature's nocturnal calm, is led 'to seek/Something, too high for Syllables to speak', and while the soul 'Joys in th'inferiour World, and thinks it like her Own' (42, 46, p. 270), that world remains inferior, the sense of likeness temporary.[10]

Some of Finch's most moving poetry is personal and concerns her struggle with the depression that affected much of her life. 'The Consolation' begins in the rapturous affirmation of 'See, Phoebus breaking from the willing skies,/See, how the soaring Lark, does with him rise', and moves to an understanding of the diurnal cycle: sun and bird must fall with night, but day will return. The speaker's need for consolation is revealed only in the final lines: 'Then lett no cloudy change, create my sorrow,/I'll think 'tis night, and I may rise tomorrow' (1–2, 15–16, p. 18). Retrospectively we realize that the speaker is cut off from the glorious day; her insistent call to see the sun came from one subject to a personal cloud, unable to obey her own instruction. The inevitability of nightfall offers a way of thinking of and bearing her condition. The final lines, quiet and sombre in comparison to the opening, carry the hope that, at some future time, she may be able to share the joy she began by only describing.

In 'The Spleen', now Finch's most famous poem, there is a much more ambitious attempt to understand the implications of this disorder. The spleen was the current term for what we would now call depression, and was a fashionable diagnosis in the eighteenth century; the malady was sometimes thought to be especially the preserve of women.[11] Finch embeds a confessional passage about her own experience of the disorder in a wide-ranging philosophical enquiry into its nature. This comprehensiveness is made possible by, and helps the reader to appreciate, Finch's refusal of the satirist's position. The spleen, both as a nervous disorder reputedly productive of delusions and as a glamorous illness supposedly adopted as an interesting explanation for bad behaviour offered rich opportunities to the satirist. Pope was to exploit these to the full in the Cave of Spleen section of *The Rape of the Lock*. His Spleen is a goddess hiding in the shade and wallowing in misery, attended by the handmaids Ill-nature, whose solemn peevishness takes the form of prayers and lampoons, and Affectation, who 'On the rich Quilt sinks with becoming Woe', obviously faking it.[12] Spleen has especial power over women and produces both their hysteria and their poetry, which by implication are very much the same thing. No wonder the four lines concerning women's writing annoyed Finch;[13] but the whole of the Cave of Spleen section might have been painful for her, given her own love of shade and prayer, and her wish to dissociate herself from lampoon. Finch's own treatment of spleen is far from Pope's satiric approach. His certainty about spleen as affectation and his mockery of the delusions it induces contrast sharply with her uncertain exploration of these possibilities.

Uncertainty is the keynote: the poem begins with the question 'What art thou, *SPLEEN*, which ev'ry thing does ape?', never definitively answered (1, p. 248). Some of her lines have a satirical cast, as sullen husbands, drunks and coquettes all claim to be afflicted by the disease. When a coquette looks melancholy, 'The Cause, indeed, is a Defect in Sense,/Yet is the *Spleen* alledg'd, and still the dull Pretence'. The poem continues:

> But these are thy fantastic Harms,
> The Tricks of thy pernicious Stage,
> Which do the weaker Sort engage;
> Worse are the dire Effects of thy more pow'rful Charms. (110–15, p. 251)

This apparently sets up a contrast between false and true spleen: my suffering is real, they are putting it on. The distinction fails to hold. Because spleen deals in fantasy and illusion, it is itself the 'Patron' of 'ev'ry gross Abuse' of its own name (90, p. 250): those who pretend to suffer from it must really be affected by it by virtue of the very pretence. At the same time the speaker, suffering from deceptive spleen, cannot be sure of the reality of the things that pain her. When she cries:

> O'er me alas! thou dost too much prevail:
> I feel thy Force, whilst I against thee rail;
> I feel my Verse decay, and my crampt Numbers fail (774–6, p. 250),

the position of the satirist, the one who rails, breaks down: she is subject to the ailment she rails against, and this is reflected in the decay of her verse – or so she thinks. Even this is thrown into question, since one of spleen's symptoms is the false black colouring it places over everything: 'Thro' thy black Jaundice I all Objects see,/ As Dark, and Terrible as Thee' (77–8, p. 250). On one point the speaker is clear: the spleen is a spiritual, not a bodily disorder: we blame 'the Mortal Part' of ourselves quite wrongly for a disease that was 'Let . . . in' by 'the First degrading Sin' (26, 29, 28, p. 249). Spleen is a consequence of the Fall. It is also to blame for our sense of guilt:

> By Thee *Religion*, all we know,
> That shou'd enlighten here below,
> Is veil'd in Darkness, and perplext
> With anxious Doubts, with endless Scruples vext,
> And some Restraint imply'd from each perverted Text.
> Whilst *Touch* not, *Taste* not, what is freely giv'n,
> Is but thy niggard Voice, disgracing bounteous Heav'n. (251)

These lines have been glossed as an attack on Puritanism.[14] They are followed by lines that, calling those 'in Cells reclus'd' 'Mistaken Vot'ries to the Powers Divine', seem rather an attack on monasticism (124–5, p. 251). Perhaps Finch means to attack both extremes and imply that her own Anglicanism is the best, middle way; but this reading underestimates the force of Finch's use of the pronoun 'we'. The speaker has already emphatically included herself among spleen's victims. We all, she suggests, feel the command '*Taste* not'; it was, of course, the original command broken in Eden. Spleen exists because of the Fall, but it is also spleen's false influence that leads us to believe Heaven is prohibiting us the enjoyment of our senses. What art thou, Spleen? Not only can we not get a full answer, to pose the question at all seems to be to acknowledge spleen and fall into its power, just as Richard Lower, the physician of the poem's closing lines, fell a prisoner to the disease he tried to investigate.[15] The indecipherability of spleen means that there is no way of making a clear distinction between true and false suffering from the disease, and therefore no way to maintain the position of the satirist, who needs to be sure what is right and what wrong. There is no way, either, to achieve the detachment of the satirist, who judges follies without sharing them: Finch is too aware of being herself caught in the toils of the indefinable monster. Refusing satire, 'The Spleen' reaches a wide vision of human folly and suffering in which the poet is not detached from what she reveals.

Finch's poetry was well received by her contemporaries, but fell into obscurity in the second half of the eighteenth century. Her revival by Wordsworth, whose supplementary essay in the 1815 *Lyrical Ballads* famously praised 'A Nocturnal Reverie' as one of the very few eighteenth-century poems written with the poet's eye on the object, distorted her reputation. For over a century she was considered a Romanticist before her time, and this view still has some influence, especially as it is repeated in what is still the most complete edition of her work, Reynolds's 1904 volume.[16] Reuben Brower's 1945 essay restored a sense of her roots in the poetic traditions of the seventeenth century, and more recent work has explored her relation to the culture and society of her own time from various angles. In the 1970s and 1980s readings by Gilbert and Gubar, Katharine Rogers and Ruth Salvaggio emphasized her anxieties as a female poet and her sense of displacement within eighteenth-century culture, Salvaggio reading Finch's shade as a radical feminine space disrupting dualist oppositions and Enlightenment systems. Criticism in the 1990s, including that by Barbara McGovern in her landmark biography, turned to considering Finch in the national political context, reading her displacement as that of a defeated Jacobite. Her religious concerns have also begun to receive attention. Carol Barash combined consideration of gender and national politics in her reading of Finch as creating a feminine poetic identity out of a Jacobite retreat. Despite a rich growing body of Finch criticism, though, much basic work is still to come. There is an urgent need for a critical edition of Finch's complete poems which will correct the Reynolds edition and allow the poet's work to be seen as a whole. The plays have received hardly a critical mention. The relation between her creativity and her illness is a tricky but important subject for further investigation: so far her 'spleen' has been viewed in relation to her position as a woman and as a Jacobite, both important contexts but neither providing an exhaustive explanation. It is to be hoped that editorial work now in progress will lead to much more attention being given to the entire range of a poet who deserves it for the individuality, interest and beauty of her work.

Notes

1. 'The Introduction', 1–2; *The Poems of Anne, Countess of Winchilsea*, ed. Myra Reynolds (Chicago: University Press of Chicago, 1903), p. 4. Further references to Finch's poems are to the Reynolds edition unless otherwise stated.

2. The ark of the covenant is brought by the Levites to Zion in 1 Chronicles 15–16, which describe the joy of 'all Israel', expressed in singing and with harps, cymbals, cornets and trumpets. This seems the likeliest source for Finch's lines: 'The Levites do the sacred Charge convey,/Whilst various Instruments, before itt play' (28–9, p. 5). Though women are evidently included in the rejoicing, since after the ark has been set down David gives bread and wine 'to every one of Israel, both man and woman' (1 Chronicles 16.3), their singing is not specifically mentioned: Finch is adding to her source to create a specific role for female song.

3. 1 Samuel 18.6–9. The women's praise of David arouses Saul's anger and subsequent persecution of his rival; but the Lord is with David (1 Samuel 18.12, 14, 28) and he is eventually to triumph over Saul. I differ here from Carol Barash's interpretation of David as a dangerous charmer and the women of Israel as 'dangerously swayed by popular opinion': see Carol Barash, *English Women's Poetry 1649–1714: Politics, Community, and Linguistic Authority* (Oxford: Clarendon Press, 1996), p. 271.

4. Judges 4–5. The battle instigated by Deborah contains another famous example of women's action: Israel's victory is assured when Jael kills Sisera, the leader of the enemy host (Judges 5.21). Finch ignores Jael's violent action and concentrates on Deborah who, acting through prophecy, advice and song, is a model for the public poet.

5. B. McGovern, *Anne Finch and Her Poetry: a Critical Biography* (Athens, Georgia, and London: University of Georgia Press, 1992), p. 123.

6. McGovern, *Anne Finch and Her Poetry*, pp. 68–9.

7. 'On my being charged with writing a lampoon at Tunbridge', *The Anne Finch Wellesley Manuscript Poems: a Critical Edition*, ed. Barbara McGovern and Charles H. Hinnant (Athens, Georgia, and London: University of Georgia Press, 1998), p. 75.

8. McGovern, *Anne Finch and Her Poetry*, p. 137. See ibid., pp. 136–43, for a discussion of this poem as a revision of Rochester's satirical epistle 'A Letter from Artemisia in the Town to Chloe in the Country'.

9. See M. A. Doody, 'Sensuousness in the Poetry of Eighteenth-Century Women Poets', in I. Armstrong and V. Blain (eds), *Women's Poetry in the Enlightenment: the Making of a Canon, 1730–1820* (London: Macmillan now Palgrave Macmillan, 1999), pp. 3–33, esp. the discussion of 'A Nocturnal Reverie' on pp. 16–17.

10. See A. Messenger, *Pastoral Tradition and the Female Talent: Studies in Augustan Poetry* (New York: AMS Press, Inc., 2001), pp. 39–49, for a discussion of the conflict in Finch's poetry between Christian doctrine and the affinity between human and nature typical of pastoral.

11. See McGovern, *Anne Finch and Her Poetry*, pp. 159–78, and K. M. Rogers, 'Finch's "Candid Account" vs. Eighteenth-Century Theories of the Spleen', *Mosaic: a Journal for the Interdisciplinary Study of Literature* 22 (1989), pp. 17–27, for discussions of Finch's writing in the context of contemporary ideas about the spleen.

12. Alexander Pope, *The Rape of the Lock*, Canto IV, 1. 35; *The Poems of Alexander Pope*, ed. John Butt (London: Methuen, 1965), p. 233.

13. See the discussion in 'Imagining the Woman Poet', below, p. 104–5.

14. McGovern, *Anne Finch and Her Poetry*, p. 176.

15. Richard Lower (1631–91) was a fashionable London physician who, as assistant anatomist to Dr Thomas Willis at Oxford, contributed to groundbreaking research on the physiology of the nerves.
16. See McGovern, *Anne Finch and Her Poetry*, pp. 79–83, for a discussion of the misrepresentation of Finch as precursor of Romanticism.

Bibliography

Biographical sources

Ballard, G., *Memoirs of Several Ladies* (Oxford: W. Jackson, 1752).
Biographia Britannica (London, 1763).
Birch, T., et al., *The General Dictionary*, 10 vols (London: G. Strahan, 1734–41).
Cameron, W. J., 'Anne, Countess of Winchilsea: a Guide for the Future Biographer', thesis (Victoria College, Wellington, NZ, 1951).
Cibber, T., *The Lives of the Poets of Great Britain and Ireland* (London: R. Griffiths, 1753).
Hughes, H. S., 'Lady Winchilsea and Her Friends', *London Mercury* 19 (1929), pp. 624–35.
McGovern, B., *Anne Finch and Her Poetry: a Critical Biography* (Athens, Georgia, and London: University of Georgia Press, 1992).

Library and modern editions

Anne Finch has received little editorial attention and there is still no complete collected edition of her works; Germaine Greer is currently working on a full edition.

Octavo MS 'Poems on Several Subjects, Written by Ardelia', Finch-Hatton ms. 283, Northamptonshire Record Office.
Folio MS 'Miscellany Poems with Two Plays by Ardelia', Folger Shakespeare Library.
MS 'Countess of Winchilsea's Poems', Wellesley College, Margaret Clapp Library.
An Elegy on The Death of K. James, By a Lady (London: 1701).
A New Miscellany of Original Poems, On Several Occasions (London: 1701).
The Spleen, a pindarique ode, by a lady (London: 1709).
Miscellany Poems, on Several Occasions. Written by a Lady (London: printed for J. B. and sold by Benj. Tooke, William Taylor and James Round, 1713).
Colman, George, and Bonnell Thornton (eds), *Poems by Eminent Ladies*, 2 vols (London: R. Baldwin, 1755).
The Poems of Anne, Countess of Winchilsea, ed. Myra Reynolds (Chicago: University of Chicago Press, 1903).
Selected Poems of Anne Finch, Countess of Winchilsea, ed. Katharine Rogers (New York: Ungar, 1979).
Selected Poems, ed. Denys Thompson (Manchester: Carcanet, 1987).
The Wellesley Manuscript Poems of Anne Countess of Winchilsea, ed. Jean M. Ellis d'Alessandro (Florence: privately printed, 1988).
The Anne Finch Wellesley Manuscript Poems: a Critical Edition, ed. Barbara McGovern and Charles H. Hinnant (Athens, Georgia, and London: University of Georgia Press, 1998).

Selected secondary sources

Barash, Carol, 'The Political Origins of Anne Finch's Poetry', *Huntington Library Quarterly* 54 (1991), pp. 327–51.

Baresh, Carol, *English Women's Poetry, 1649–1714: Politics, Community, and Linguistic Authority* (Oxford: Clarendon Press, 1996).

Brower, R. A., 'Lady Winchilsea and the Poetic Tradition of the Seventeenth Century', *Studies in Philology* 42 (1945), pp. 61–80.

Doody, M. A., 'Sensuousness in the Poetry of Eighteenth-Century Women Poets', in I. Armstrong and V. Blain (eds), *Women's Poetry in the Enlightenment: the Making of a Canon, 1730–1820* (London: Macmillan now Palgrave Macmillan, 1999), pp. 3–32.

Gilbert, S. M., and S. Gubar, 'Introduction: Gender, Creativity and the Woman Poet', *Shakespeare's Sisters: Feminist Essays on Women Poets* (Bloomington: Indiana University Press, 1979).

Hellegers, D, ' "The Threatening Angel and the Speaking Ass": the Masculine Mismeasure of Madness in *The Spleen*', *Genre* 26 (1993), pp. 199–217.

Hinnant, C. H., 'Song and Speech in Anne Finch's "To the Nightingale" ', *Studies in English Literature 1500–1900* 31 (1991), pp. 499–513.

Hinnant, C. H., *The Poetry of Anne Finch: an Essay in Interpretation* (Newark: Delaware, 1994).

Mallinson, J., 'Anne Finch: a Woman Poet and the Tradition', in A. Messenger (ed.), *Gender at Work: Four Women Writers of the Eighteenth Century* (Detroit: Wayne State University Press, 1990), pp. 34–76.

Mermin, D., 'Women Becoming Poets: Katherine Philips, Aphra Behn, Anne Finch', *English Literary History* 57 (1990), pp. 335–55.

Messenger, A., 'Selected Nightingales: Anne Finch, Countess of Winchilsea, et al.', *His and Hers: Essays in Restoration and Eighteenth-Century Literature* (Lexington: University Press of Kentucky, 1986).

Messenger, A., *Pastoral Tradition and the Female Talent: Studies in Augustan Poetry* (New York: AMS Press, Inc., 2001).

Rogers, K., 'Anne Finch, Countess of Winchilsea: an Augustan Woman Poet', in Gilbert and Gubar, *Shakespeare's Sisters*, pp. 32–46.

Rogers, K., 'Finch's "Candid Account" vs. Eighteenth-Century Theories of the Spleen', *Mosaic: a Journal for the Interdisciplinary Study of Literature* 22 (1989), pp. 17–27.

Salvaggio, R., *Enlightened Absence: Neoclassical Configurations of the Feminine* (Urbana: University of Illinois Press, 1988).

Williamson, M. L., *Raising Their Voices: British Women Writers, 1650–1750* (Detroit: Wayne State University Press, 1990).

7
Elizabeth Singer Rowe (1674–1737): Politics, Passion and Piety

Sarah Prescott

Elizabeth Singer Rowe was one of the most influential, well-known and respected women writers of the late seventeenth and early eighteenth centuries. After Rowe's death in 1737, for example, the poet Elizabeth Carter, herself extremely respected as a writer, lamented the loss of Rowe as the demise of 'our sex's ornament and pride!' (8).[1] For eighteenth-century readers in general, Rowe's image as a writer was bound up with the popular success of her elegy 'On the death of Mr. THOMAS ROWE' in which she laments the unseasonably early death of her beloved husband in the following terms:

> FOR thee all thoughts of pleasure I forego,
> For thee my tears shall never cease to flow;
> For thee at once I from the world retire,
> To feed, in silent shades, a hopeless fire. (88–91)[2]

This sentimental image of the lamenting widow who eschews all worldly pleasures for a life of contemplative retirement was to prove remarkably enduring and doubtless added to Rowe's success as a poet. In addition, Rowe's equally well-known image as a pious Christian did much to establish her as a respectable female author. However, like many women writers, Rowe's life and reputation has tended to overshadow any critical engagement with her writing. In Rowe's case, her pious and sentimental persona may have secured her a place in the history of women's writing as a modest exemplar, but it has also led to an almost wholesale neglect of her poetry. What the accepted view of Rowe leaves out, however, is not only the remarkable range of Rowe's poetry but also the political, religious and social contexts in which she wrote and which provide a framework for thinking about her poetry in ways that go beyond a mere enforcement of her image of saintly piety.

Elizabeth Singer Rowe was born in Ilchester on 11 September 1674 into a strongly dissenting family. The Singers moved to Frome in Somerset in about 1692 when Rowe was in her late teens. After her marriage to Thomas Rowe in 1710, she lived in London until her husband's death in 1715, at which time she returned to Frome and lived there until her death in 1737. Rowe was to be associated with the West Country and Frome throughout her literary career and the connection was often used as a way of enforcing her image as one of pious retirement. Her biographers, Henry Grove and Theophilus Rowe, suggest that, after the death of Thomas, Rowe 'indulged her unconquerable inclinations to solitude, by returning to Frome in Somersetshire . . . to conceal the remainder of her life in absolute retirement'.[3] In terms of her literary reputation, her association with a location geographically distant from London, the centre of the book trade and print industry, meant that she could also symbolically distance herself from the London literary world and all it represented. Yet despite this reputation for seclusion, Rowe interacted extensively with other writers and inhabited a number of different literary and social contexts. She began her career by publishing her early poetry in a popular 1690s periodical, the *Athenian Mercury*, under the pseudonym of the Pindarick Lady. In 1696, John Dunton, the editor of the *Mercury*, published a single-volume collection of her 'Athenian' verse as *Poems on Several Occasions*, under another pseudonym, Philomela, which alluded to the poetic implications of her maiden name Singer, as opposed to the more gruesome implications of the Ovidian source.

In contrast also to her accepted image as modest and apolitical, Rowe's Athenian verse and Philomela collection clearly demonstrate her Whiggish allegiances. Her poem, 'Upon King William Passing the Boyn', for example, represents the victory of William over James II as both a military triumph and an example of divine intervention on the part of William and his supporters. She describes the 'kind Aethereal Powers' as watching over William as he battles against his French and Jacobite enemies and asks these powers to guide and protect 'the *Hero and the King*' (4):

> All the Ill Fate that threatens him oppose;
> Confound the Forces of his Foreign Foes,
> *And Treacherous Friends less generous than those;*
> May Heaven success to all his Actions give,

And long, and long, and long, let WILLIAM live. (38–42)[4]

Her antipathy to Jacobite resistance to the 1688–89 Revolution is even more strongly expressed in a 'Poetical Question' she posed to the *Mercury* in the issue for 29 May 1694, in which she asks incredulously:

> Resolve me, then, *Athenians*, what are those,
> (Can there be any such?) You call his Foes?
> His Foes! Curst word; and why they'd pierce his Breast,
> Ungrateful Vipers! Where they warmly rest? (9–12)

Despite these explicitly partisan poems, the political side to Rowe's authorial identity has, until recently, been almost completely ignored.

As a nonconformist, Rowe would have welcomed the increased tolerance shown towards religious dissent in the years following 1688 and the accession of William to the throne. As well as revealing her political allegiance, her poetry has a strong religious element which is evident in her juvenile verse and continued to be a major theme in her mature writing. In 1736, for example, she published an eight-book verse narrative *The History of Joseph*.[5] Rowe's devotional verse was not, however, divorced from her political beliefs. In addition to serving as demonstrations of personal faith, religious themes in poetry were often used to signal patriotic loyalty to William and the Revolution principles of 1688–89. As Rowe's early poem on William showed, the overthrow of the Catholic James II was often figured as evidence of divine intervention in support of the Protestant religion and the 1688–89 Revolution. Many of Rowe's religious poems can be read from the context of this approach which was advocated by writers such as John Dennis, Richard Blackmore and, more pertinently in the case of Rowe, the nonconformist poet and hymn writer Isaac Watts. Watts and Rowe not only shared a literary and social network of other nonconformist writers and figures but also a common approach to writing poetry. Like many Whig-oriented poets, both writers advocated the use of biblical themes as suitable material for contemporary poetry. Rowe and Watts shared a belief that biblical verse could serve a social and moral function to reform an increasingly profligate world by fully depicting the horrors of damnation, a sentiment shown in the following lines from 'The Conflagration: An Ode':

> SUPINE as men before the deluge lay,
> In melting joys and luxury dissolv'd,

'Till swift destruction swept them all away,
    The stupid world will then be found;
In all licentiousness and sin involv'd,
    When loud to judgment the last trumpets sound. (1–6)

After her early Philomela poems, Rowe did not produce another single-authored volume until the publication of her extremely success-ful prose work, *Friendship in Death. In Twenty Letters from the Dead to the Living* (1728). Her miscellaneous works were posthumously collected by a family friend and her brother-in-law in 1739, and in 1737 Isaac Watts published a collection of her devotional writing as *Devout Exercises of the Heart.* This lack of single-authored volumes does not mean that Rowe was out of the public eye. In her lifetime, she appeared in a number of prestigious miscellanies throughout the early eighteenth century. Some of these collections, such as *Divine Hymns and Poems on Several Occasions* (1704), showcase her religious verse and draw on her involvement in nonconformist literary circles. Other appearances, such as those in Jacob Tonson's *Poetical Miscellanies: The Fifth Part* (1704) and Matthew Prior's *Poems on Several Occasions* (1709), were a result of more extensive social links, often with her social superiors. Most prominent among these social connections was Rowe's friend and patron, Frances Thynne, the Countess of Hertford, whom Rowe met at the family estate at Longleat, seven miles from Frome. Lady Hertford was to become a well-known literary patron and her association with Rowe continued from the early days at Longleat throughout the author's life. Indeed, Rowe's popular *Letters Moral and Entertaining* (1729–33) are based on a genuine correspondence between the Countess and the middle-class dissenter. The influence of this social network, and of Lady Hertford in particular, can be seen in the many occasional poems Rowe addressed to members of this circle. Poems such as 'To Mr. PRIOR on his SOLOMON', 'To Mr. THOMSON. On the Countess of —'s praising his POEMS' and 'On the death of the Honourable Mrs. THYNNE' may seem excessively narrow and private in concern to a modern reader, but it must be remembered that occasional verses such as these were a staple of early eighteenth-century poetic production.

Despite her huge popularity in the eighteenth century itself and the comparative wealth of biographical detail we have about her, Rowe's poetry has attracted very little critical commentary. Twentieth-century work on Rowe is divided between those critics who have centred on the exemplary portrait of femininity she offered and those who have suggested that this persona masks Rowe's cultural and sexual repression.[6] A common early approach to Rowe was to claim that, particularly after the death of Thomas Rowe, she sublimated her sexual passion in ecstatic religious verse.[7] Certainly, passages such as the following from her biblical paraphrase of 'Canticles. II. Viii, ix' invite such speculation:

> Is it a dream? Or does my ravish'd ear
> The charming voice of my beloved hear?
> Is it his face? Or are my eager eyes
> Deluded by some vision's bright disguise? (1–4)
> [. . .]
> O welcome, welcome, never more to part!
> I'll lodge thee now for ever in my heart;
> My doubtful heart, which trembling scarce believes,
> And scarce the mighty ecstasy receives. (13–16)

Rather than read poems such as this as evidence of Rowe's sublimation of sexual desire, it is more plausible to place her writing in a long tradition of eroticized divine poetry, especially the Canticles, of which the above is a paraphrase. Indeed, Rowe's use of the poetic voice of the Spouse in the Canticles was particularly enabling as it allowed her to experiment with the use of a female poetic persona within a recognizable and established biblical precedent. As Madeleine Forell Marshall points out, 'Divine love in this context was neither particularly mystical nor evidence of psychological confusion. It suggests, rather, a forthright recognition that God is love and love metaphors are legitimate in religious poetry.'[8]

For modern readers, however, the tradition of Christian poetry can seem alien and uninteresting. As a result, Rowe's poetry is seldom taught and no modern accessible critical edition exists of her work. Furthermore, Rowe's poetic expressions of her religious belief have often served to enforce her pious image which, by the same token, has made her a less than attractive figure to feminist literary history in its early stages. Unlike the image of Aphra Behn, for example, Rowe's exemplary reputation has made her a difficult figure to incorporate into a model of women's literary history which insists on isolation and/or embattlement as symptomatic of female literary endeavour. In fact, Rowe's literary career reveals a woman writer who was accepted and applauded by the male critical establishment and who wrote and published her work from within the context of a supportive network of like-minded friends and acquaintances. More recent scholarship on Rowe and patterns of authorship for women has started to focus on these supportive networks and has tended to emphasize a model of women's literary production in this period as more sociable and integrative than has previously been acknowledged. In the course of an essay on Rowe's use of both print and manuscript as media for her poetry. Kathryn R. King has, for example, called for a reassessment of Rowe's significance in the light of 'a theoretical framework that accounts for the complexity and variousness of women's writing in early print culture without recourse to moralized dichotomous models'.[9] In my own recent work on Rowe, I have also emphasized the need to recognize Rowe's lively and active involvement in the various literary cultures and contexts of her day. The challenge now is to use this new contextual work to precipitate in-depth studies of Rowe's poetry. Such a process has been set in motion by Ann Messenger's treatment of Rowe's Christian pastoral verse. In her *Pastoral Tradition and the Female Talent*, Messenger places Rowe's work in relation to both male and female contemporaries, such as Richard Blackmore, Isaac Watts, John Dennis, Sarah Dixon and Elizabeth Carter.[10] As with many of the women poets discussed in this book, however, what is needed is an accessible and authoritative edition of Rowe's poems which represents the full range of her writing. Without such a basic necessity, even a poet as influential and popular as Rowe will continue to be sidelined to the margins of literary history.[11]

Notes

1. Elizabeth Carter, 'On the Death of Mrs. [Elizabeth] Rowe', in Roger Lonsdale, *Eighteenth-Century Women Poets* (Oxford: Oxford University Press, 1990), p. 167.
2. The elegy was first printed with the second edition of Pope's *Eloisa to Abelard* (London: 1720).
3. *The Miscellaneous Works in Prose and Verse of Mrs. Elizabeth Rowe*, eds Henry Grove and Theophilus Rowe, 2 vols (London: 1739), p. xxxiii.
4. In *Poems on Several Occasions* (1696).
5. A ten-book version was published in 1737.
6. See Marlene R. Hansen, 'The Pious Mrs. Rowe', *English Studies* 1 (1995), pp. 34–51, for an analysis of Rowe as exemplar.
7. This approach can be found in Henry F. Stecher, *Elizabeth Singer Rowe, the Poetess of Frome: a Study in Early English Pietism* (Frankfurt: Peter Lang, 1973).
8. Madeleine Forell Marshall, *The Poetry of Elizabeth Singer Rowe (1674–1737)*, Studies in Women and Relgion, Vol. 25 (Lewiston/Queenston: The Edwin Mellen Press, 1989), p. 16.
9. Kathryn R. King, 'Elizabeth Singer Rowe's Tactical Use of Print and Manuscript', in George Justice and Nathan Tinker (eds), *Women's Writing and the*

Circulation of Ideas: Manuscript Publication in England, 1550–1800
(Cambridge: Cambridge University Press, 2002), pp. 158–81 (174). See also,
Margaret J. M. Ezell, *Social Authorship and the Advent of Print* (Baltimore and
London: The Johns Hopkins University Press, 1999), p. 82.

10. See Chapter 7 in particular, ' "The Lord is my Shepherd": Pastoral Elements in Christian Verse', in Ann Messenger, *Pastoral Tradition and the Female Talent* (New York: AMS Press, INC., 2001). See also Chapter 5 of my *Women, Authorship and Literary Culture, 1690–1740* (Basingstoke: Palgrave Macmillan, 2003).

11. As Forell Marshall points out in her selection of Rowe's work, such a critical edition would have to take into account the various 'editorial interference' practised by Rowe's original editors: John Dunton, Grove and Rowe, and Isaac Watts (*The Poetry of Elizabeth Singer Rowe*, pp. 95–6).

Bibliography

Biographical sources

'The Life of Mrs. Elizabeth Rowe', in *The Miscellaneous Works in Prose and Verse of Mrs. Elizabeth Rowe*, ed. Henry Grove and Theophilus Rowe, 2 vols (London: 1739).

Lonsdale, Roger, *Eighteenth-Century Women Poets* (Oxford: Oxford University Press, 1990), pp. 45–6.

Maison, Margaret, 'Elizabeth Rowe', entry in Janet Todd (ed.), *Dictionary of British Women Writers* (London: Routledge, 1989), pp. 582–4.

Napier, Elizabeth R., 'Elizabeth Rowe' entry in Martin C. Battesin (ed.), *Dictionary of Literary Biography*, British Novelists, 1660–1800 (Detroit: Gale Research, 1985), Vol. 39, pp. 409–13.

Prescott, Sarah, and David E. Shuttleton, 'Mary Chandler, Elizabeth Rowe, and "Ralph's Miscellany": Coincidental Biographical and Bibliographical Findings', *Notes and Queries* N.S. 48.1 (March 2001), pp. 31–4.

Some of the original correspondence between Lady Hertford and Elizabeth Rowe can be found in the archives of Alnwick Castle, Northumberland. Alnwick MS 110. Edited versions of their letters can also be found in the two-volume *Miscellaneous Works*.

Library and modern editions

Marshall, Madeleine Forell, *The Poetry of Elizabeth Singer Rowe (1674–1737)*, Studies in Women and Religion, Vol. 25 (Lewiston/Queenston: The Edwin Mellen Press, 1989).

Selections in Roger Lonsdale (ed.), *Eighteenth-Century Women Poets* (Oxford: Oxford University Press, 1989), pp. 47–52.

Poems on Several Occasions. Written by Philomela (London: 1696).

Divine Hymns and Poems on Several Occasions (London: 1704).

The History of Joseph: A Poem (London: 1736), 8 books; a second edition was published in 1737 in ten books.

Poems on Several Occasions. By Mrs Elizabeth Rowe, ed. Edmund Curll (London: 1736/37).

Devout Exercises of the Heart, In Meditation and Soliloquy, Prayer and Praise, ed. Isaac Watts (London: 1737).

The Miscellaneous Works in Prose and Verse of Mrs. Elizabeth Rowe, ed. Henry Grove and Theophilus Rowe, 2 vols (London: 1739); reprinted and expanded as *The Works of Mrs. Elizabeth Rowe*, 4 vols (London: 1796).

Selected secondary sources

Clarke, Norma, 'Soft Passions and Darling Themes: From Elizabeth Singer Rowe, (1674–1737) to Elizabeth Carter (1717–1806)', *Women's Writing* 7.3 (2000), pp. 353–71.

Curran, Stuart, 'Romantic Women Poets: Inscribing the Self', in Isobel Armstrong and Virginia Blain (eds), *Women's Poetry in the Enlightenment: the Making of a Canon, 1730–1820* (Basingstoke: Macmillan now Palgrave Macmillan, 1999), pp. 145–66.

David, Alun, ' "The Story of Semiramis": an Oriental Tale in Elizabeth Rowe's *The History of Joseph*', *Women's Writing* 4.1 (1997), pp. 91–101.

Fairchild, Hoxie Neale, *Religious Trends in English Poetry*, 6 vols (New York: Columbia University Press, 1939), Vol. 1.

Hansen, Marlene R., 'The Pious Mrs. Rowe', *English Studies* 1 (1995), pp. 34–51.

Hughes, Helen Sard, 'Elizabeth Singer Rowe and the Countess of Hertford', *PMLA* 59 (1944), pp. 726–46.

King, Kathryn R., 'Elizabeth Singer Rowe's Tactical Use of Print and Manuscript', in George Justice and Nathan Tinker (eds), *Women's Writing and the Circulation of Ideas: Manuscript Publication in England, 1550–1800* (Cambridge: Cambridge University Press, 2002), pp. 158–81.

Lund, Roger D., '*Bibliotecha* and "the British Dames": an Early Critique of the Female Wits of the Restoration', *Restoration: Studies in English Literary Culture* 12.2 (1988), pp. 96–105.

Marshall, Madeleine Forell, 'Teaching the Uncanonized: the Examples of Watts and Rowe', in Christopher Fox (ed.), *Teaching Eighteenth-Century Poetry* (New York: AMS Press, 1990), pp. 1–24.

Messenger, Ann, *Pastoral Tradition and the Female Talent* (New York: AMS Press, Inc., 2001).

Prescott, Sarah, 'Provincial Networks, Dissenting Connections, and Noble Friends: Elizabeth Singer Rowe and Female Authorship in Early Eighteenth-Century England', *Eighteenth-Century Life* 25, n.s., 1 (Winter 2001), pp. 29–42.

Prescott, Sarah, 'Elizabeth Singer Rowe: Gender, Dissent and Whig Poetics', in Abigail Williams and David Womersley (eds), *Cultures of Whiggism* (Delaware: University of Delaware Press, forthcoming 2003).

Prescott, Sarah, *Women, Authorship and Literary Culture, 1690–1740* (Basingstoke: Palgrave Macmillan, 2003).

Stecher, Henry F., *Elizabeth Singer Rowe, the Poetess of Frome: a Study in Early English Pietism* (Frankfurt: Peter Lang, 1973).

Wright, H. Bunker, 'Matthew Prior and Elizabeth Singer', *Philological Quarterly* 24.1 (1945), pp. 71–82.

8
Lady Mary Wortley Montagu (1689–1762): Haughty Mind, Warm Blood and the 'Demon of Poesie'

Jennifer Keith

Lady Mary Wortley Montagu (1689–1762) is better known for her life and letters than for her poetry. Scholars of the eighteenth century are familiar with this aristocrat's life as traveller, proponent of the small-pox inoculation, and associate of prominent writers of her day, including Alexander Pope and Mary Astell.[1] Her poetry is only gradually gaining the attention it deserves, however. From her satires to her lyrics, Montagu's poetry not only shows a fluent command of formal features and classical erudition valued by a male-dominated poetic elite but also delineates a woman's experience inside and outside a poetic discourse that has been associated with the 'masculine' world of the 'Augustans'.[2] To appreciate Montagu's contributions to the course of English poetry, we must attend to her skilled use of forms associated with the canon and her exploration of poetic personas and lyric passion in relation to these forms.

Mary Pierrepoint began writing poetry as a child, 'haunted', as she later described it, by the 'Demon of Poesie'.[3] Primarily educating herself in her father's extensive library – as a girl, albeit of an aristocratic family, she would not have received the formal education her brother did – she not only read widely in English and French literature but also taught herself Latin. In other words, as an autodidact, Mary acquired something like the elite education considered the sine qua non of Restoration and early eighteenth-century poetry.

It was after Mary eloped with Edward Wortley Montagu that she became acquainted with the male literati of London – including William Congreve and John Gay.[4] In 1715 began her complicated relationship with Alexander Pope, a friendship that ended in hatred. With her husband's appointment as the British ambassador to Turkey, Lady Mary embarked on her voyage to Constantinople in 1716, with her travels including Rotterdam, Cologne, Prague, Budapest, Belgrade, Lesbos, Porto Farina, Italy and France. Although they would return to England in 1717, Lady Mary would later live much of her life abroad. Her position as an aristocrat and, often, an expatriate emboldened her trenchant wit and search for an independence rare for women of this time period.[5]

Her first publication was a rolicking satire in *The Spectator* (No. 573, Wednesday, 28 July 1714) by 'Mrs. President'. In this reply to Addison's *Spectator* No. 561, which satirizes a club of widows led by Mrs. President, Montagu's wit turns on both the widows' penchant for remarriage and the insufficiencies of their past and future husbands.[6] Her political journal, *The Nonsense of Common Sense*, appeared in print from 1737 to 1738. The best known of her works, *Letters . . . Written during her Travels in Europe, Asia and Africa*, would be published posthumously in 1763. While several of her poems were published in her lifetime (many of them without her consent), as a woman and an aristocrat she disdained the public, commercial forum of the press.[7] Precisely because of her dislike of publication and the complex nature of the 'social authorship' inherent in manuscript circulation, the attribution of her poems is difficult and probably incomplete.[8] Isobel Grundy concludes that much of Montagu's work is lost to us, either because she destroyed it, failed to claim it, or its authorship is irretrievably obscured. Montagu wrote to her friends the Steuarts, 'All my works are consecrated to the fire for fear of being put to more ignoble uses, as their betters have before them.'[9]

The reception of her work that did circulate, whether in manuscript or in print, was often conflated with a reception of her person, particularly her violation of gender decorum.[10] Along with other women writers of her era, 'it was hard to distinguish response to her writing (even admiration) from response to her as a person', observes Grundy.[11] But one of the most significant aspects of Montagu's poetry is less how she was received by her contemporaries than how she received *their* work. Her bold critiques, whether her comments to Addison on his *Cato*, some of which he incorporated in his revisions,[12] or her stinging returns to Pope's attacks on her and Swift's 'The Lady's Dressing-Room', are examples of pointed judgements by a woman writer of this era upon the works of her male contemporaries. Such were the results, perhaps, of her class privilege trumping the constraints of her gender. In 'Verses Address'd to the Imitator of the First Satire of the Second Book of Horace' (w. with Lord Hervey 1733, pub. 1733) she identifies Pope's high-mindedness as hatred:

Neither to Folly, nor to Vice confin'd;
The Object of thy Spleen is Human Kind:
It preys on all, who yield or who resist;
To Thee 'tis Provocation to exist. (32–5)

But as thou hate'st, be hated by Mankind,
And with the Emblem of thy crooked Mind,
Mark'd on thy Back, like *Cain*, by God's own Hand;
Wander like him, accursed through the Land. (109–12)

Montagu's aggressive poetic attacks, focusing especially on the bodies of her male victims, are rare examples of a woman poet in this era participating in the typically masculine arena of satire.

Her poetry shows the fruits of an intensive self-education, including fluency in Latin, gained from studying in her family's extraordinary library. Ovid and Horace were to prove important models for her poetry. She demonstrates a facility in elements often considered 'Augustan': the couplet, verse epistle, satire and wit. But the label of Augustan, one increasingly losing its hold on characterizing Restoration and early eighteenth-century poetry, brings with it a misleading assessment of Montagu's poetry as 'masculine'. Such an assessment frequently underpins studies that compare her poetry with that of her male contemporaries. Montagu's poetry may be read fruitfully in relation to several contexts and literary movements, but it is in her juxtaposition and modulation of categories usually seen as opposite, such as the satirical and lyrical, that she contributes uniquely to the course of eighteenth-century poetry. Introducing tonal variations that oppose the urbane structures she uses, Montagu revises poetic kinds, creating a complex emotional range in her work still insufficiently explored by critics. Her representation of women's experience in many of her poems revises inherited models and subgenres: from the perspective of a female speaker or character she reworks the topographical poem (e.g. 'Epistle [to Lord Bathurst]'), recasts Greek myths in relation to female desire (e.g. 'Apollo and Daphne') and revises the Horatian ode (e.g. 'The 5th Ode of Horace Imitated').

Among the notable poems published in her lifetime are her *Six Town Eclogues*, including 'Satturday. The Small Pox: Flavia' (w. 1716, pub. 1747), a poem that achieves Montagu's trademark complexity of tone. Expressing through the character of Flavia Montagu's own sorrow over the loss of her beauty after smallpox, the poet balances sympathy for Flavia with a condemnation of the vanity of physical beauty.[13] As the

poem draws to a close, Flavia's self-pity is transformed when she up-
braids her own attachment to worldly things:

> Cease hapless Maid, no more thy Tale persue,
> Forsake Mankind, and bid the World Adieu.
> Monarchs, and Beauties rule with equal sway,
> All strive to serve, and Glory to obey,
> Alike unpity'd when depos'd they grow,
> Men mock the Idol of their Former vow. (83–8)

Montagu's characteristic use of shifting tones and multiple perspectives underpins her remarkable transformations of classical conventions such as the topos of *beatus ille* – the 'happy man'. Instead of
Horace's happy man who treasures his own small farm in his own
country, in her poem 'Constantinople' (w. 1717; pub. 1720), the
speaker yearns for 'a Little Farm' not in her native England but in
Constantinople where 'Summer reigns with one Eternal Smile' (20).
The first part of the poem combines philosophical contentment and a
feeling of being *depaysagé* – unlanded – which the speaker finds desirable. From this beautiful, un-English landscape, her eyes turn towards
the women enclosed in the city's Greek quarter:

> One Little Spot the small Fenar contains,
> Of Greek Nobillity, the poor remains,
> Where other Helens show like powerfull Charms
> As once engag'd the Warring World in Arms,
> Those Names which Royal Auncestry can boast
> In mean Mechanic arts obscurely lost,
> Those Eyes a second Homer might inspire,
> Fix'd at the loom, destroy their useless Fire. (68–75)

Rather than develop a view of the larger landscape, the poem locates
the fixed eyes of these women in an interior of domestic limitation
and imperial defeat. The happy man yields place to unhappy women,
remnants of a displaced nobility.

Montagu's poetic range includes mordant satires on men and
women, lyrical renderings of the torments of love and critiques of the
double standards placed on women in love and marriage. Her 'Epistle
from Mrs. Y[onge] to her Husband. 1724' (w. 1724, pub. 1972) defends
Mrs. Yonge's affair with another man after enduring her husband's
numerous affairs:

From whence is this unjust Distinction grown?
Are we not form'd with Passions like your own?
   Nature with equal Fire our Souls endu'd,
   Our Minds as Haughty, and as warm our blood,
O're the wide World your pleasures you persue,
The Change is justify'd by something new;
But we must sigh in Silence–and be true. (25–31)

In 'Ye soft Ideas leave this tortur'd Breast' (w. 1736 or 1739) Montagu explores the pain of passion, which extends to thoughts of suicide in the poem '1736. Address'd To' (w. 1736, pub. 1749):[14] 'Why then not hasten that decisive Hour,/Still in my view, and ever in my power?' (20–1). 'Whence this misterious bearing to exist', she asks, 'When every Joy is lost, and every Hope dismist?' (24–5).

In the meditative 'Hymn to the Moon' (w. before August 1740; pub. 1750), the speaker delicately confides in the moon, an intimacy expressed by the moonbeams that softly gild the trees:

By thy pale beams I solitary rove,
   To thee my tender Greife confide,
Serenely sweet you gild the silent Grove,
   My Freind, my Goddess and my Guide.

And yet in the next stanza confiding intimacy turns to protective self-restraint:

Even thee fair Queen from thy amazing height
   The Charms of young Endimion drew,
Veil'd with the Mantle of concealing Night,
   With all thy Greatness, and thy Coldness too. (5–12)

This shift from warmth to coldness can turn on a single line, as in her brief 'Answer to an impromptu Song Address'd to me at Avignon by the Count' (w. 1742–46):

Chantez, chantez vostre tendresse,
   Arachez moi mon Coeur par Force ou par Adresse,
Tachez de le gagner, pour moi je le permets,
   Je n'ai point encore fait d'Efforts pour le defendre,
Mais vous n'avez pas scu le prendre
   Et ferez aussi bien de m'en parler jamais.[15]

The wit and indirection of Augustan lyric are broken down by a lyricism that features the vulnerable heart. Despite the increasing attention given to eighteenth-century women writers in the last decades, Montagu's poetry has received far less critical attention than her prose. Studies of her poems have thus far been concerned with problems of attribution and collaboration with her male contemporaries, biographical and historical information conveyed in her verse, and her poems' representations of gender identity and women's experience. Scholars of Lady Mary are indebted to Isobel Grundy and Robert Halsband for their biographies and scholarly editions of her work. In her scholarly edition of Montagu's poetry, Isobel Grundy has recounted the problems faced by the modern editor in attributing poems to Montagu in the context of manuscript circulation and collaborative authorship. Many of Montagu's poems are probably lost to us. As Lady Mary Pierrepont and then Lady Mary Wortley Montagu, wife of Edward Wortley Montagu, she enjoyed an elite social position that, along with her gender, made the prospect of publishing her poetry abhorrent to her. Still, with the admirable foundation provided by Halsband and Grundy, readers of her poetry are in a position to interpret and evaluate the nuances of Montagu's achievements: her representations of the self through the lenses of gender, class, orientalism and poetic forms.

Notes

1. On Lady Mary's friendship with Astell, see Isobel Grundy, *Lady Mary Wortley Montagu* (Oxford, New York: Clarendon Press, 1999), p. 193ff.
2. I use 'Lady Mary' for the person and 'Montagu' for the writer. See Grundy's *Lady Mary Wortley Montagu*, p. xviii.
3. In Robert Halsband and Isobel Grundy (eds), *Essays and Poems and* Simplicity, *a Comedy* (Oxford: Clarendon Press, 1977, 1993), p. 171. All citations are from this edition.
4. Grundy, *Lady Mary Wortley Montagu*, p. 63
5. 'Montagu epitomizes the expatriate adventurer, whose aristocratic rank enabled her independence but also meant she could only really practice it abroad' (Donna Landry, 'Alexander Pope, Lady Mary Wortley Montagu, and the Literature of Social Comment', in Steven N. Zwicker (ed. and introd.), *The Cambridge Companion to English Literature 1650–1740* (Cambridge: Cambridge University Press, 1998), pp. 307–8).
6. Montagu's Mrs President explains her reasons for accepting to be Lord Friday's *third* wife: 'I could not resist the Delight I took in shewing the young Flirts about Town, it was yet in my Power to give pain to a Man of Sense: This and some private hopes he would hang himself, and what a Glory would it be for me, and how I should be envy'd, made me accept of

being third Wife to my Lord Friday' (Halsband and Grundy, *Essays and Poems and* Simplicity, *a Comedy*, p. 72).

7. Isobel Grundy describes the prevailing atmosphere for women writers of Montagu's generation: '[I]t was not fitting for a well-born woman to publish verses except in circumstances of the most careful decorum and discretion.' See Grundy's 'The Politics of Female Authorship: Lady Mary Wortley Montagu's Reaction to the Printing of Her Poems', *The Book Collector* XXXI (Spring 1982), pp. 19–37 (19).

8. See Margaret J. M. Ezell, *Social Authorship and the Advent of Print* (Baltimore: Johns Hopkins University Press, 1999).

9. Quoted in Grundy, 'The Politics of Female Authorship', p. 37.

10. See Grundy's 'The Politics of Female Authorship' for a detailed account of Montagu's reaction to the printing of her poems and her possible participation in seeing some of her work published.

11. See Isobel Grundy's 'Introduction', p. ix, to her edition of Montagu's *Romance Writings* (Oxford: Clarendon Press, 1999): ' "Lady Mary . . . shines like a comet," wrote Joseph Spence in 1741; "she is all irregular, and always wandering . . . born with fine parts enough for twenty men" [*Letters from the Grand Tour*, ed. Slava Klima (1975), pp. 356–7]. Spence, a scholarly, professional man, was able to muster literary as well as personal admiration, and to translate this into action: he was instrumental in the appearance of Montagu's poems in Dodsley's immensely successful *Collection* [1748] and so – for the moment – in the literary mainstream. Meanwhile their more famous publicizer, Horace Walpole, whose relation to social norms was more tortuous than that of Spence, first judged them "too Womanish," and later noted that they "don't please, though so excessively good" [*Correspondence*, ed. W. S. Lewis et al. (1937ff.), xiiii.234, xix.450]' (Grundy, p. ix).

12. Grundy, *Lady Mary Wortley Montagu*, p. 63.

13. Grundy has described the poem's fine 'equipoise between earnestness and irony' (*Lady Mary Wortley Montagu*, p. xi). Lady Mary had contracted smallpox by December 1715 (p. 99).

14. Grundy notes that 'Lady Mary must have addressed this poem to either Algarotti or Hervey during the period of despair which followed the former's departure'; see *Essays and Poems and* Simplicity, *a Comedy*, Halsband and Grundy, p. 290.

15. Halsband and Grundy's translation (from *Essays and Poems and* Simplicity, *a Comedy*, p. 394) follows:

Sing, sing of your tenderness,
Steal my heart away by force or by guile,
Try to win it, you may, as far as I'm concerned,
I've made no attempt to defend it so far,
But you've been unable to capture it,
And you'll do just as well never to speak of it again.

Bibliography

Biographical sources

Barash, Carol, 'Lady Mary Wortley Montagu', in John Sitter (ed.), *Dictionary of Literary Biography*, Eighteenth-Century British Poets, First Series (Detroit: Gale Research, 1990), Vol. 90, pp. 145–59.

Barry, Iris, *Portrait of Lady Mary Wortley Montagu* ([London]: E. Benn, 1928).

Benjamin, Lewis Saul, *Lady Mary Wortley Montagu: Her Life and Letters (1689–1762)* (London: Hutchinson, 1925).

Gibbs, Lewis [pseud.], Cove, Joseph Walter, *The Admirable Lady Mary: the Life and Times of Lady Mary Wortley Montagu (1689–1762)* (London: J. M. Dent, 1949).

Grundy, Isobel, *Lady Mary Wortley Montagu* (Oxford, New York: Clarendon Press, 1999).

Halsband, Robert, *The Life of Lady Mary Wortley Montagu* (Oxford: Clarendon Press, 1956 [i.e. 1957]).

Paston, George [pseud], *Lady Mary Wortley Montagu and Her Times* (London, New York: Putnam, 1907).

Library and modern editions

The Complete Letters of Lady Mary Wortley Montagu, ed. Robert Halsband (Oxford: Clarendon Press, 1965–67).

Essays and Poems and Simplicity, a Comedy, ed. Robert Halsband and Isobel Grundy (Oxford: Clarendon Press, 1977, 1993).

The Letters and Works of Lady Mary Wortley Montagu, ed. by her great-grandson, Lord Wharncliffe. With additions and corrections derived from original manuscripts, illustrative notes, and a memoir by W. Moy Thomas, new edn, rev. (London: G. Bell and Sons, 1887).

Romance Writings, ed. Isobel Grundy (Oxford: Clarendon Press, 1996).

The Selected Letters of Lady Mary Wortley Montagu, ed. Robert Halsband (Harmondsworth: Penguin, 1986, 1970).

Turkish Embassy Letters, introd. Anita Desai and ed. and annot. Malcolm Jack (Athens, Georgia: University of Georgia Press, 1993).

Selected secondary sources

Campbell, Jill, 'Lady Mary Montagu and the "Glass Revers'd" of Female Old Age', in Helen Deutsch and Felicity Nussbaum (eds), *'Defects': Engendering the Modern Body* (Ann Arbor: University of Michigan Press, 2000), pp. 312–51.

Campbell, Jill, 'Lady Wortley Montagu and the Historical Machinery of Female Identity', in Beth Fowkes Tobin (ed.), *History, Gender and Eighteenth-Century Literature* (Athens, Georgia: University of Georgia Press, 1994), pp. 64–85.

Grundy, Isobel, 'Books and the Woman: an Eighteenth-Century Owner and Her Libraries', *English Studies in Canada* XX (March 1994), pp. 1–22.

Grundy, Isobel, ' "The Entire Works of Clarinda": Unpublished Juvenile Verse by Lady Mary Wortley Montagu', *Yearbook of English Studies* VII (1977), pp. 91–107.

Grundy, Isobel, 'Lady Mary Wortley Montagu and the Theatrical Eclogue', in Carol Gibson-Wood and Gordon D. Fulton (eds), *Theatre of the World/Theatre du Monde* (Edmondton, AB: Academic, 1998), pp. 63–75.

Grundy, Isobel, 'A Moon of Literature: Verse by Lady Mary Wortley Montagu', *New Rambler: Journal of the Johnson Society of London* XI (1972), pp. 6–22.

Grundy, Isobel, 'New Verse by Lady Mary Wortley Montagu', *Bodleian Library Record* X (February 1981), pp. 237–49.

Grundy, Isobel, 'Ovid and Eighteenth-Century Divorce: an Unpublished Poem by Lady Mary Wortley Montagu', *Review of English Studies* XXIII (1973), pp. 417–28.

Grundy, Isobel, 'The Politics of Female Authorship: Lady Mary Wortley Montagu's Reaction to the Printing of her Poems', *The Book Collector* XXXI (Spring 1982), pp. 19–37.

Grundy, Isobel, 'Verses Address'd to the Imitator of Horace: a Skirmish between Pope and Some Persons of Rank and Fortune', *Studies in Bibliography: Papers of the Bibiographical Society of the University of Virginia* XXX (1977), pp. 96–119.

Halsband, Robert, ' "The Lady's Dressing Room" Explicated by a Contemporary', in Henry K. Miller, Eric Rothstein and George S. Rousseau (eds), *The Augustan Milieu: Essays Presented to Louis A. Landa* (Oxford: Clarendon Press, 1970), pp. 225–31.

Landry, Donna, 'Alexander Pope, Lady Mary Wortley Montagu, and the Literature of Social Comment', in Steven N. Zwicker (ed. and introd.), *The Cambridge Companion to English Literature 1650–1740* (Cambridge, England: Cambridge University Press, 1998), pp. 307–29.

Landry, Donna, 'Reading the Rape and To a Lady with Texts by Swift, Wortley Montagu, and Yearsley', in Wallace Jackson and R. Paul Yoder (eds), *Approaches to Teaching Pope's Poetry* (New York: Modern Language Association of America, 1993), pp. 134–41.

Lerner, Laurence, 'Subverting the Canon', *British Journal of Aesthetics* XXXII (October 1992), pp. 347–58.

Lowenthal, Cynthia, *Lady Mary Wortley Montagu and the Eighteenth-Century Familiar Letter* (Athens, Georgia: University of Georgia Press, 1994).

McLaverty, James, ' "Of Which Being Publick the Publick Judge": Pope and the Publication of "Verses address'd to the Imitator of Horace" ', *Studies in Bibliography: Papers of the Bibliographical Society of the University of Virginia* LI (1998), pp. 183–204.

Sherbo, Arthur, and Isobel Grundy, 'A "Spurious" Poem by Lady Mary Wortley Montagu?', *Notes and Queries* XXVII (1980), pp. 407–10.

Snyder, Elizabeth, 'Female Heroism and Legal Discourse in Lady Mary Wortley Montagu's "Epistle from Mrs. Y(onge) to Her Husband" ', *English Language Notes* XXXIV, 4 (June 1997), pp. 10–22.

Thomas, Claudia N., *Alexander Pope and His Eighteenth-Century Women Readers* (Carbondale and Edwardsville: Southern Illinois University Press, 1994), pp. 121–30.

9
Mary Leapor (1722–46): Menial Labour and Poetic Aspiration

Valerie Rumbold

Mary Leapor was born in 1722 at Marston St Lawrence, Northamptonshire, the daughter of Philip Leapor, a gardener, and his wife Anne, née Sharman.[1] Her short life was constrained by poverty and menial labour; but she was to produce a body of work of remarkable accomplishment. Although her poems were until recently very little known, their gradual reappearance in anthologies has been greeted with particular acclaim. Reviewers have singled her out as one of the most impressive voices among the recently rediscovered women poets of the eighteenth century; academic feminist criticism has responded enthusiastically to her engagement with issues of social and gender inequality; and students have often been delighted by the freshness of her wit and the forceful expression of her analysis of injustice and oppression.[2] For Isobel Grundy, she is 'perhaps the most complex and rewarding of all the women labouring-class poets of the eighteenth century'; while for Margaret Anne Doody, 'she delineates the possibilities of some kind of solidarity among women of different classes' and 'is one of the cleverest, most uncompromising, even outrageous' of the women poets in her writing about personal appearance.[3] She speaks to concerns central for many readers today; and though her poems may seem quirky (and in some cases may not have been finished as they would have been if she had lived to prepare them for the press), the quirkiness is arguably inseparable from their particular kind of effectiveness, and is supported by an acute ear for rhythm and expressive emphasis. Leapor is particularly interested in appropriating the heritage of elite poetry to her own purposes; and the boldness and sophistication of her approach to a literary culture to which she was born an outsider is remarkable. A handful of her most anthologized poems has become a staple of the new canon of women's poetry;

but the range of her work is wide, and most of it remains little explored.

Most of what is known of Leapor's education and the writing of her poetry is either inferred from the poems themselves, or is related in a letter by her friend Bridget Freemantle that was printed in the second volume of her poems in 1751.[4] Leapor's father, who at the time of her birth was in service to a local landowner, took a step towards relative independence when in the later 1720s he moved to Brackley, where he ran a market garden and provided gardening services to local gentry.[5] Leapor herself may have attended the local free school: Freeman recorded from Philip Leapor's recollections that 'she was always fond of reading every thing that came in her way', and 'had learnt to write tolerably . . . at about ten or eleven Years old'.[6] Conflict ensued, however, when her parents became concerned that her interest in writing was standing in the way of the manual skills by which she would need to earn her livelihood:

> She would often be scribbling, and sometimes in Rhyme; which her Mother was at first pleas'd with: But finding this Humour increase upon her as she grew up, when she thought her capable of more profitable Employment, she endeavour'd to break her of it; and that he likewise, having no Taste for Poetry, and not imagining it could ever be any Advantage to her, join'd in the same Design: But finding it impossible to alter her natural Inclination, he had of late desisted, and left her more at Liberty.[7]

Leapor's mother died, however, in about 1742; and after this Leapor had two posts as kitchen maid for nearby gentry families. In the first, Weston Hall, she was encouraged in her writing by Susanna Jennens, the widowed mistress of the house, who seems to have given her access to her library, and went so far as to hail her in a humorous poem as 'The successor of Pope'.[8] Her second known post, probably at Edgcote House, home of the Chauncy family, was less congenial, and the house has been plausibly identified as the original of Crumble Hall.[9] Here, to judge by an incident narrated in 'An Epistle to Artemisia. On Fame', she quarrelled with a superior about her writing and was dismissed. In the poem Sophronia calls her a 'thoughtless Baggage', and reminds her of her destiny as a labouring woman:

> Go, ply your Needle: You might earn your Bread;
> Or who must feed you when your Father's dead?[10]

After her dismissal 'she was engaged in her Father's Affairs, and the Business of his House, in which she had nobody to assist her', a situation that although 'she was always chearful' was nevertheless 'some Mortification to a Person of her Turn'.[11] Freemantle, the unmarried daughter of a former rector, became acquainted with Leapor little more than a year before her death; but in this short time she transformed Leapor's prospects; and in poems addressed to Freemantle (alias 'Artemisia') Leapor (using the persona 'Mira') was able to confront some of her most crucial and difficult conflicts.

Freemantle reported that Leapor often wrote 'the humorous Parts of her Poems . . . when cross Accidents happen'd to disturb her', and that this 'generally had the intended Effect, by putting her in a good Humour'.[12] For a woman poet of the lower orders, 'cross Accidents' were arguably structural, not in many cases truly accidents at all; but Freemantle was clearly aware of the need to present Leapor to potential readers as one of the cheerful and unpretending poor. She suggested and largely organized a subscription for a volume of Leapor's verse, and described how prolific Leapor became in what would turn out to be the last months of her life:

> It was really amazeing to see how fast she advanc'd in it; her Thoughts seeming to flow as fast as she could put them upon Paper; and I am persuaded, that many beautiful ones have been lost for want of Leisure to write them.[13]

To judge by the range and ambition of the poems she left behind her, Leapor was at this point maturing fast, gaining confidence to experiment with a wide range of genres and subjects as she glimpsed the possibility of a life freed from the conflict between intellectual ambition and manual obligations.

In 1746, however, all such prospects were cut short when Leapor died of measles. Freemantle reported that shortly before Leapor died she expressed concern for her aged father, and gave her 'the Key of my Buroe', asking her 'to promote a Subscription for his Benefit, which you so kindly have propos'd for mine'.[14] Proposals for her poems, including her 'Ode on Mercy' as a sample, were published in 1747, and attracted nearly 600 subscribers, including several of the nobility as well as influential local families.[15] The 'Ode' is far distant both in form and in theme from the incisive couplets for which Leapor is best known today; and the poems that the subscribers received were a rather cautious selection that avoided potentially controversial satire.[16]

The volume appeared in 1747, with a prefatory notice presenting her as markedly less subversive than the full range of her work would have borne out. A second volume, whose smaller subscription seems to have been supported principally by the circle of the printer and novelist Samuel Richardson, was printed by him in 1751; and it is this volume that contains the satirical verse, largely in couplets, that has been most frequently anthologized and discussed since the rediscovery of Leapor's work in the 1980s and 1990s.[17]

Much of her work, however, remains very little known. Although she studied and imitated Pope and Swift, and worked confidently in the heroic and octosyllabic couplets associated with their familiar epistles, philosophical poems and satires, she was also exploring stanzaic and lyric forms and experimenting with drama.[18] Moreover, alongside the political implications of her writing on landownership, cultural power and gender relations, she was developing a poetry of devout religious enquiry and celebration. Her contemporary readers very probably ranked these currently less fashionable aspects of her work more highly than recent readers have done. Indeed, Lonsdale has suggested that the mid-century taste for poetry that was 'stanzaic, self-consciously elevated and refined, polished in diction, and earnest in moral import' would soon have made poetry like Leapor's seem 'dated and earthbound'; and it may be that the organizers' decision to offer a devotional ode as sample to prospective subscribers was an attempt not only to soothe the social anxieties of Leapor's superiors but also to appeal to a perceived shift in polite taste.[19]

There is room for much more close study of Leapor's art, not only in relation to the themes for which she is currently celebrated but also, potentially, in relation to lesser-known areas of her work. Particularly impressive – especially in relation to her position outside the main stream of educational and occupational privilege – is her confident appropriation of a wide range of forms, genres and topics from a literary culture to which she remained in important respects an outsider: her ability to drop in on a debate with a long history with the casual authority of one who has been following it all along is continually a surprise and a delight.[20] She is a poet with a fine ear for the articulation of emphasis, whether in rendering colloquial exchanges, or in adjusting the impact of discursive argument; and, at her best, she integrates her ideas in teasing and suggestive ways with the structure and movement of her poems, using form in an expressive way that obviates over-explicit statement. Thus, in *Crumble Hall*, it is left to the reader to interpret the placement of the genteel sleeper in the unused library at the central point of the poem; or to meditate on the violent swiftness of the poem's transition from the 'gay Prospect' visible from the 'hot Leads' down to 'the nether World' occupied by Leapor's former colleagues; or to weigh the significance of an account of the house's 'People' that focuses entirely on the occupants of the kitchen.[21]

The initial reception of Leapor's verse was broadly positive; and her reputation was to an extent kept alive throughout the eighteenth century, assisted by praise in John Duncombe's *Feminiad*: she was accorded a representation in George Colman and Bonnell Thornton's *Poems by Eminent Ladies* more generous than that of any other writer, Anne Finch included.[22] However, the fact that her poems were never reprinted in anything like their entirety, and that the second volume in particular is extremely rare, has meant that it has never been easy for later readers to form a balanced estimate of her achievement. She has sometimes been linked with John Clare; but the rapid changes in rural politics, in constructions of gender and in literary taste over the period that separates them means that it is not as straightforward to make meaningful comparisons as might at first appear.[23]

The foundations for the current revival of interest in Leapor's work were laid in the 1980s, with Betty Rizzo's investigations of the publication and reception of her poems. In 1984 Roger Lonsdale's groundbreaking *New Oxford Book of Eighteenth-Century Verse* included three Leapor poems (as many as allocated to Addison or Parnell, but more than the two each allotted to Anne Finch and Mary Barber).[24] In 1990 Lonsdale went on to include an extensive selection of Leapor's work in his *Eighteenth-Century Women Poets: an Oxford Anthology*, prefaced by a judicious and densely researched headnote. Lonsdale's selection favoured the satirical and subversive poems from the second volume; and this element in Leapor's work was also fundamental to Donna Landry's 1990 *The Muses of Resistance: Laboring-Class Women's Poetry in Britain, 1739–1796*. This, the first major monograph to take Leapor as one of its key figures, gained wide attention for its bold and provocative reading in terms of class and gender issues – precisely the aspects of her work that had been played down by Leapor's contemporary promoters, but topics that would be enthusiastically taken up in many of the discussions that followed.

Meanwhile, Richard Greene was working on a doctoral thesis later to be revised and published in 1993 as *Mary Leapor: a Study in Eighteenth-Century Women's Poetry*. Greene provided rich archival detail for her biography, and readings sensitive both to the particularities of a specific time and place in rural England, and to a range of current literary, moral and religious contexts. Leapor was now evidently important enough for critics to disagree about: Landry and Greene implied different answers to the question of how to understand Leapor's writing on social and gender inequality, and to the larger underlying question of how much importance such topics as economic protest or female community should be given in the interpretation of her work as a whole. What was still lacking, however, was a full, annotated modern edition. Only readers prepared to travel to rare book collections, or to resort to microfilm or electronic texts, could make themselves familiar with her whole output; and only those with a thorough knowledge of eighteenth-century contexts could feel even moderately confident of reading Leapor's language, allusions and formal techniques appropriately. Most students remained dependent on the few poems popularized in anthologies.

This will change with the publication of a full edition of Leapor's works, edited by Richard Greene and the late Ann Messenger, expected from Oxford University Press in late 2003. Students will at last have ready access to the full range of her poems and be able to engage in a more thoroughly grounded debate about their significance. It is an exciting prospect.

Notes

1. Richard Greene, *Mary Leapor: a Study in Eighteenth-Century Women's Poetry* (Oxford: Clarendon Press, 1993), p. 4; Mary Leapor, *Poems on Several Occasions*, 2 vols (London: 1748–51), Vol. 2, p. xxix.
2. For reviewers' responses, see Greene, *Mary Leapor*, pp. 35–6; for academic feminism, see Donna Landry, *The Muses of Resistance: Laboring-Class Women's Poetry in Britain, 1739–1796* (Cambridge: Cambridge University Press, 1990), and Kate Lilley, 'Homosocial Women: Martha Sansom, Constantia Grierson, Mary Leapor and Georgic Verse Epistle', in Isobel Armstrong and Virginia Blain (eds), *Women's Poetry in the Enlightenment: the Making of a Canon, 1730–1820* (London: Macmillan now Palgrave Macmillan, 1998), pp. 167–83.
3. Isobel Grundy, '(Re)discovering Women's Texts', in Vivien Jones (ed.), *Women and Literature in Britain, 1700–1800* (Cambridge: Cambridge University Press, 2000), pp. 179–96 (188); Margaret Anne Doody, 'Women Poets of the Eighteenth Century', in Jones, *Women and Literature in Britain, 1700–1800*, pp. 217–37 (224).
4. Leapor, *Poems on Several Occasions*, 2 vols (London: 1748–51), Vol. 2, pp. xvii–xxxii.
5. Greene, *Mary Leapor*, pp. 5–8.
6. Ibid., pp. 8–9; Leapor, *Poems on Several Occasions*, Vol. 2, pp. xxix–xxx.
7. Leapor, *Poems on Several Occasions*, Vol. 2, p. xxx.

8. Greene, *Mary Leapor*, pp. 10–14.
9. Ibid., pp. 15–17.
10. Leapor, *Poems on Several Occasions*, Vol. 2, p. 52.
11. Greene, *Mary Leapor*, pp. 10–18; Leapor, *Poems on Several Occasions*, Vol. 2, p. xxii.
12. Leapor, *Poems on Several Occasions*, Vol. 2, p. xxvii.
13. Ibid., pp. xx, xxiii.
14. Ibid., p. xxviii.
15. Greene, *Mary Leapor*, p. 24.
16. The 'Ode on Mercy' can also be found in Leapor, *Poems on Several Occasions*, Vol. 1, pp. 12–15. A copy of the proposal is preserved in the Bodleian Library, Ballard MS 42: see Greene, *Mary Leapor*, p. 10, n.
17. Greene, *Mary Leapor*, pp. 26–9. The most rounded impression is given by Fairer and Gerrard: David Fairer and Christine Gerrard (eds), *Eighteenth-Century Poetry: an Annotated Anthology*, Blackwell Annotated Anthologies (Oxford: Blackwell, 1999), pp. 289–91.
18. For Pope, see Claudia N. Thomas, *Alexander Pope and His Eighteenth-Century Women Readers* (Carbondale and Edwardsville: Southern Illinois University Press, 1994); for Swift, see Margaret Doody, 'Swift among the Women', *YES* XVIII (1988), pp. 68–92.
19. Roger Lonsdale (ed.), *Eighteenth-Century Women Poets: an Oxford Anthology* (Oxford: Oxford University Press, 1990), p. xxxi.
20. See, for example, her engagement with theories of political origins in 'Man the Monarch': Leapor, *Poems on Several Occasions*, Vol. 2, pp. 7–10.
21. Leapor, *Poems on Several Occasions*, Vol. 2, pp. 116–18.
22. Greene, *Mary Leapor*, pp. 29–31.
23. Ibid., pp. 33–5.
24. Roger Lonsdale (ed.), *The New Oxford Book of Eighteenth-Century Verse* (Oxford: Oxford University Press, 1984), nos 269–71.

Bibliography

Library and modern editions

Leapor, Mary, *Poems on Several Occasions*, 2 vols (London: 1748–51).
Greene, Richard, and Ann Messenger (eds), *The Works of Mary Leapor* (Oxford: Oxford University Press, 2003).
Selections in anthologies include: Roger Lonsdale (ed.), *Eighteenth-Century Women Poets: an Oxford Anthology* (Oxford: Oxford University Press, 1990), pp. 194–217, with a particularly useful biographical headnote; David Fairer and Christine Gerrard (eds), *Eighteenth-Century Poetry: an Annotated Anthology*, Blackwell Annotated Anthologies (Oxford: Blackwell, 1999), pp. 284–304, with detailed headnotes on individual poems.

Selected secondary sources

Chaden, Caryn, 'Mentored from the Page: Mary Leapor's Relationship with Alexander Pope', in Donald C. Mell (ed.), *Pope, Swift, and Women Writers* (London: Associated University Presses, 1996), pp. 31–47.

Doody, Margaret Anne, 'Swift among the Women', *YES* XVIII (1988), pp. 68–92.

Doody, Margaret Anne, 'Women Poets of the Eighteenth Century', in Vivien Jones (ed.), *Women and Literature in Britain, 1700–1800* (Cambridge: Cambridge University Press, 2000), pp. 217–37.

Greene, Richard, *Mary Leapor: a Study in Eighteenth-Century Women's Poetry* (Oxford: Clarendon Press, 1993).

Griffin, Dustin, *Literary Patronage in England, 1650–1800* (Cambridge: Cambridge University Press, 1996).

Grundy, Isobel, '(Re)discovering Women's Texts', in Jones (ed.), *Women and Literature in Britain, 1700–1800*, pp. 179–96.

Landry, Donna, *The Muses of Resistance: Laboring-Class Women's Poetry in Britain, 1739–1796* (Cambridge: Cambridge University Press, 1990).

Lilley, Kate, 'Homosocial Women: Martha Sansom, Constantia Grierson, Mary Leapor and Georgic Verse Epistle', in Isobel Armstrong and Virginia Blain (eds), *Women's Poetry in the Enlightenment: the Making of a Canon, 1730–1820* (London: Macmillan now Palgrave Macmillan, 1998), pp. 167–83.

Mandell, Laura, 'Demystifying (with) the Repugnant Female Body: Mary Leapor and Feminist Literary History', *Criticism* XXXVIII (1991), pp. 551–82.

Messenger, Ann, *Pastoral Tradition and the Female Talent: Studies in Augustan Poetry* (New York: AMS Press, 2001).

Rizzo, Betty, 'Christopher Smart, the "C.S." Poems, and Molly Leapor's Epitaph', *The Library*, series 6–5 (1983), pp. 21–31.

Rizzo, Betty, 'Molly Leapor: an Anxiety for Influence', *Age of Johnson* IV (1991), pp. 313–43.

Rizzo, Betty, 'The Patron as Poet Maker: the Politics of Benefaction', in *Studies in Eighteenth-Century Culture* XX, Proceedings of the American Society for Eighteenth-Century Studies (East Lansing: Colleagues Press, 1990), pp. 241–66.

Rumbold, Valerie, 'The Alienated Insider: Mary Leapor in "Crumble Hall" ', *British Journal for Eighteenth-Century Studies* XIX (1996), pp. 63–76.

Thomas, Claudia N., *Alexander Pope and His Eighteenth-Century Women Readers* (Carbondale and Edwardsville: Southern Illinois University Press, 1994).

Part II
Contexts

10
Imagining the Woman Poet: Creative Female Bodies

Jane Spencer

As women poets grew in numbers during the years 1660–1750, the web of writing discussing the woman poet grew too, a necessary accompaniment, offering ways of imagining her existence. The poet had always been generally understood to be male, his muse or inspiration female. The Renaissance had emphasized the poet's masculinity through his writing on the female beloved and the implicit femininity of the text he produced.[1] The idea that poetic authorship was grounded in a hierarchical heterosexual relation remained strong in later periods, and made the notion of the woman writer problematic. One solution was to think of the muse as writer instead of inspiration. In 1700, when a group of women wrote poems to commemorate the death of Dryden, thus claiming for female poets a place in the national literary culture, they did so as 'the Nine Muses'. Such attempts aroused some opposition. 'Chagrin', a fictional critic in a 1702 pamphlet, may have the Nine Muses' poems in mind when he complains about women writing for the stage:

> What a Pox have the Women to do with the Muses? I grant you the Poets call the Nine Muses by the Name of Women, but why so? not because the Sex had anything to do with Poetry, but because in that Sex they're much fitter for prostitution.

His companion immediately scolds him for being 'abusive', but his rudeness draws attention to something generally understood: that the female role in poetry is as sexual partner and inspiration of the male poet. On that basis, he sees the woman writer as a contradiction in terms: 'I hate these Petticoat-Authors; 'tis false Grammar, there's no Feminine for the *Latin* word, 'tis entirely of the Masculine Gender, and

99

the Language won't bear such a thing as a She-Author'.[2] Satires on women writers during this period express something similar, though covertly: the woman is a poet, but she is a bad, or affected, or ridiculous, or immoral one, hence not really a true poet.

Some defenders of the woman poet understood that to imagine her fully required a radical revision of the relationship between sexuality and poetry. One admirer of Katherine Philips, known by her pseudonym 'Philo-Philippa', rewrote the familiar myth of Daphne and Apollo, in which poetic achievement comes from the sublimation of male sexual aggression. Apollo, god of poetry and figure for the poet, pursues Daphne with intent to rape, till she foils him by turning into a laurel tree. Forever unable to attain the object of his desires, the poet gets the bays, the crown of poetry, instead. Philo-Philippa dismisses Apollo: he does not rule poetry in general, only male poets. Her own muse will be Orinda (Philips) herself, one female poet as muse for another. True poetry, she contends, comes from such a relationship: all-female and non-aggressive:

> He [Apollo] could but force a Branch, *Daphne* her Tree
> Most freely offers to her Sex and thee,
> And says to Verse, so unconstrain'd as yours,
> Her Laurel freely comes, your fame secures:
> And men no longer shall with ravish'd Bays
> Crown their forc'd Poems with as forc'd a praise.[3]

Both male poetry and its fame are seen as the result of sexual violence, while Orinda's poetry has the freedom of her consensual relationship with inspiration. Not all writers on the woman poet offered so bold a rethinking of existing terms; but there was no lack of figures in which to show that the language could, in fact, bear a She-Author. The woman poet was imagined not only as muse but as angel, Amazon, nightingale, whore, mother, amorous woman, domestic matron, virgin, hermaphrodite. Whether positive or negative in intention, whether created in hyperbolic praise, anxious self-justification, or satiric detraction, these images dealt in their various ways with one all-pervasive problem, recently theorized as the mismatch within patriarchal society between female embodiment and full human subjectivity.[4] How could the poet's writing come from a woman's body?

This question was tackled in a dazzling variety of ways by Abraham Cowley in his commendatory ode to Katherine Philips, printed in the unauthorized edition of her *Poems* in 1664. Reprinted in the posthumous 1667 edition, and in successive editions of Cowley's own works, this poem helped establish Philips's high reputation. Orinda has added to the conventionally feminine beauty the conventionally masculine wit; she is an Amazonian fighter who deposes man with his own weapons; and poetry, figured as a kingdom ruled by Apollo, must now admit women to the succession, as the 'Salick Law' keeping them out is cancelled.[5] Her poetry is equated with her feminine physical attractions, her gentle numbers likened to her smooth forehead; yet her work is 'manly', or better still 'Angelical', for her verses, like angels, unite man's strength and woman's sweetness (Stanza 3, sig. C1r). The Greek poet Sappho is here, as so often in this period, invoked to indicate the ancient precedent for women's poetry; but, again as is often the case, she is a shamed ancestor: 'Ill Manners soil the lustre of her fame'. Orinda outdoes Sappho because of her 'inward Vertue', imagined as a light shining through her paper. Her works teach honour and friendship (Stanza 4, sig. C1r–C1v). Finally, the Amazonian reference is softened: Orinda reigns over men, but hers is 'Wit's Mild Empire'; and she is a national heroine, her existence prophesied by Merlin. 'Boadicia', the female warrior who tried to defend Britain against the Romans, now rejoices to see a new British heroine defeat her old enemies in art (Stanza 5, sig. C1v).

Cowley's terms for Orinda were repeatedly echoed in later commentary on women poets. Her union of wit and beauty was also ascribed to Aphra Behn, of whom George Granville wondered whether her 'Wit' or her 'Eyes' were more captivating.[6] The female poet as heroic warrior deposing man is frequently invoked, especially among the feminist writers and the new female playwrights of the turn of the century. 'Thou Champion of our Sex go on and show/Ambitious Man what Womankind can do', Sarah Fyge Egerton was urged.[7] 'Our *Salique* Law of wit you have destroy'd,/Establish'd female claim, and triumph'd o'er our pride', Catharine Trotter was told.[8] Like Katherine Philips, Aphra Behn was praised for linked physical and poetical attractions, her 'charming Lines' being 'smooth, as Beauty's Face';[9] conversely, attacks on her poetry could always invoke 'the Ruin of her Face'.[10] Behn, like Philips, was seen to unite masculine and feminine qualities: 'A Female Sweetness and a Manly Grace'.[11] As Cowley saw Orinda surpassing Sappho through her virtue, Elizabeth Singer was similarly seen to surpass the ancient Greek and the more recent precursor, Behn: 'Sapho and Behn reform'd, in thee revive', declared one encomiast[12] of her 1696 volume (*Philomela: Or, Poems*). 'Wit's Empire' is once more claimed for a 'Female Reign' in Sarah Fyge's poem 'The Emulation'; and Behn and Philips together are invoked to demonstrate the strength of the native poetic tradition when Nahum Tate announces that 'Greece *boasts one* Sappho; *two* Orinda's, *we*'.[13]

However, one cluster of images used by Cowley is very rarely invoked with positive connotations in subsequent discussions of the woman poet. In the second stanza of his ode, he turns to the ancient and familiar analogy between poetic creativity and human procreation, confronting the idea of the poet in the maternal body:

> Women, as if the Body were the whole
>   Did that, and not the Soul,
>   Transmit to their posterity;
>   If in it sometimes they conceiv'd,
>   Th'abortive issue never liv'd.
> 'Twere shame and pity, *Orinda*, if in thee
> A spirit so rich, so noble, and so high,
>   Should unmanur'd or barren lie.
> But thou industriously hast sow'd and till'd
>   The fair and fruitful field:
> And 'tis a strange increase that it doth yield.
>   As when the happy Gods above
>   Meet all together at a Feast,
> As secret joy unspeakably does move
> In their great Mother *Cybeles* contented breast:
> With no less pleasure thou, methinks, shoud'st see
> This thy no less immortal Progeny,
> And in their Birth thou no one touch dost find,
>   Of th'ancient Curse to Woman-Kind;
>   Thou bring'st not forth with pain,
> It neither Travel is, nor *Labour* of thy Brain.
>   So easily they from thee come,
>   And there is so much room
> In the unexhausted and unfathom'd womb;
> That, like the *Holland* Countess, thou might'st bear
> A Child for ev'ry day of all the fertile year. (Stanza 2, sig. B2v–C1r)

It is an old idea to figure a writer's poems as his children, and in the Renaissance a well-known conceit that the (male) poet labours in childbirth as he tries to write.[14] The metaphor, while applying feminine imagery to the poet, draws attention to the perceived difference between male and female creativity: in analogy to the Aristotelian view of procreation, in which the female provides only the matter, the male the spiritual principle of generation, the (male) writer's poem is understood as a spiritual child in contrast to the bodily child the mother bears. On this view spiritual or poetic creativity is hard to imagine in a woman, who is or should be confined to literal childbearing. Cowley's poem concedes this to have been the case before Orinda: women, defined by and confined to the body, could not produce conceptions of the soul, or if they did, these would not develop. Orinda, unlike other women, has spiritual offspring. Thus Cowley allows woman, in Orinda, to transcend the body and transmit the soul; but the insistent use of the imagery of fertility, easy birth and unfathomed womb, literalized by our consciousness that it applies here, not to a man's writing, but to the poetry of a mother, keeps returning the reader to the female body. To rescue Orinda from the merely passive reproductive role understood as woman's, Cowley adapts ancient metaphors: the female body as earth to be ploughed and sown by man is now the female spirit that needs to be made fertile; and Orinda herself, turned hermaphrodite, tills the field. Fertilizing herself, she is next compared to the mother goddess Cybele, her poems to the immortal gods who were Cybele's sons. That Cybele, goddess of fertility, was also identified with Agdistis, originally a hermaphrodite, may be relevant here. Orinda's poetic fertility requires that the usual understanding of reproduction be reimagined. While this stanza makes her vividly a mother, it equally sets her apart from other mothers: unlike other women, she is free from Eve's curse, and feels no pain in childbirth. Like the Virgin Mary she is a singular, dazzling exception among women.

Cowley's stanza offers a rare example of maternal fecundity favourably invoked in discussion of women's poetry. Others praised Orinda's shining virtue, and her strength and sweetness, but not her womb. This is not surprising, given the seventeenth- and eighteenth-century association of monstrosity with motherhood. The excessive fertility of monstrous mothers, from Spenser's Errour to Milton's Sin and Pope's Dulness, is associated with darkness and chaos, antitheses of the light and order of divine creation.[15] When the female writer is figured as mother, it is usually to degrade her by the implicit contrast between real (male) spiritual creativity and the merely bodily acts of female creation. The prolific writer Eliza Haywood is placed in *The Dunciad* as an animal mother, 'with cow-like udders', and her books are 'Two babes of love close clinging to her waste'.[16] In Gay's *Three Hours After Marriage*, the fictional poet Phoebe Clinket is innocent of bearing the literal bastard child introduced towards the end of the farce, but a running joke is made of the confusion between such a child and 'the Offspring of [her] Brain'. The more she announces with pride that 'for Fertility and Readiness of Conception, I will yield to nobody', the more the woman poet is reduced to a comic maternal body.[17] The mother's body is by no means the only image to be used against the woman poet, but it is a crucial one. An implicit contrast between female procreation and the true poetic creation of which men are capable underlies hostile reactions to the woman poet, which return obsessively to imagining her in terms of her body.

One unfavourable image is of the female poet as subject to, and produced by, particularly female mental and physical disorders. In *The Rape of the Lock* the goddess Spleen is greeted as the

> Parent of Vapours and of Female Wit,
> Who give th' *Hysteric* or *Poetic* Fit,
> On various Tempers act by various ways,
> Make some take Physick, others scribble Plays . . .

Hysteria, believed to be a particularly female malady caused by the wandering womb, makes the woman write, and is itself caused by spleen, a mental illness particularly associated with women. Pope links it especially to the woman of childbearing age: spleen is said to 'rule the Sex to Fifty from Fifteen'.[18] Pope's lines on spleen and women's writing offended the poet Anne Finch, Countess of Winchilsea; they must have struck her with peculiar force, since she was herself the author of a Pindaric poem on the spleen in which she confessed her own susceptibility to the disorder (see above, p. 65). She complained to him about the lines, and he answered her with a gallant poem, praising her by separating her from all other women writers: it is of no use for her to defend them, for she surpasses them all – an idea he expresses by detaching her from images of the female body and associating her with a symbol of masculine spirit:

> To write their Praise you but in vain essay;
> Ev'n while you write, you take that Praise away:
> Light to the Stars the Sun does thus restore,
> But shines himself till they are seen no more.[19]

In her answer, Finch refused to be detached from other women, and playfully advised Pope to 'shock the sex no more' if he did not wish, like Orpheus, to be torn to pieces by avenging women.[20] The exchange between them was good humoured, but still made it clear that only the exceptional woman poet could escape the association with the disorderly female body.

A very common hostile image of the woman poet as sexualized body was the whore. This figure expresses anxieties not only about women's writing but also about the debasement of all writing in a developing commercial culture. Robert Gould makes the connection between hack writing and prostitution clear in his lines attacking Aphra Behn and 'Ephelia' as *'Hackny Writers'*, who:

> . . . when their Verse did fail
> To get 'em Brandy, Bread and Cheese, and Ale,
> Their Wants by Prostitution were supply'd,
> Shew but a *Tester*, you might up and Ride;
> For *Punk* and *Poetess* agree so pat,
> You cannot well be *This* and not be *That*.[21]

An earlier version links *'Punk* and *Poesie'*, showing that poetry itself, not only its female practitioners, is implicated in the charge.[22] If the anxiety is general, though, women are seen particularly to embody it. The efforts expended by women poets and their supporters to present a counter-image of the woman poet as chaste show how damaging the whore image was felt to be. The emphasis laid on the woman poet's modest reserve, her reluctance to publish, her higher than commercial motives, is there to avoid her association with the whore. By the beginning of the eighteenth century, the tradition was well established of using earlier women poets to provide example and counter-example. Behn, the most prominent and successful of the women writing professionally up to that time, was admired and imitated by many female poets, but she was increasingly invoked as an example of the impure female writer. Katherine Philips, understood in terms of chastity and apparent reluctance to publish, was a safer model for emulation. The women writers of the eighteenth century have therefore been described as dividing into professional 'daughters of Behn' and genteel, amateur 'daughters of Orinda',[23] a division which tells us a good deal about women writers' self-presentation, but much less about their practice. In fact, during the first half of the eighteenth century the counter-image of the modest, retiring, virtuous poetess became so successful that it became a means to market women's poetry to subscribers and other buyers, in a discreet form of professionalization.[24]

The valorization of the woman poet in terms of her sexual virtue was one attempt to deal with the question of poetry and the female body, by de-emphasizing the body of the woman poet. This tendency was seen early in the period in praise of women writers, especially when, like Anne Killigrew, they were virginal and dead. Dryden's ode on Anne Killigrew associates her with various human figures but not the mature woman: 'Her Wit was more than Man, her Innocence a Child!' Even on the subject of love Killigrew was considered pure: 'Ev'n love (for Love sometimes her Muse exprest)/Was but a Lambent-flame which play'd about her Brest'.[25] Till the end of the seventeenth century, however, it was still possible to write favourably of the woman poet in terms of her sexual power and sexual feeling. The amorous female poet was a positive counterpart to the negative stereotype of the whore. 'Ephelia', echoing Dryden's rhymes but not his sentiments, wrote that Behn's poetry depicted 'passions so gentle, and so well exprest,/As needs must be the same fill your own Breast'.[26] Behn was praised for seducing her readers: her 'Pen disarms' the male reader, so that he yields to the next woman he meets, and turns female readers 'Love-sick', their bodies expressing an eroticism transferred to them directly from the female poet:

> Within their Breasts thy warmth and spirit flows,
> And in their Eyes thy streaming softness flows;
> Thy raptures are transfus'd through every vein.[27]

Such positive views of the link between poetry and the sexually aroused body always coexisted with negative images of eroticism; but it was from the 1690s onwards that there was a decisive turn against the figure of the amorous woman poet. The poetry of Elizabeth Singer (later Rowe) was early associated with this turn. Elizabeth Johnson introduced Singer's *Poems on Several Occasions* (1696) to the reader with a preface praising earlier women poets as champions of women, but acknowledging that some poetesses had been corrupted by sexual love. This 'fall' is compared to the fall of the angels. Men tried

> to *Corrupt* that *Virtue* which they can no otherwise *overcome*: and sometimes they prevail'd: But, if some *Angels* fell, others remained in their *Innocence* and *Perfection* . . . *Angels Love*, but they love *Virtuously* and *Reasonably* . . . and if all our *Poetesses* had done the same, I wonder what our *Enemies* cou'd have found out to have objected against us.[28]

This image of the virtuous poetess as unfallen angel offers a feminized version of a figure that in Cowley's ode to Philips had signified androgyny. The stress now is not on the union of masculine and feminine, but that of purity and femininity, as the feminine is spiritualized. The virgin is one figure for the woman poet used to express the severing of the connection between poetry and the sexual life. In Dryden's ode to her Anne Killigrew is 'the much lamented Virgin', Heaven's '*Vestal*', who atones for the sins of those who have 'Prophan'd' the 'Heav'nly Gift of Poesy', and 'Made prostitute and profligate the Muse' (Dryden, *Works*, III, 111). One of Catharine Trotter's encomiasts linked the virgin poetess to the moral reform of the stage, remarking that Trotter's '*virgin* voice offends no *virgin* ear'.[29] The most thorough attempt to build up the image of the poetess as virgin was undertaken by Jane Barker. From the poems circulating in manuscript in the 1670s to the late novels – the final one published in 1726 – centred on the poet-heroine Galesia, she linked the virgin life with dedication to both Apollo's arts, medicine and poetry. Sometimes, as in the poem 'A Virgin Life', she celebrates virginity; at other times she represents Galesia's loss of Bosvil's love, her avoidance of sundry marital prospects, and her vow to remain a virgin as more curse than blessing. In one early poem, first published in her *Poetical Recreations* in 1688 and included in the short novel *Bosvil and Galesia* in 1713, Galesia is told:

> Since, since thou hast the muses chose,
> Hymen and fortune are thy foes,
>   Thou shalt have Cassandras fate,
>   In all thou sayst unfortunate.[30]

The image of the faithful virgin also informs Barker's other poetic persona, Fidelia, in whose name she wrote Jacobite verses presented in a manuscript book to James II's son. Little notice was taken of Fidelia's verse in the Jacobite court-in-exile, however, and Barker seems to have felt that the virgin poet's voice, like Cassandra's, was not heard.[31] Certainly the virgin did not become a dominant image for the woman poet during the eighteenth century, which was more interested in integrating its ideals of women's writing with its ideals of marriage and domesticity.

While Barker spent years in exile in St Germain, another Jacobite poet, Anne Finch, Countess of Winchilsea, remained in England, retiring from the court after the 1688 Revolution to live in rural Kent. Political retreat was transformed in her poetry into a willed poetic solitude, in which the laurel is rejected and the muse prefers the shade. Finch's poetry of 'solitude, inwardness, darkness', which 'relegates party politics to the underworld of poetic discourse', has even been seen as creating not just an image of the specifically female poetic speaker, but a powerful figure for the 'poetic psyche' generally.[32] The images of retirement so common in her work are also found in the poetry of several women of the late seventeenth and early eighteenth centuries. Based on a Horatian model of retirement from the urban political scene to rural virtue, and influenced by Cowley's and Pope's poetry of retirement, women's praises of a country retreat both partake of a common, classically authorised image of the virtuous (male) poet, and adapt it to imply the especially feminine virtues of an authorship removed from urban commerce.[33] The image of the retired poet was adopted by many women and used to create poems in various moods. 'When all alone in some belov'd Retreat', Mary Chudleigh writes of enjoying a calm and religious introspection in which she can:

> Enlarge my Knowledge, and each Error find;
> Inspect each Action, ev'ry Word dissect,
> And on the Failures of my Life reflect.[34]

Lady Mary Wortley Montagu transformed her window overlooking Constantinople into a 'retreat, secure from Human Kind', from which she could write as a satirist glad to escape such worldly follies as:

> Impertinence with all her tattling train,
> Fair-sounding Flattery's delicious bane,
> Censorious Folly, noisy Party rage,
> The thousand Tongues with which she must engage
> Who dare have Virtue in a vicious Age.[35]

Jean Adams, in a more homely address 'To the Muse', described the neat boundaries of a virtuous rural poetic ideal:

> Come hither to the hedge, and see
> The Walks that are assigned to thee:
> All the bounds of Virtue shine,
> All the plain of Wisdom's thine,
> All the flowers of harmless Wit
> Thou may'st pull, if thou think'st fit,
> In the fair field of History.

All the plants of Piety
Thou mayst freely thence transplant:
But have a care of whining Cant.[36]

This verse has the unpretentious air admired in the retired female
poet, especially when, like Adams, she was of humble origins. It establishes a confident and humorous relationship with the muse at the
expense of circumscribing her.

The retiring, rural female poet could be especially appropriately
imaged in the figure of the nightingale. Famed for the sweetness of its
song, sometimes taken to express love, sometimes seen as an outpouring of grief, this bird was used by Petrarch and extensively in the Renaissance as a figure for the lyric poet. Its reputation as a solitary singer fed
ideas of the poet's solitude, while the artlessness of birdsong provided
the occasion for meditation on the relationship between poetic art and
untutored nature. Early in the eighteenth century Anne Finch, Countess
of Winchilsea, contributed to this tradition in 'To the Nightingale'. The
speaker addresses the nightingale with a promise to imitate it, to 'set my
Numbers to thy Layes', in order to produce a song 'Free as thine'; but
though poets were originally 'wild as thee', they cannot return to that
natural state. The muse cannot find words to fit the bird's 'Accents',
whether her notes of harmony or 'Division'; so the speaker asks the bird
to stop singing, ending in a comment on her own peevishness:

Thus we Poets that have Speech,
Unlike what thy Forests teach,
    If a fluent Vein be shown
    That's transcendent to our own,
Criticise, reform, or preach,
Or censure what we cannot reach.[37]

The poem is notable for its reversal of earlier contests in which poetic
art is construed as superior to the outpourings of nature.[38] Finch, traditionally, makes the bird female and the generalized 'unhappy Poet'
male, but complicates this pattern by including herself among the
'Poets that have Speech'. Finch here refuses the identification of
woman poet with feminine nature in the body of the nightingale.
Others in her time and earlier used such an identification as one way
of imagining a specifically feminine woman poet.

In the late sixteenth century, the nightingale had been seen as an
image for the female poet because of its associations with artlessness,

sweetness and the expression of feeling; and the bird's reputed reclusiveness enabled the woman poet to avoid charges of boldness and self-display. Moreover, the nightingale was understood as female because of its identification with Philomela, of classical myth, who was raped by Tereus, had her tongue cut out, and was eventually transformed into a bird. Philomela's sweet song thus voices the complaints that were silenced in the woman. Mary Ellen Lamb has shown how Renaissance readings of Philomela concentrated on her as the victim of Tereus, expressing her grief, ignoring the more vengeful aspect of her story, when she and her sister Procne kill Tereus and Procne's son and serve him as a meal to his father.[39] In the Restoration and eighteenth century the figure of Philomela was still further removed from the violence of the classical myth, her specific complaint about rape being softened to a more general melancholy. The key association between woman poet and nightingale in this period was made by Elizabeth Singer, whose poems were published under the pseudonym Philomela in the 1690s. The pseudonym made an oblique reference to her real surname, and in 1739 her biographer suggested that the name was given by her friends at the time of publication:

> her modesty not consenting that her own name should appear [as the author of her poems], this was substituted in the room of it, as bearing a very easy allusion to it, and happily expressing the softness and harmony of her verses, not less soothing and melodious than the strains of the nightingale, when from some leafy shade she fills the woods with her melancholy plaints.

He also emphasized her 'love of solitude, which seems almost inseparable from a poetic genius', and the artlessness of her verse: 'her exquisite wit, and delicate imagination, were scarce any thing indebted to the assistance of art or labour'.[40] Singer Rowe's Philomela, then, had the associations of natural song, sweetness and retiring modesty that had led to the adoption of the figure for the female poet. By the time this biography of her was written, moreover, this early adopted poetic pseudonym had acquired some added resonance from the circumstances of her later life and writings. After the death of her husband, Elizabeth Rowe returned to live in her father's house in Frome, Somerset. She represented this as a retirement from the world, prompted by natural temperament and by grief, and expressing her carelessness of this world and devotion to the next. One of this Philomela's most admired poems was 'On the death of Mr. Thomas Rowe', in which she addresses her husband's departed soul:

For thee, all thoughts of pleasure I forego,
For thee, my tears shall never cease to flow;
For thee at once I from the world retire,
To feed, in silent shades, a hopeless fire.[41]

This nightingale, mourning her husband's death rather than complaining of Tereus' rape, builds altogether gentler associations for the female poet of the eighteenth century.

While Rowe's grief and rural retirement consolidated her image as Philomela, her religious writing, with its exalted strain of dissenting piety, added a heavenly connotation to the meaning of the nightingale. For Isaac Watts, Philomela's wings were the means for lifting his own thoughts heavenwards:

Let all my powers with awe profound,
    While PHILOMELA sings,
Attend the rapture of the sound,
And my devotion rise on her seraphic wings.[42]

Her two prose works *Friendship in Death*, in which departed souls describe heaven's joys to their friends left behind on earth, and the posthumously published *Devout Exercises of the Heart*, expressing eager desire for God and immortal life, furthered the image of Rowe as a writer transcending the mortal body. Watts saw her prose devotional writing as poetic in its expression of

a Spirit dwelling in Flesh, elevated into divine Transport, congenial to those of Angels and unbodied Minds . . . I scarce ever met with any devotional Writings which give us an Example of a Soul, at Special Seasons, so far raised above every thing that is not immortal and divine.[43]

In one poem of posthumous praise, the image of Philomela is associated with the poet's aspiration towards heaven:

Thus PHILOMELA sung, on earth detain'd,
While cumb'rous clay the rising soul restrained:
Now the freed spirit, with th'angelic choir,
In fields of light attunes th'immortal lyre,
And hymns her God in strains more soft, more strong;
There only could she learn a loftier song.[44]

This nightingale partakes of the idea of the soaring bird as emblem for the rising spirit: Philomela, restrained by the body but aspiring to the condition of spirit, is the point where mortal and immortal meet. Praise of Rowe exalts the female poet through her transcendence of the 'cumb'rous clay' of the female body.

The 'rising soul' of the religious poet forms a counter-image to the amorous woman whose poems express and arouse sexual feeling; but the amorous woman threatens to return in the passionate language of Rowe's devotions, which address God as absent lover. Isaac Watts felt the need to defend her by insisting that there was 'no secret panting after a mortal Love' in her divine meditations.[45] More orthodox writers were a little wary of the excess of Enthusiasm expressed by the pious dissenter. The Anglican Jane Brereton admired Rowe's work and evidently found her an enabling model for her own role as a poet, but expressed one reservation: 'I confess, that in my Opinion, there breathes too much of the Air of Enthusiasm in her Letters'.[46] The contrast between religious Enthusiasm and a calmer, rational piety corresponds to that between two images for the woman poet active at this time: we could call them the ecstatic soul and the domestic matron. As ecstatic soul, the woman poet could partake of the divine spirit long associated with poetry; but in an Augustan age suspicious of such claims, the domestic matron, earthbound as she was, made a more generally acceptable figure. Rowe somehow managed to encompass both images. It is telling that Watts's defence of her from the charge that her devotional ecstasy was displaced sexuality was not made in terms of her transcendence of bodily desires. Instead, he argued that she had known married love, and therefore did not need to seek it in her religion.[47] In effect he suggested that Rowe was both ecstatic soul and domestic matron.

To imagine the woman poet as domestic matron is to see her as writing from a life embedded in family, service to others, and in household concerns. This was a widespread model of the good woman writer by the 1730s, and indicates that eighteenth-century culture had come to some accommodation between the ideas of poet and female body. The woman poet as domestic matron is not disembodied; rather, a regulated female body is seen as the legitimate source of a certain kind of poetry, informal, modest, often comic, concerned with everyday life. Not all women writing such poetry were married, of course, nor was marriage necessary to gain the kind of domestic authority on which this image was based. Samuel Johnson's famous praise of the unmarried Elizabeth Carter for making puddings as well as translating

Epictetus is one example of the aura of domesticity surrounding the good woman poet in the later eighteenth century. Nevertheless 'matron' seems the appropriate word to encapsulate the sense of household authority and family orientation that seems central to the self-image of many women poets, and to the ideal of the woman poet most current in the middle years of the century. Mary Barber offers a good example of the woman poet as domestic matron. Her work, published by subscription in 1734, was introduced with Jonathan Swift's recommendation that:

> she seemeth to have a true poetical Genius, better cultivated than could well be expected, either from her Sex, or the Scene she hath acted in, as the Wife of a Citizen. Yet I am assured, that no Woman was ever more useful to her Husband in the way of his Business. Poetry hath only been her favourite Amusement.[48]

The poems themselves corroborate this in their concern to deflect possible criticisms of writing as a dereliction of wifely duty. In 'Conclusion of a Letter to the Rev. Mr. C—', Barber makes verse out of her ostensible refusal to continue writing. The speaker begins the poem by declaring she is ending her letter, significantly because of the interruption of family duties in the shape of her son:

> 'Tis time to conclude; for I make it a Rule,
> To leave off all Writing, when *Con.* comes from School. (*Poems*, p. 58)

Con, however, encourages her to continue her letter in verse, which she does, in the form of a self-cancelling refusal to write verse to Mr C—because he disapproves of writing wives. His supposed reaction to her verses is one of her main themes:

> She has Wisdom enough, that keeps out of the Dirt,
> And can make a good *Pudding*, and cut out a *Shirt*.
> What Good's in a Dame, that will pore on a Book?
> No! – Give me the Wife, that shall save me a Cook. (p. 60)

This verse is typical of the 1730s and 1740s in its replacement of the older anxiety about the woman poet as whore with worry about her as failed housewife. The speaker's son plays a crucial role in her effort to refute this charge. Not only does he suggest that she writes the verse, in the final section he becomes the recipient of her maternal advice on his own choice of wife. Here she opposes Mr C— by insisting on the compatibility of intellectual and domestic life, and, more unusually, by focusing on a husband's duty as well as a wife's. Particularly notable is her concern that the husband as well as the wife should take care to be physically attractive to his partner: if she should be 'In the Care of her Person, exact and refin'd', he is advised to 'Let your Person be neat, unaffectedly clean' (pp. 61–2). Most importantly, though, the good wife will combine proper 'Family Cares' with 'her principal Care', her mind, and will be:

> By Learning made humble, not thence taking Airs,
> To despise, or neglect, her domestick Affairs:
> Nor think her less fitted for doing her Duty,
> By knowing its Reasons, its Use, and its Beauty. (p. 61)

Such claims would be made repeatedly by women in the mid-eighteenth century and later, as domesticity became the standard against which they would be measured.

The image of the woman poet projected in Barber's volume also anticipates later concerns in the stress laid on her public benevolence. The preface explains that she came to public attention as a writer through the verse-petition she wrote to Lady Carteret on behalf of an officer's widow. The petition was well received, the widow was helped, and the author discovered and patronised (pp. xviii–xix). In a poem included in the volume, Constantia Grierson praises Barber for moving beyond the old heroic themes and imitating 'Beneficence divine' (p. lxii). Barber herself explains that such public activity came second, her first reason for writing coming in the course of private family duty:

> My Aim being chiefly to form the Minds of my Children, I imagin'd that Precepts convey'd in Verse would be easier remember'd . . . nor was I ever known to write upon any other Account, till the Distresses of an Officer's Widow set me upon drawing a Petition in Verse, having found that other methods had proved ineffectual for her Relief' (pp. xvii/xviii).

Exactly this transition, from maternal duty within the family to a nurturing role in a wider society, was to authorize women's writing, and women's public activity generally, throughout the eighteenth century and beyond it.

Her maternal identity was central to Barber's development of a poetic voice. In many of her poems she adopts the persona of her own son, writing verses supposedly expressing his feelings on being breeched or on aspects of school life, which were intended for him to recite. She is defensive about publishing 'Verses written between a Mother and her Son', but justifies them on the grounds that educating the young is 'the best Apology a Woman could make for writing at all'. (pp. xxv/xxvi). She is unusual in her concentration on the poet as mother, but ideas of maternal care and authority were active in other eighteenth-century images of the woman poet. In the 1740s Jane Brereton was even seen as passing on a poetic legacy to her daughter. Charlotte Brereton wrote a poem, '*To the* MEMORY *of a* MOTHER', published in the *Gentleman's Magazine* and later in Jane Brereton's *Poems on Several Occasions*. Here she mourned her mother, placed her in heaven with her poetic predecessor Rowe, and implicitly claimed to be herself carrying on their tradition of female poetry.[49] A poem '*To Miss* CHARLOTTE BRERETON' emphasizes her likeness to her lost mother, who is revived in the daughter: 'MELISSA's better Part remains,/MELISSA lives in YOU'.[50]

The maternal public images of Mary Barber and Jane Brereton worked against the monstrosity of the creative mother as imagined in Augustan satire. This rehabilitation, however, depended on a maternity construed in social and moral terms, downplaying both physical reproduction and its metaphorical connection to poetic fertility: in contrast to Cowley writing on Orinda, Barber's and Brereton's supporters do not celebrate the teeming womb that produces poems.

By the middle decades of the eighteenth century the modest, retired, domestic writer was the dominant positive image of the woman poet. Negative images still circulated, of course: the woman poet as whore still surfaced at times, as did the related stereotype of the slovenly woman poet, her dirty clothes and ink-stained fingers standing for the sexual contamination she supposedly introduced to the literary world. Women's repeated attempts, however humorously expressed, to dissociate themselves from the image of the slattern suggest its continuing power. Yet the idea that many women, not just dazzling exceptions, could unite womanly virtue and a poetic identity was gaining ground. This helped to make writing poetry respectable over a wider social range than before. In Mary Collier's work, for example, the image of the working woman poet is created by adapting the virtues generally ascribed to the good woman writer. The required modesty about her achievements is expressed in a complaint about injustice: 'No Learning ever was bestow'd on me', she reminds her reader.[51] The labouring woman's retirement differs from that of the Horatian speaker withdrawing from political life, or the lady shunning town frivolity in favour of rural contemplation: her seclusion from the public world is part of her class condition. Her focus on domesticity also differs from that of the middle-class matron concerned with the moral management of her family affairs: Collier writes of the 'Drudgery' of women's lives spent in the service of their own poor families and in washing linen for ladies.[52] Mary Collier thus has some of the 'matron's' authority that had developed in a middle-class context, and uses it to offer social critique from her own class perspective.[53] Nevertheless the image of her promoted in the Advertisement to her work indicates the limits of her authority. Her value, it is implied, was largely curiosity value: 'her Friends are of Opinion that the Novelty of a *Washer-Woman*'s turning Poetess, will procure her some Readers'.[54]

Another woman celebrated for her lowly class origins was Mary Leapor, whose posthumously published poems were presented as the 'first Productions of a young unassisted Genius . . . in their native Simplicity'.[55] Despite this her poetry offers a sophisticated imitation and revision of many of the themes and attitudes of neoclassical poetry, responding especially to the work of Pope.[56] Leapor's poetic persona, Mira, addresses Artemisia (Leapor's patron, Bridget Freemantle) in a Popean verse-epistle which details the many interruptions and criticisms which threaten her poetic vocation, until Artemisia frees her 'laughing Muse'. Mira's various unsympathetic visitors remind her of some of the negative images that threaten the woman poet. Parthenia greets her with: 'Still poking o'er your what-d'ye-call – your Muse,/But prithee, Mira, when dost clean thy shoes?' Sophronia reminds her of the specific constraints on a lower-class woman: 'Go, ply your needle: you might earn your bread:/Or who must feed you when your father's dead?'[57] 'The proclamation of Apollo' revises the old theme of Apollo's judgement of the best poet to imagine a democratization of the realm of poetry. Apollo's conclusion is:

> Let none presume to fret and squabble,
> Nor curse the dirty rhiming Rabble:
> For see the Beams of *Phoebus* strike
> The Meadows, Hills, and Dales alike:
> So shines the Muse on ev'ry Creature,
> Who tags his humble Lines with Metre.[58]

The middle years of the century, then, saw some widening of the social range of the woman poet, and the creation of some more democratic versions of the poet's image. However, the social conditions that meant that a labouring-class writer could not gain 'a literary livelihood without a radical deracination' remained,[59] and the introduction to Leapor's poems suggested that the poet would have been raised by her merit to a higher social sphere if she had lived longer.[60]. In a sense, she was so raised, gaining honorary lady's status when a selection of her poems was reprinted in the 1755 anthology *Poems By Eminent Ladies*. This was one of a number of publications during the 1750s which consolidated the notion that the good woman poet belonged in the English literary canon – but in a special section reserved for 'ladies'.[61] George Ballard's *Memoirs of Several Ladies of Great Britain* (1752) ranged more widely, treating intellectual ladies whether poets or not, but still contributed to the growing fame of several female poets. John Duncombe's *The Feminiad* (1754) balanced high praise for virtuous women poets with criticism of such 'bold, unblushing' writers as 'Manley, Centlivre and Behn', further establishing a combination of sexual purity, personal modesty and (apparent) freedom from commercial taint as the criterion for the good woman poet.[62] Such works helped create a special cultural niche for female poets. The problem of recognizing that poetry could come from a woman's body had been – temporarily – solved by means of an Augustan compromise. Though the woman could no longer be celebrated in the way Cowley had celebrated Philips, as the fertile body bringing forth poems, the woman poet was not disembodied. Rather, good women's poetry came from a tamed, domesticated body, and could involve, indeed, a distinctive sensual response to animal and everyday life.[63] However, the modest verse of the domestic matron was not expected to aspire to the sublime regions which were soon to be understood as the only place for true poetry. Women of the Romantic era would have to face the same questions again, and search for new ways of imagining the woman as poet.

Notes

1. Wendy Wall, *The Imprint of Gender: Authorship and Publication in the English Renaissance* (Ithaca, NY, and London: Cornell University Press, 1993), pp. 65–9.
2. *A Comparison Between the Two Stages* (London: 1702), pp. 25–6.
3. 'To the Excellent *Orinda*', *Poems by the Most Deservedly Admired Mrs. Katherine Philips the Matchless Orinda* (London: 1667), sig. C2r.
4. See Elizabeth Grosz, *Space, Time and Perversion: Essays on the Politics of Bodies* (New York and London: Routledge, 1995). For a good survey of the question of female embodiment and writing, see Ashley Tauchert, *Mary Wollstonecraft and the Accent of the Feminine* (Basingstoke: Palgrave Macmillan, 2002), pp. 1–16.

5. Cowley, 'Upon Mrs. *K. Philips* her Poems', Stanza 1, in Philips, *Poems* (1667), sig. B2v.
6. George Granville, 'To Mrs. Afra Behn', *The Genuine Works* (London: 1736), Vol. 1, 42.
7. 'S.C.' [Susanna Carroll?], '*To Mrs. S.F. on her incomparable Poems*', in [Sarah Fyge Egerton], *Poems on Several Occasions* (London: 1703), sig. A7r.
8. John Hughes, 'To the ingenious Author, on her Tragedy called, Fatal Friendship', in *The Works of Mrs. Catharine Cockburn* (London: 1751), Vol. 2, p. 471.
9. Charles Cotton, '*To the Admir'd* Astrea', in Aphra Behn, *La Montre* (London: 1686), sig. A7r.
10. Matthew Prior, 'A Satire on the Modern Translators', *Dialogues of the Dead and Other Works*, ed. A. R. Waller (Cambridge: Cambridge University Press, 1907), p. 50.
11. J. Adams, '*To the excellent Madam* Behn, *on her Poems*', in Aphra Behn, *Poems Upon Several Occasions* (London: 1684), sig. A7r.
12. Anon, 'Verses to the Author', in *Philomela: Or, Poems By Mrs. Elizabeth Singer*, 2nd edn (London: 1737), p. xiii.
13. [Sarah Fyge Egerton], *Poems on Several Occasions*, p. 109; Nahum Tate, 'To the Incomparable Author', in Behn, *La Montre*, sig. A8r.
14. See Susan Stanford Friedman, 'Creativity and the Childbirth Metaphor: Gender Difference in Literary Discourse', *Feminist Studies* 13/1 (1987), pp. 49–82; Terry J. Castle, 'La'bring Bards: Birth *Topoi* and English Poetics', *JEGP* 78 (1979), pp. 193–201.
15. Marilyn Francus, 'The Monstrous Mother: Reproductive Anxiety in Swift and Pope', *ELH* 16 (1994), pp. 829–52.
16. *The Dunciad Variorum* II, ll. 156, 150; *The Poems of Alexander Pope*, ed. John Butt (London: Methuen, 1965), p. 385.
17. John Gay, *Three Hours After Marriage*, Act III, ll. 497,483, *Dramatic Works*, ed. John Fuller, 2 vols (Oxford: Clarendon Press, 1983), Vol. 1, 259.
18. *The Rape of the Lock*, Canto IV, ll. 59–62, 58, *The Poems of Alexander Pope*, p. 234.
19. Alexander Pope, '*To the Right Hon:ble ANN Countess of WINCHILSEA*', in *The Anne Finch Wellesley Manuscript Poems*, ed. B. McGovern and Charles Hinnant (Athens, Georgia, and London: University of Georgia Press, 1998), p. 68.
20. 'To Mr Pope', *The Anne Finch Wellesley Manuscript Poems*, p. 69.
21. Robert Gould, *The Poetess: A Satyr* (London: 1707), pp. 3–4.
22. *A Satyrical Epistle to the Female Author of a Poem, call'd Silvia's Revenge* (London: 1691), p. 5.
23. Marilyn Williamson, *Raising Their Voices: British Women Writers 1650–1750* (Detroit: Wayne State University Press, 1990).
24. I am indebted here to the discussion in Sarah Prescott, *Women, Authorship and Literary Culture, 1690–1740* (Basingstoke: Palgrave Macmillan, 2003).
25. *The Works of John Dryden* (Berkeley and Los Angeles: University of California Press, 1967–89), Vol. 3, pp. 111, 112.
26. 'To Madam Bhen [sic]', *Female Poems on Several Occasions. Written by Ephelia* (London: 1679), p. 72.

27. 'To the Author, on her Voyage to the Island of Love', in Behn, *Poems Upon Several Occasions*, sig. A7v, A8r.
28. *Poems on Several Occasions, by Philomela* (London: 1696), sig. A4r.
29. *Works of Mrs. Catharine Cockburn*, Vol. 2, 471.
30. *The Poems of Jane Barker: the Magdalen Manuscript*, ed. Kathryn R. King (Oxford: Magdalen College, 1998), p. 40; the lines also appear in *Love Intrigues: Or, the History of the Amours of Bosvil and Galesia* (London: 1713), p. 33.
31. Kathryn R. King, *Jane Barker, Exile: a Literary Career 1675–1725* (Oxford: Clarendon Press, 2000), pp. 127–9.
32. Carol Barash, *English Women's Poetry 1649–1714: Politics, Community, and Linguistic Authority* (Oxford: Clarendon Press, 1996), p. 261.
33. See Sarah Prescott, *Women, Authorship, and Literary Culture, 1690–1740* (Basingstoke: Palgrave Macmillan, 2003), and Claudia Thomas, *Alexander Pope and His Eighteenth-Century Women Readers* (Carbondale and Edwardsville: Southern Illinois University Press, 1994).
34. 'To *Clorissa*', *The Poems and Prose of Mary, Lady Chudleigh*, ed. Margaret J. M. Ezell (Oxford: Oxford University Press, 1993), p. 68.
35. Lady Mary Wortley Montagu, 'Constantinople. To —', *Essays and Poems and Simplicity, a Comedy*, ed. R. Halsband and I. Grundy (Oxford: Clarendon Press, 1977), pp. 209, 210.
36. *Eighteenth-Century Women Poets: an Oxford Anthology*, ed. Roger Lonsdale (Oxford: Oxford University Press, 1989), p. 145.
37. 'To the Nightingale', ll. 4, 5, 7, 17, 24, 30–5, *The Poems of Anne, Countess of Winchilsea*, ed. Myra Reynolds (Chicago: University of Chicago Press, 1903), pp. 267–8.
38. C. H. Hinnant, 'Song and Speech in Anne Finch's "To the Nightingale"', *Studies in English Literature 1500–1900* 31 (1991), pp. 499–513.
39. Mary Ellen Lamb, *Gender and Authorship in the Sidney Circle* (Madison: University of Wisconsin Press, 1990), pp. 195, 210–11.
40. *The Miscellaneous Works in Prose and Verse of Mrs Elizabeth Rowe* (London: 1739), Vol. 1, pp. xvi, lvi, liii–liv.
41. Ibid., Vol. 1, p. 115.
42. 'To Mrs. Elizabeth Singer', in Rowe, *Miscellaneous Works*, Vol. 1, p. xcix.
43. Watts, *Devout Exercises of the Heart in Meditation and Soliloquy, Prayer and Praise* (London: 1738), Preface, p. xii.
44. Rowe, *Miscellaneous Works*, Vol. 1, p. cxxviii.
45. Watts, *Devout Exercises*, p. xvi.
46. Jane Brereton, *Poems on Several Occasions* (London: 1744), p. xxx.
47. Watts, *Devout Exercises*, p. xv–xvi.
48. Mary Barber, *Poems on Several Occasions* (London: 1734), pp. vi–vii.
49. Brereton, *Poems*, p. lxiii.
50. Barber, *Poems*, p. lxiv.
51. *The Woman's Labour: An Epistle to Mr. Stephen Duck* (London: 1739), p. 6.
52. Collier, *Woman's Labour*, pp. 7, 12–13.
53. For an analysis of this critique and its limitations see Donna Landry, *The Muses of Resistance: Laboring-Class Women's Poetry in Britain, 1739–1796* (Cambridge: Cambridge University Press, 1990), pp. 56–77.
54. Collier, *Woman's Labour*, sig. A2r.

55. Mary Leapor, *Poems upon Several Occasions* (London: 1748), sig. A2r.
56. See Landry, *Muses of Resistance*, pp. 78–106.
57. Leapor, 'An Epistle to Artemisia', in *Eighteenth-Century Women Poets*, ed. Lonsdale, p. 206.
58. Leapor, *Poems*, p. 46.
59. Landry, *Muses of Resistance*, p. 76.
60. Leapor, *Poems*, sig. A2v.
61. For a discussion of the eighteenth-century anthologies of ladies' verse, see Margaret Ezell, *Writing Women's Literary History* (Baltimore: Johns Hopkins University Press, 1993).
62. John Duncombe, *The Feminiad* (London: 1754), p. 15.
63. Margaret Doody, 'Sensuousness in the Poetry of Eighteenth-Century Women Poets', in I. Armstrong and V. Blain (eds), *Women's Poetry in the Enlightenment: the Making of a Canon, 1730–1820* (London: Macmillan now Palgrave Macmillan, 1999), pp. 3–32.

11
Rank, Community and Audience: the Social Range of Women's Poetry

Valerie Rumbold

The social and economic structures and perceptions of the late seventeenth and early eighteenth centuries were in some ways very different from ours. They are difficult to describe not only because they are alien, and because they varied from one place and community to another, but also because they were undergoing major change. In reading the women poets of the time we therefore need to be particularly wary of any rush to assimilate their constructions to our own. Women poets of earlier centuries often began to be rediscovered and anthologized in the later twentieth century as part of an explicitly feminist quest for subversive foremothers and role models, which attached particular value to elements that could be construed as resistance to gender and class oppression. Thanks to such advocacy, seventeenth- and eighteenth-century women poets have swiftly become an established part of the literary landscape, and it is now possible to think in terms of a wider and deeper contextualization of their writing, moving debate beyond the well-established anthology pieces and attempting to read these women poets not only in relation to modern agendas but also in relation to the specific social and economic issues and assumptions of their times.[1]

At the beginning of this period, the complex stratifications in society were described using a variety of terminologies, among them 'rank', 'order', 'degree', 'estate', or 'sort' of people.[2] There was no general agreement even as to how many basic groups made up the whole, for society was changing, and attempts at description were always to an extent trying to adapt older concepts to fit new realities.[3] Also lacking, it has been argued, except at the uppermost levels of the social spectrum, was any nationally unified sense of shared status that we would recognize as a social class.[4] Thus, although social resentment was rife, it seems to have been articulated principally within a context of individual or local relationships.[5] The language of rank, order and degree, moreover, had potentially comforting implications: hierarchy implied mutual relationship; and it was a commonplace that the monarch's subjects were all, no matter how lowly, members of the body or family of the nation.[6] Although social structures and notions of status continued to evolve during the period from the late seventeenth to the mid-eighteenth century, moving closer to the later eighteenth-century and nineteenth-century world in which the discourse of class would become more central, this chapter focuses instead on the concepts by which people in the period 1660–1750 routinely structured their understanding of the social world and their place in it.[7]

The most highly placed members of late seventeenth-century society were the titled nobility (or 'persons of quality'), whose rank put them on terms of sociability with the monarch. For many purposes the nobility could be seen as a privileged element within the larger category of the gentry, who ranged from substantial landowning families to those with unsustainably small or unprofitable properties, whose female unmarried members in particular might be worse off financially than women of trading families. Placed somewhat ambiguously on the lower fringes of the gentry were at least some members of the learned professions (who might themselves be of the gentry by birth, though arguably somewhat lowered in rank by the commercial exercise of their skills), although some clergy and lawyers, for example, fell well short of the income and associated gentility of lifestyle that would have enabled them to stake a convincing claim to the status of gentlemen. Ranged below the self-conscious distinction of birth that elevated nobility and gentry above the rest came 'the middling sort', an important group whose nature and extent is much contested.[8] This seems to have had at its heart the more substantial and independent of the urban trading communities (whose menfolk might also come of gentry stock, or have married gentry wives in an exchange between rank and wealth; or who might equally have made their own way up from lower stations by their own or their fathers' diligent enterprise or apprenticeship, perhaps confirmed by marriage with a master's daughter or widow).[9] Rural society, meanwhile, presented the case of the yeomen, a relatively independent and wealthy group that occupied a position between gentry and peasantry, but was in serious decline in the period.[10] At the base of the social pyramid were the common people, often called 'low' or 'mean' and conceived of by superiors as an undistinguished mass, but in reality an intricately stratified group, largely comprising servants and various kinds of manual ('mechanick') workers. Differences within this group could be related to differences between urban and rural livelihoods, to different degrees of independence from wage-labour (notably those associated with access to smallholdings), and to changes of occupation over the span of a lifetime, with many adolescents, for example, working as live-in servants while they saved towards setting up a more independent household on marriage. From the ranks of the lower orders, some might make their way by talent or opportunity towards commercial or professional success; and imprudent or unfortunate members of more privileged groups could easily, over a couple of generations, take their descendants down into these lower ranks. Finally, at the very bottom of the structure, and hardly seen as a legitimate part of society at all, were the poor who lived hand to mouth, devoid of reliable subsistence, and a thorn in the flesh to the respectable.

The older conception of divinely ordered estates was under pressure in this period from the increasing importance of occupation and wealth. Gradations of social status could be both subtle and constraining; but financial, marital and other circumstances could decisively alter an individual's position in the social order. The social worlds of the city merchant's daughter and the rural gentleman might seem utterly distinct, even if her father had been wealthier than his; but he might seek, by a proposal of marriage, to join her wealth to his status, while her parents might welcome the chance to see their grandchildren born into the gentry. Again, a successful professional might provide for his daughters a haven of privileged security; but if he died without leaving them enough to live on, they could easily find themselves reduced to domestic service or worse. At the same time, the impact of such life-changing circumstances was potentially enhanced by the growth of an ideology responsive to the increasing importance of wealth and lifestyle in defining status, typified at the beginning of the eighteenth century in the *Tatler* and the *Spectator* written by the Whigs Richard Steele and Joseph Addison. These periodicals sought to persuade their readers that to be a gentleman was in effect to be accomplished in polite sociability: while this opened the way for cultivated merchants to consider themselves on a level with the gentry, it erected new barriers in the way of impoverished or unsophisticated gentry, and made a more divisive distinction between prosperous and less prosperous merchants and tradesmen.[11] Rank was, in effect, increasingly renegotiated around a polite sociability that required property to sustain it: towards the middle of the eighteenth century the word 'class' begins to be used, particularly to refer to the 'lower class'; and as we move into the second half of the century there are increasing signs of the changes that were to lead to a social world construed less in terms of rank and order and more in terms of class. Throughout our period, issues of social discrimination remained vital to the self-constructions of individuals and communities; yet the system proved complex, shifting and often contested; and if this was true for men, it was arguably even truer for the women whose status was to a large extent contingent on theirs. Indeed, towards the end of our period, it has been argued that women of the more privileged groups were increasingly denied the security of sharing intrinsically in the status of their birth families, as they came to be perceived as ciphers given status only by their husbands. This was bad news for spinsters and those who married beneath them, however convenient it may have been for those who married up the social scale.[12]

One of the most interesting issues emerging from recent attempts to understand women poets' construction of social and political identities is the question of why, particularly at the beginning of the period, so many women poets expressed passionate attachment to conservative social and political ideologies, and to the Anglican or Roman Catholic models of piety that supported them. If, as has often been assumed, writing was a potentially subversive act for women, why would women poets not only tolerate but also even strenuously advocate a Tory ideology of divinely authorized subordination? For Catherine Gallagher, the highflying Tory conception of the monarch's absolute power presents an attractive model for the creative autonomy to which women poets aspire.[13] For Carol Barash, the increasingly old-fashioned cult of the monarch's mystic body is also a factor, especially in the context of Stuart queens' function as focus of court rituals, and their potential as symbols of female linguistic authority capable of sustaining loyal women in their authority as poets.[14] One of the most suggestive responses to this question, however, is that of Paula McDowell, which moves beyond poetry and beyond the social elite to take a wider view of women's agency in print culture. In considering middling and lower-class women's engagement with mainstream politics, McDowell develops the view that the more traditional ideologies, which figured society as a body with the monarch as its head, and the self 'as social, collective, and essentially unsexed', allowed non-gentry women, however lowly, to figure themselves as intrinsic members of the body politic.[15] This, she argues, assured them of their connectedness with those in authority, and enabled them to evade the inhibitions on political intervention that a focus merely on their subordination as women might have entailed: indeed, in a nation figured as family, they found specific opportunities in the hortatory roles of mother and sister.

In contrast with such traditional hierarchy and collectivity, modernizing Whig views of society and the self could be seen as tending to atomize society, insisting increasingly on gender as radically constitutive of the self, and relying increasingly on commerce and contract to organize and connect a world of unique individuals. Although such changes have often been seen as marking progress towards a more open, democratic and entrepreneurial society, they could from this point of view be seen as marginalizing some as surely as they enabled others. Moreover, although Whig ideology can be seen as in some ways deriving from the Parliamentary ideology of the Civil War, and from a pragmatic rejection on the grounds of his Roman Catholicism of a king, James II, whose right in terms of male primogeniture was beyond question, it would be dangerous to assume that to be a Whig – particularly a Whig aristocrat – in the late seventeenth and early eighteenth centuries necessarily meant being less committed in practice to the importance of distinctions of rank and status. Whatever the ideologies professed by the women writers of this period, their texts need to be read with sensitivity to the complexities of their social and political contexts, and with a detachment that respects the sometimes unbridgeable differences that separate their subjectivities from ours.

When we attempt to reconstruct the social contexts within which women poets composed and circulated their work, we also need to take account of the physical objects, the manuscripts and books, through which the work was passed from writer to reader. Here there is much to be gained from the current revival of interest in bibliographical studies, with its commitment to the history of the book as a physical object, and its illumination of the gradual transition from manuscript to print culture, along with its analysis of the processes of manuscript circulation, print and marketing as agents of cultural transformation.[16] Through the work of David Foxon and James McLaverty, Pope has emerged as the standard exemplar in this period of a new concern with typography, format and marketing: although the relation of women poets to these processes may be complicated by factors that in many cases limited their control over the publication of their work, they too need to be understood in relation to the physical format and circulation of their writing.[17] Recent work has explored several such areas, all crucial to women's sense of their relation to community and society, notably circulation of manuscripts, subscriptions for collections of verse, and the search for and management of patronage.[18]

Just on the threshold of the period covered by the present volume, and affording a useful perspective on constructions of social order at its beginning, stand Margaret Cavendish, Duchess of Newcastle, and Katherine Philips, 'the matchless Orinda'. Both were royalists, the former born a gentlewoman and recruited by marriage into the aristocracy and the latter born a merchant's daughter and promoted by marriage into the gentry. Both, therefore, knew from experience how personal and political contingency could temper strict notions of rank; yet Philips's poetry continues to embrace images of monarchy as the touchstone of human fulfilment and potency; and Cavendish too, writing of her mother's sufferings during the Civil War, recurs to a deeply felt sense of the sanctity of hierarchy:

> She was of a grave Behaviour, and had such a Magestick Grandeur, as it were continually hung about her, that it would command respect from the rudest, I mean the rudest of civiliz'd people, I mean not such Barbarous people, as plundered her, and used her cruelly, for they would have pulled God out of Heaven, had they had power, as they did Royaltie out of his Throne.[19]

Yet the wider structure within which such views made sense could never again, after the Civil War and the Revolution of 1688, seem quite as impregnable as it might once have done. Whig doctrine, with its pragmatic assessment of the qualifications required to render a monarch fit to enter into a contract with the nation, was, despite the elitist spirit of its grandees, sapping at the foundations of conceptions of the nation as a body or family structured by rank and incorporated under the monarch as head; and commerce, as exemplified in the growing market for print, was becoming a transforming power noticeably out of alignment with traditional assumptions about the location of social authority. When Cavendish or Philips circulated their work in manuscript to a select circle, they were doing what poets of the gentry and aristocracy had traditionally done; but when Cavendish took the novel step of having her work printed, or Philips found her work published without her authority, they were in touch with a future of proliferating print whose momentum, generated by commerce, might easily outrun the authorial control of elite writers like themselves, while at the same time evolving new opportunities for some writers of less privileged background.[20] Yet whether the women poets of the gentry and aristocracy circulated their work primarily in manuscript to a coterie (like Katherine Philips, Lady Mary Wortley Montagu and Judith Cowper), published it at their own expense (like Cavendish), arranged for its publication by a bookseller (like Anne Finch, Countess of Winchilsea), saw it published without their consent (like Philips and Wortley Montagu), or incorporated their poems into prose narrative deliberately marketed for profit (like Jane Barker), they all benefited from various combinations of the educational resources, social networks and relative financial security associated with their rank. In the light of such advantages, the striking prominence of women from the upper levels of society among the women poets of this period and the relatively late appearance and small number of women poets who came from labouring backgrounds are hardly surprising.

A range of issues relevant to the poets of the gentry and aristocracy intersect in the work of Mary Lady Chudleigh (1656–1710). Chudleigh, a gentlewoman married to a baronet, identified firmly with the gentry; but her world-view is strongly inflected by individual concerns. One is commitment to a very particular kind of Christian philosophical otherworldliness that despises worldly advantages as a mere gift of fortune; and another is a strongly articulated resentment, consistent with the early exposure of elite women to newer, more strictly gendered notions of identity, of the privileges that men in her society enjoyed at women's expense.[21]

Her essay 'Of Justice' sets out a social ideal structured by rank: from the position that human beings 'are all parts of one great Community' she reminds readers of their duties to inferiors ('Acts of Charity'), to equals ('Kindness', 'Affection' and 'Esteem') and to superiors ('Services', 'dutiful Concern', 'Respect'); and she recommends devoting 'Room in their Prayers' to superiors so elevated as to be beyond their personal acquaintance.[22] The negative reflex of such a hierarchical view of society is shown by Mellissa, the favoured speaker in *The Ladies Defence*, who, when she refers to 'Tradesmen' and 'the Mob', characterizes the former as people who 'wealthy by their Cheats and Flatteries grow' and the latter as 'those Dregs of Humanekind,/Those Animals': when she berates her male peers for their severity to her sex, it is by contrast with what she decries as their overindulgence to the pretensions of such inferiors.[23]

Yet if such social views are likely to prove unattractive to modern readers, Chudleigh's frank denunciations of gender inequalities have given her something of an exemplary status in the study of women writers: thus a selection from *The Ladies Defence*, beginning "Tis hard we should be by the men despised,/Yet kept from knowing what would make us prized', stands first in Lonsdale's *Eighteenth-Century Women Poets*; and is immediately followed by 'To the Ladies', beginning 'Wife and servant are the same,/But only differ in the name'.[24] Unlike the lowlier women whose empowerment through obsolescent assumptions of participation in a hierarchical body is discussed by McDowell, Chudleigh repeatedly confronts the subordination of female selves defined by gender, and makes common cause with other ladies – if not with other women.

At the conclusion of 'To the *Queen*'s most Excellent *Majesty*', addressed to Queen Anne, Chudleigh declares that if she 'cou'd the best of Queens attend', her time would be spent 'In glad Attendance, and in grateful Lays'.[25] This aspiration bears out Barash's contention that rituals of female power centred on queens were crucial to the productive experiments of many of the women poets of the period.[26] In 1710, moreover, Chudleigh dedicated her *Essays upon Several Subjects in Prose and Verse* to the Electress Sophia, who, since the death of the Duke of Gloucester, had been heir to the throne. Had Sophia survived until Anne's death in 1714, her high level of cultivation might well have ensured a British court supportive of women writers and thinkers. However Sophia, who corresponded briefly with Chudleigh before her death in 1710, predeceased Anne, leaving her distinctly uncultured son George I to set up a court without a queen (since his marriage had been dissolved on the grounds of his wife's adultery), and to pass the throne in 1727 to a son, George II, who made a virtue of thinking literature beneath him.[27] George II's highly intelligent wife, Caroline of Anspach, soon learned that unremitting flattery and sexual assiduity, not any parade of her intellectual interests, were the keys to power.[28] Such courts were not to prove any kind of enabling context for women poets.

Chudleigh's social orientation in fact presents an intriguing blend of old and new. Her identity as a person of rank is supported by a network of largely genteel friends, relations and correspondents, along with such writers of middling or minor gentry origin as Dryden, Elizabeth Thomas and Mary Astell.[29] Yet she is also, as an elite female in touch with newer currents of thought, adapting to increased emphasis on the gendered self by advocating education to encourage her sex in the proper performance of its duty; while her reliance on female community and her readiness to address her publications to a female audience can make a poem like 'To the Ladies' appear truly radical. Yet this is the same author whose principal preoccupation is detachment from the world and preparation for the life to come, and whose advice to unhappy wives is principled submission. She is also astute enough to venture beyond co-terie circulation into the expanding world of print, and bold enough to dedicate her work to female rulers capable of lending authority to those concerns.

Other well-connected poets of the early part of the period include Anne Finch, Countess of Winchilsea (1661–1720), a gentlewoman privi-leged in being chosen to serve the queen of James II, Mary of Modena, but forced into impoverished internal exile by the Revolution of 1688.[30] Solaced by solidarity with her husband and the brother-in-law who had offered them a home, she often projected muted themes of political dissent onto motifs of pastoral retreat, idealizing a circle of sympathetic acquaintance, and in particular the support and friend-ship of other women; but while it is unsurprising that she was later involved, when she returned to court under Anne, in exchanges of poems with the Tory circle of Swift, Pope and Prior, it is also note-worthy that the Whig Charles Gildon had included four of her poems in his *New Collection of Poems on Several Occasions* (1701), and that the Whig poet and playwright Nicholas Rowe had been prepared to pref-ace them with a lengthy and effusive commendatory poem, suggesting that her poetry, though produced within a coterie in political eclipse, could appeal to readers outside that coterie.[31] Elizabeth Rowe (no rela-tion) was another Whig poet with whom she was on good terms; and this may suggest not only the relative mildness of the political climate under Anne but also a recognition among female poets that they had common interests that should not be eclipsed by political differences. In 1713, perhaps in an attempt to keep closer personal control over the form in which her work appeared, Finch acted decisively to move into the world of print, and published *Miscellany Poems on Several Occasions*; but it may be a sign of her caution about presenting herself to the public as an author that the volume at first appeared without her name on the title.[32]

Two somewhat later poets from distinguished Whig families were Lady Mary Wortley Montagu (1689–1762) and Judith Cowper (later Madan: 1702–81): born too late to seek patronage from the queens of the late Stuart courts, their backgrounds would in any case probably have made such strategies uncongenial. For Lady Mary, daughter of the Duke of Kingston, poetry was only one of the kinds of writing in which she might intervene, often in collaboration with fellow wits or political accomplices, in a whole range of cultural, philosophical or party political issues. As one of the most socially distinguished of the women poets of the period, she was particularly sensitive to the decorum that dictated aloofness from the vulgar commerce of print, and specified manuscript circulation among a select audience as the proper means of sharing verse: even when Lady Mary seems to have designed work for the press, notably lampoons on her former friend Pope, she would not publicly profess authorship, however obvious it might be to an informed audience.[33] A somewhat similar pattern, of manuscript circulation occasionally breaking through into print publication (though at a markedly lower pitch of intensity), characterized Lady Mary's acquaintance Judith Cowper, for a time a member of Pope's circle, and on occasion a target of Lady Mary's satire in this connection.[34] Cowper, a member of a gentry family that included a former Lord Chancellor, was an altogether more decorous and less confident writer.[35] In her lifetime only a few items were published, though manuscript circulation gained her a minor reputation for the quality and ambition of her work. Yet this was a vulnerable stance to adopt in the context of a book trade expanding through the activities of entrepreneurs like Curll: on the death of William Pattison, a young poet reduced to accepting lodgings in Curll's house, it was all too easy for Curll to include her substantial reply to Pope's *Eloisa to Abelard* in his posthumous edition of Pattison's works, starting a trail of misattribution that lasted well into the twentieth century.[36]

In strong contrast with such women both socially and politically was Jane Barker (1652–1732), a daughter of minor gentry whose experience was of decisively downward mobility, and whose political allegiance was not to Sophia or her son George I, but to the exiled James II. What makes Barker so interesting in terms of social orientation and mediation of her work to audiences, however, is the combination of traditional and innovative elements in her varied career. As a young woman she depicted herself as empowered by the circle of Cambridge students she knew through her brother; and at this stage in her life she found her poems printed without her permission.[37] She also practised medicine, taking advantage of print culture to circulate advertisements for her gout treatment, and she exulted over being mistaken for a doctor.[38] At the Revolution of 1688, however, having converted to Catholicism, she went into exile with the Stuarts; and at this stage she embarked on an ambitious cycle of poems constituting a Jacobite history of recent times, which she crafted into a presentation manuscript, apparently using it to make an unsuccessful bid for patronage from the court in exile.[39] Returning to England, she turned to professional writing for her livelihood, producing prose fiction replete with Jacobite implication into which she inserted versions of earlier poems; and the audience targeted by these texts was, at least in part, a conservative rural elite specifically singled out by Curll's entrepreneurial shrewdness.[40] Barker's career thus illuminates not only an intriguing blend of ideological steadfastness and commercial flexibility, but also the paradoxical workings of the new commercial world of print, aligned in essentials with modernizing Whig commercialism, but, in its quest for viable markets, prepared to procure and promote even the most reactionary doctrine where a demand could be established.

Among women poets of the middling sort, different kinds of networks, typically involving the management of patrons or of subscription projects, were more likely to be called upon. Yet the careers of women poets at this social level not only display some of the same strategies as those of the gentry and aristocracy, particularly the coterie circulation of manuscripts and the publication of printed collections, but also reveal supportive networks that were not bounded by strict notions of rank, nor always reducible to simple patronage of inferior by superior. Moreover, the cultural aspirations of the more prosperous of the middling sort meant that increasingly valuable support could be found within the professional and commercial classes themselves.

At the beginning of the period, Aphra Behn (1640–89) has come to stand as exemplar of women's capacity to earn a livelihood as professional writers, adapting herself to the exigencies of the market by turning as occasion demanded from plays to poetry and prose fiction, as well as working for the government as a spy.[41] Such traits and occupations might seem to connect her with the middling sort, although what evidence there is of her actual origins suggests that her father was a barber with financially unsustainable aspirations to upwards mobility: the issue is also – probably strategically – clouded by various claims of gentry background, and even of relationship to the aristocracy.[42] Whatever the rank to which she was born, however, she held firm to hierarchical principles: she promoted a high Tory view of the monarchy, depicted Catholicism with sympathy, and despised Whig innovation. Behn's public persona remained one of poise and capability: she addressed her work to male as well as female patrons, and engaged robustly with affairs of state. For her, Tory emphasis on hierarchy, with its emphasis on the incorporation even of women in the body politic, proved enabling in ways that would increasingly be denied to women who interiorized the implications of the gendered female sphere and the discreet but expensive gentility promulgated by Whig doctrines of politeness.

A more cautionary tale, however, might be told of Mary Pix (1666–1709), a far less talented writer, but a lively apologist for the values of enlightened merchant culture, whose plays enjoyed some theatrical success, and who also composed verse and prose fiction.[43] She was more clearly identified with the middling sort by birth and marriage, being the daughter of a clergyman and the wife of a merchant; but she was later reduced to being the only support of her family; and her published work furnishes a salutary example of a major and fundamental problem that could afflict writers in such a position. While elite women might feel that their purpose in writing could be largely fulfilled by coterie circulation, professional writers needed to publish, but might be unable either to ensure the competence of their printers or to control the print process.[44] A casual glance at the published texts of Pix's verse drama *Ibrahim* might suggest complete metrical incompetence, and make the reader wonder how verse so bungled could have escaped being damned in the theatre.[45] In contrast, *Violenta: Or, The Rewards of Virtue* (1704), a translation from Boccaccio, suggests a competent if pedestrian versifier, but one sabotaged at every turn by the printer's carelessness, as testified by a lengthy errata slip. Yet her contribution to *The Nine Muses* (1700), a collaborative women's volume lamenting the death of Dryden, is polished to the standard that one would expect of such a high-profile tribute. In sum, the printed texts of Pix's verse offer contradictory images of her poetic competence: much of the printed record is probably grotesquely mangled; yet it is not impossible that the relative polish of her *Nine Muses* contribution is owing to another hand. Her case is a reminder that women poets who were publishing to support themselves could not necessarily command the services of the best printers, nor intervene in the print process to ensure quality and accuracy: if our image of the author's relationship to the press in this period is dominated by Pope's strategic supervision of booksellers and printers, we may make misleading assumptions about the end products of the labour of less privileged authors like Pix.

Behn and Pix were Londoners; yet some of the interest to be found in the careers of women poets of the middling sort in this period lies in their relation to other regional centres or, as in the case of the Dubliner Mary Barber, to the other kingdoms. Sarah Prescott has described the Somerset base of Elizabeth Rowe (1674–1737), characterizing it as a positive source of strength, by which Rowe expressed her affiliation to people of similar rank and of modernizing Whig and dissenting views in Frome, a confident town riding a wave of industrial growth.[46] Rowe's work was extensively published in London; but when, as a widow, she retired to the provinces, she was able to maintain and develop her existing network through correspondence and visits. Over her lifetime she accumulated a range of contacts ranging far beyond trade and dissent: she corresponded with the Tory poet and diplomat Matthew Prior as well as with the dissenter and popular devotional poet Isaac Watts; she knew Anne Finch; and through her friendship with Frances, Countess of Hertford, once her childhood companion, she was later able to meet poets such as Thomson, and to draw upon the support of a circle of distinguished subscribers. As a Whig, a dissenter, a professional writer and a widow who needed to support herself, she could draw strength from local solidarity with a rather untraditional community; but she also benefited from links where her social skills, her literary reputation and her celebrated piety could bridge divisions of rank, politics and religious affiliation.

Mary Chandler (1687–1745), a dissenting clergyman's daughter handicapped by spinal deformity, had established herself as a milliner in the tourist centre of Bath, which gave her an ideal base for launching her celebrated poem *A Description of Bath* in 1733.[47] Chandler came to be on visiting terms with the titled and the distinguished, including the poets Elizabeth Rowe and Mary Barber and the Countess of Hertford. She also acknowledged advice from the celebrated physician Dr William Oliver, whose influence was probably responsible for a visit from Pope. Late in life, however, her self-construction in print had a surprising consequence, when a customer came into her shop to make her a proposal of marriage.[48] As she wrote in a comic rendering of the episode to a female friend, she turned him down, preferring her present lifestyle with 'No questions asked'. This was a woman who 'Though she ne'er had a lover, much friendship had met', and was sustained by it both socially and as a poet.[49]

The independence of a Bath shopkeeper also attracted Mary Barber (1690?–1757), the wife of an unsuccessful English-born Dublin woollen draper, and the mother of four children. Swift, her mentor, used his network to promote a subscription campaign for her *Poems on Several Occasions* (1734); but while the subscribers' list has all the social and literary brilliance that titles and distinguished authors can give it, the volume betrays the strain of the strategies of compliment and evasion necessary to sustain that support. Given this limitation, what is particularly impressive are the few poems where she manifests, with tact and deftness, her understanding of the intractable structures that separate merit from its reward. 'An Unanswerable Apology for the Rich' attempts to enter into the mind of a would-be patron of 'merit in distress': as his wealth increases, he can hardly believe how inexorably it is consumed by the need to 'live as others do'.[50] Barber's example reminds us of questions that need to be asked about the power relations implied by subscription projects. Was the poet in control, or was she following a programme set out by more powerful sponsors? Was the sponsors' aim to lift the poet out of the necessity of work that would interfere with her future writing? Or was it more like the charity routinely enjoined upon the devout, intended not to change its recipient's economic position, but to make it more tolerable?

Subscriptions were absolutely fundamental to the poetic careers of women of the lower orders. In this period there were two notable examples: Mary Collier (1679–after 1762), spurred into publication by the slights on women included by the thresher-poet Stephen Duck in *The Thresher's Labour*; and Mary Leapor (1722–46) who, inspired by her reading, of Pope above all, experimented in a wide range of forms.

Leapor's career reveals both the subtle gradations of rank and status in eighteenth-century England and the factors that made problematic the emergence of such a gifted writer from the ranks of manual workers. In *Crumble Hall*, for example, she takes the institution of the landed estate, the basic unit of traditional notions of social structure, and subjects the traditional poem that celebrates the virtues of its owner as lynchpin of social and cultural order to a witheringly unresponsive rewriting, in which the special features of a great house are rendered as disjointed and meaningless, or as positively repulsive, or simply as making work for servants like herself.[51] Several of her poems also address the difficulty of integrating her identity as poet with the social situation and community into which she was born.[52] Marriage was the most obvious route to social integration for an eighteenth-century woman; but the satirical bias of Leapor's commentary on men and marriage suggests that she would not have been keen to give up the independence of a single woman.[53] Even the most superficial biographical evidence demonstrates the importance to Leapor of female community and its potential for the crossing of social boundaries: a female employer, widowed and independent, encouraged her as 'the Successor of *Pope*'; her only 'intimate Companion', according to her father, was 'one agreeable young Woman in this Town, whom she mentions in her Poem upon *Friendship*, by the Name of FIDELIA'; several poems take the form of familiar epistles to female addressees; and her creative lifeline in the last year of her life was Bridget Freemantle, spinster daughter of a former rector, and organizer of the subscription project that would bring her work to the attention of a wider public.[54]

At the end of the period treated in this book, the sense of a social hierarchy modelled on a body or family was weakening, with property and gender taking on more importance in the definition of social position. Women poets made their own accommodations between what they could use of traditional modes of figuring society and what they could assimilate from newer trends. They came from different backgrounds and articulated different political views; some relied on female networks while others were sustained by male mentors; some preferred manuscript circulation and others print; but by the middle of the eighteenth century there were more of them, and they were distributed almost down to the lowest levels of society. It was a situation that seventeenth-century elite women poets like Cavendish and Philips would have found it difficult – and perhaps not altogether pleasant – to imagine.

Notes

1. Cp. Paula McDowell, *The Women of Grub Street: Press, Politics, and Gender in the London Literary Marketplace 1678–1730* (Oxford: Clarendon Press, 1998), commenting on Elinor James and other prose polemicists: 'To quote their scattered protofeminist remarks out of context is to risk misleading twentieth-century readers as to the overall nature of their works' (p. 184).

2. One of the most approachable accounts of social structure remains Peter Laslett's *The World We Have Lost* (1965, revised as *The World We Have Lost Further Explored*, 3rd edn (London: Routledge, 2000)): see particularly Chapters 1–2, pp. 1–52. See also Keith Wrightson, 'Estates, Degrees, and Sorts: Changing Perceptions of Society in Tudor and Stuart England', in Penelope J. Corfield (ed.), *Language, History and Class* (Oxford: Blackwell, 1991), pp. 30–52.

3. Keith Wrightson's *English Society 1580–1680* (London: Hutchinson, 1982) is useful for the beginning of our period: see particularly Chapters 1 and 2, pp. 17–65. See also Jonathan Barry's Introduction to Jonathan Barry and Christopher Brooks (eds), *The Middling Sort of People: Culture, Society and Politics in England, 1550–1800* (London: Macmillan now Palgrave Macmillan, 1994), pp. 1–27. For a discussion that acknowledges the closeness of some features of the period to the structures that Marx would describe in terms of class, see Peter Earle, *The Making of the English Middle Class: Business, Society and Family Life in London 1660–1730* (London: Methuen, 1989), pp. 3–13.

4. Hence Laslett speaks of 'A One-Class Society', *World We Have Lost Further Explored*, Chapter 2, pp. 22–52; but see also Earle, *Making of the English Middle Class*, pp. 3–13.

5. See Paul Langford, *A Polite and Commercial People: England, 1727–1783*, New Oxford History of England (Oxford: Oxford University Press, 1989), p. 654, for social conflict conceived in terms of 'interest'.

6. For related themes, see McDowell, *Women of Grub Street*, Chapter 4, 'Metaphors of Being and Modes of Empowerment', pp. 180–214.

7. For the early uses of 'class', see Raymond Williams, *Culture and Society 1780–1950* (London: Chatto & Windus, 1958), p. xv; Langford, *Polite and Commercial People*, pp. 652–5. David Cannadine, *Class in Britain* (Yale: Yale University Press, 1998), cites feminist critique as one of the factors responsible for the recent shift away from class-based historical analysis: his coverage, however, is weighted towards the Hanoverian period (pp. 1–23; xi, 11, 24–56). For an attempt to recuperate the concept of class in relation to a range of texts from the Middle Ages to the present, see Gary Day, *Class*, The New Critical Idiom (London: Routledge, 2001).

8. See Earle, *Making of the English Middle Class*, and Barry and Brooks (eds), *Middling Sort of People*.

9. See Amanda Vickery, *The Gentleman's Daughter: Women's Lives in Georgian England* (London: Yale University Press, 1999), pp. 13–37, on the overlap between gentry and prosperous trading and professional groups.

10. Laslett, *World We Have Lost Further Explored*, pp. 43–4.

11. For politeness and Whig ideology, see Lawrence E. Klein, *Shaftesbury and the Culture of Politeness: Moral Discourse and Cultural Politics in Early Eighteenth-Century England* (Cambridge: Cambridge University Press, 1994), pp. 1–14.

12. Ruth Perry, 'Women in Families: the Great Disinheritance', in Vivien Jones (ed.), *Women and Literature in Britain, 1700–1800* (Cambridge: Cambridge University Press, 2000), pp. 111–31.

13. Catherine Gallagher, 'Embracing the Absolute: the Politics of the Female Subject in Seventeenth-Century England', *Genders* I (1988), pp. 24–39.

14. Carol Barash, *English Women's Poetry, 1649–1714: Politics, Community, and Linguistic Authority* (Oxford: Clarendon Press, 1996), pp. 12–24 and *passim*.

15. McDowell, *Women of Grub Street*, p. 19 and *passim*.

16. See Margaret J. M. Ezell, *The Patriarch's Wife: Literary Evidence and the History of the Family* (Chapel Hill and London: University of North Carolina Press, 1987), Chapter 3, pp. 62–100; and the same author's *Social Authorship and the Advent of Print* (London: Johns Hopkins University Press, 1999), particularly pp. 37–40. See also Harold Love, *The Culture and Commerce of Texts: Scribal Publication in Seventeenth-Century England* (Amherst: University of Massachusetts, 1998: originally published as *Scribal Publication in Seventeenth-Century England* (Oxford: Clarendon Press, 1993)), especially pp. 54–8; and the essays in George Justice and Nathan Tinker (eds), *Women's Writing and the Circulation of Ideas: Manuscript Publication in England, 1550–1800* (Cambridge: Cambridge University Press, 2002).

17. See particularly David Foxon's 1975–76 Lyell Lectures at Oxford, published as *Pope and the Early Eighteenth-Century Book Trade*, revised and edited by James McLaverty (Oxford: Clarendon Press, 1991); and James McLaverty, *Pope, Print, and Meaning* (Oxford: Oxford University Press, 2001).

18. For Pope's early use of manuscript circulation, see Julian Ferraro, 'From Text to Work: the Presentation and Re-presentation of *Epistles to Several Persons*', *Proceedings of the British Academy* XCI (1998), pp. 111–34; Ezell, *Social Authorship*, Chapter 3, pp. 61–83. For his use of print, see note 17 above. Comparable perspectives on individual women poets include:

Margaret J. M. Ezell's introduction to *The Poems and Prose of Mary, Lady Chudleigh* (Oxford: Oxford University Press, 1993), pp. xxviii–xxxiv; Kathryn R. King, *Jane Barker, Exile: a Literary Career 1675–1725* (Oxford: Clarendon Press, 2000), particularly Chapter 1, pp. 29–67; Richard Greene, *Mary Leapor: a Study in Eighteenth-Century Women's Poetry* (Oxford: Clarendon Press, 1993), pp. 18–29.

19. Cavendish's 'A True Relation of my Birth, Breeding, and Life', cited in Sylvia Bowerbank and Sara Mendelson (eds), *Paper Bodies: a Margaret Cavendish Reader* (Peterborough, Ontario: Broadview Press), p. 48.

20. Patrick Thomas (ed.), *The Collected Works of Katherine Philips: the Matchless Orinda*, 2 vols (Stump Cross: Stump Cross Books, 1990), pp. 19–20; see also Ezell, *Patriarch's Wife*, pp. 85–7; and for Philips as 'an author at odds with changing literary culture and technology', see Ezell, *Social Authorship*, pp. 52–4.

21. On the novelty of gendered subjectivity, see McDowell, *Women of Grub Street*, pp. 291–3 and *passim*.

22. Ezell, *Poems and Prose of Mary, Lady Chudleigh*, pp. 307–8.

23. Lines 785, 788–9: Ezell, *Poems and Prose of Mary, Lady Chudleigh*, p. 38.

24. Roger Lonsdale (ed.), *Eighteenth-Century Women Poets: an Oxford Anthology* (Oxford: Oxford University Press, 1990), pp. 2–3. Lonsdale's headnotes on individual poets are hereafter referred to without further acknowledgement.

25. Lines 123–32: Ezell, *Poems and Prose of Mary, Lady Chudleigh*, p. 165.

26. Before Anne, the court of James II's queen, Mary of Modena, had also nurtured female poets: see Barash, *English Women's Poetry, 1649–1714*, pp. 149–52.

27. Ezell, *Poems and Prose of Mary, Lady Chudleigh*, p. xxii. For George I's marriage, see Ragnhild Hatton, *George I: Elector and King* (London: Thames and Hudson, 1978), pp. 54–64.

28. For the relationship between George II and Queen Caroline, see Valerie Rumbold, *Women's Place in Pope's World* (Cambridge: Cambridge University Press, 1989), pp. 216–18.

29. Ezell, *Poems and Prose of Mary, Lady Chudleigh*, Introduction.

30. For Finch's relation to the court and politics of James II and, after 1688, to the Jacobite cause, see Barbara McGovern and Charles H. Hinnant (eds), *The Anne Finch Wellesley Manuscript Poems: a Critical Edition* (London: University of Georgia Press, 1998), pp. xvii–xxiii.

31. Lonsdale (ed.), *Eighteenth-Century Women Poets*, pp. 4–6.

32. For the relation between Finch's manuscript and printed poems, see Barash, *English Women's Poetry, 1649–1714*, pp. 262–78; McGovern and Hinnant (eds), *Anne Finch Wellesley Manuscript Poems*, pp. xv–xviii. The standard edition, Myra Reynolds (ed.), *The Poems of Anne Countess of Winchilsea* (Chicago: University of Chicago Press, 1903), was prepared without knowledge of the Wellesley Manuscript.

33. Robert Halsband and Isobel Grundy (eds), *Lady Mary Wortley Montagu: Essays and Poems and Simplicity, a Comedy*, paperback reprint of 1977 edition with new Preface (Oxford: Clarendon Press, 1993), pp. 172–3.

34. Isobel Grundy, *Lady Mary Wortley Montagu: Comet of the Enlightenment* (Oxford: Oxford University Press, 1999), pp. 353–4.

35. Valerie Rumbold, 'The Poetic Career of Judith Cowper: an Exemplary Failure?', in Donald C. Mell (ed.), *Pope, Swift, and Women Writers* (London: Associated University Presses, 1996), pp. 48–66.
36. For Cowper's relationship with Pope, see ibid. and the same author's *Women's Place in Pope's World*, pp. 145–50. For Pattison, see p. 146, note 33.
37. King, *Jane Barker, Exile*, pp. 32–6.
38. Ibid., pp. 69–79.
39. Kathryn R. King (ed.), *The Poems of Jane Barker: the Magdalen Manuscript*, Magdalen College Occasional Paper 3 (Oxford: Magdalen College, 1998), pp. 1–17.
40. King, *Jane Barker, Exile*, pp. 147–217; for Curll's marketing, see particularly p. 171.
41. See Margaret J. M. Ezell, *Writing Women's Literary History* (London: Johns Hopkins University Press, 1993), pp. 45–7, 53, for a critique of the Woolf-inspired tradition, still found in several standard accounts, according to which women's literary history pivots around Behn's supposed status as pioneer.
42. Janet Todd, *The Secret Life of Aphra Behn* (London: André Deutsch, 1996), pp. 12–16; Janet Todd (ed.), *The Works of Aphra Behn*, 7 vols (London: Pickering, 1992–96), Vol. 1, pp. ix–xviii.
43. For Pix, who figured in a discarded draft of Pope's 1728 *Dunciad*, see Valerie Rumbold, 'Cut the Caterwauling: Women Writers (not) in Pope's *Dunciads*', *RES*, New Series 52, No. 208 (2000), pp. 524–39 (532–4).
44. Though not directly relevant to Pix's situation, it is also worth noting McDowell's account of how in this period women of printing families tended to be removed from direct participation in the business, thus being deprived of the unmediated access to print that some of them had previously exploited.
45. Rumbold, 'Cut the Caterwauling', pp. 532–4.
46. Sarah Prescott, 'Provincial Networks, Dissenting Connections, and Noble Friends: Elizabeth Singer Rowe and Female Authorship in Early Eighteenth-Century England', *Eighteenth-Century Life* XXV (2001), pp. 29–42.
47. See David E. Shuttleton, 'Mary Chandler's *Description of Bath* (1734): the Poetic Topographies of an Augustan Tradeswoman', *Women's Writing* 7, 3 (Spring 2000), pp. 447–67.
48. Lonsdale (ed.), *Eighteenth-Century Women Poets*, pp. 153–5.
49. Ibid., pp. 152–3.
50. Ibid., p. 121.
51. For contrasting readings of the poem, see for example Donna Landry, *The Muses of Resistance: Laboring-Class Women's Poetry in Britain, 1739–1796* (Cambridge: Cambridge University Press, 1990), pp. 107–19 (and pp. 78–107 for Landry's general rationale); Greene, *Mary Leapor*, pp. 137–42; Valerie Rumbold, 'The Alienated Insider: Mary Leapor in "Crumble Hall" ', *British Journal for Eighteenth-Century Studies* XIX (1996), pp. 63–76; Dustin Griffin, *Literary Patronage in England, 1650–1800* (Cambridge: Cambridge University Press, 1996), pp. 191–203.
52. Mary Leapor, *Poems on Several Occasions*, 2 vols (1748–51), Vol. 2, pp. 68–71, 294–8, 43–54.

53. See, for example, 'Man the Monarch', 'An Essay on Woman' and 'Mira to Octavia' (*Poems*, Vol. 2, pp. 7–10, 64–7, 100–10).
54. Leapor, *Poems*, Vol. 2, pp. 97, xxx. See also Landry, *Muses of Resistance*, pp. 83–99; and Kate Lilley, 'Homosocial Women: Martha Sansom, Constantia Grierson, Mary Leapor and Georgic Verse Epistle', in Isobel Armstrong and Virginia Blain (eds), *Women's Poetry in the Enlightenment: the Making of a Canon, 1730–1820* (London: Macmillan now Palgrave Macmillan, 1999), pp. 167–83.

12
From Manuscript to Print: a Volume of Their Own?

Margaret J. M. Ezell

Thinking about the mechanics of how early modern English women's poetry moved from manuscript to print offers us the opportunity to examine the material culture of writing and reading in earlier times, but it also invites us to ponder the ways in which audience and authorship have been conceived in other generations and the assumptions about each which we ourselves bring to the study of early modern women's texts. Does the media – manuscript or printed page – determine the audience, or does the author? Why would writers, male or female, want to transform their manuscripts into print? Having made that decision, how could it happen and did it happen differently depending on the sex of the writer?

When thinking about early modern women writers, our assumptions about class, literacy, ethnicity and women's participation in the material side of textual production have recently been brought under increasing scrutiny. Some of the primary assumptions about early modern female literary figures were that she was aristocratic, privileged, pious, married and English. Elite social status was typically deemed the primary position from which an early modern woman writer could both read and write. As Helen Wilcox wittily observed, most of us on being asked to imagine an early modern woman, 'will probably visualize one of the many portraits of Elizabeth I . . . [or] the Renaissance mother heading ranks of children in descending order of height'.[1] And, indeed, as we shall see, the texts of such women with extended families had a greater chance of survival in the archives and of moving from manuscript into print than a woman who had no library or closet in which to store her writings, and no family to preserve her papers. However, as Margo Hendricks has suggested, 'feminist historiography cannot afford to generate totalizing narratives about women's existence in Renaissance and early modern England, particularly when a number of these women were from diverse ethnic and social backgrounds'.[2]

This holds true for the textual analysis of early modern women's writings as well. The work of the Perdita Project to document manuscript texts by early modern women and the resulting electronic database has made women's manuscripts more clearly visible as part of our field of investigation; its contents have brought into question our assumptions about the supposedly restricted and aristocratic nature of manuscript circulation. The most recent anthologies of early modern women writers instead of apologizing for, or omitting, women's manuscript texts draw them in without textual comment as part of their design to represent 'the sheer energy and diversity of women's cultural activity in the British islands and in the communities of exiles from those islands'.[3] 'From the beginning', Stevenson and Davidson declare, 'women's writing was not homogeneous in terms of class, language, subject-matter, or intention'.[4]

The audience for women's writing, both printed and in script, is also being redefined as we consider the grounds on which literacy has traditionally been measured, a reassessment greatly enhanced by the expansion in interest in the history of reading practices in general.[5] Finally, the implications of class as well as gender as a factor shaping the extent and the ways in which a woman could participate in the literary culture of her times have been raised into question in several sharply contrasting studies, for example, Carol Barash's *English Women's Poetry, 1649–1714: Politics, Community, and Linguistic Authority* (1996) and Paula McDowell's *The Women of Grub Street: Press, Politics, and Gender in the London Literary Marketplace 1678–1730* (1998) and McDowell's ongoing work with women's participation in oral literary culture. All of these studies, from anthologies and databases to critical interpretations and the recovery of the material culture of reading and writing, invite us to look more closely at what we believe 'being an author' and in particular what 'being a poet' meant then – and now.

Some audiences for early modern women's writing obviously did not require a printed text to achieve the author's intended goals or to reach her intended audience. Elizabeth Bury (1644–1720), for example, rose at 4 a.m. to have the time to pursue her studies in Hebrew, divinity, philosophy, history, medicine, French and mathematics and to record her responses in her voluminous diaries and to share her thoughts in her widespread correspondence that extended to 'very distant Countries', recorded her husband.[6] Clearly, getting into print was not important in her self-fashioning as either an intellectual or a writer. Of her primary readership, neither God nor her intellectual network relied on print medium to exchange ideas, only to provide the raw materials on which to speculate. After her death, however, her husband oversaw the publication of selections from her diaries to reach a very different type of reader than she had sought; this secondary readership experienced her thoughts in edited selections, framed by commentary from Isaac Watts and her grieving husband.

Elizabeth Bury, of course, was not a poet and this raises the question of whether there were different motivations and intended readers for women who expressed themselves in verse rather than prose, desires which print could satisfy better than script. Women writers such as Damaris, Lady Masham (1658–1708) and Mary Astell (1661–1731) actively pursued publication for their prose treatises, but not for their poetry. Mary Astell gained a public reputation as a controversialist with her treatises on marriage and education, but she chose to keep her poetry in manuscript. That she valued it is without question – she had a manuscript volume carefully prepared with complete textual apparatus, including a dated title page and a letter of dedication to William Sandcroft, Archbishop of Canterbury – but her poems were not printed until the twentieth century.[7]

Masham apparently considered printing her verse, but decided against it. She wrote wryly to her partner in poetry, the philosopher John Locke, that among contemporary women poets the fashion seemed to be for posthumous publication: 'perhaps you may see me in Print in a little While', she wrote, but, 'I confess it has not much of my Approbation because (Principally) the Mode is for one to Dye first'.[8] In this comment she draws our attention to what may seem an uncomfortable path for getting into print for a modern writer, but one we find frequently among earlier social authors of both sexes – posthumous publication.

Like Elizabeth Bury's diaries, much of the verse written by early modern women was devotional in nature. Often it takes the form of self-examination at times of spiritual trial, and the initial readership was private and personal, the author, her God and her family, a readership requiring no printed aides. The careful preservation of such manuscript texts, however, often invited the posthumous publication of them by friends and family as spiritual models for future unknown print readers, unknown in a personal sense, but united with the writer and her family through issues of faith. The Quaker poet Mary Mollineux (1651–95) originally wrote her verses for a select group of family and friends, for whom there was no need of a printed text. As her recent editors have noted, like many poets male and female, she began her poetic career at an early age, starting around age 12 to versify 'pious exhortations to members of her family'.[9] After her marriage she wrote less, but she still sent verses in Latin to her husband Henry, imprisoned for his refusal to pay tithes; after her death, he along with other family members translated them and, along with her other English verses, had them published by the Quaker woman printer Tace Sowle as *Fruits of Retirement or Miscellaneous Poems Moral and Divine* (1702).

Thus, women's manuscripts intended by the author only for private reading could find their way into print without her assistance. Octavia Walsh (1677–1706), the sister of William Walsh (himself a published poet, critic and mentor of the young Alexander Pope), managed her own poetry so privately that her poems were 'found among her Papers after her death, till which time none of her nearest Relations knew that she was an Author'.[10] The note on the manuscript volume describes the contents as 'the Private Entertainment of Mrs. Octavia Walsh In her Vacant Hours From the Age of Fifteen to Twenty-Nine, At which Time it pleas'd Almighty God by ye Small Pox to take her out of this World'. Her family apparently compiled the volume itself after her death, but it is unclear whether she circulated her separate verses circumspectly among friends, since there is reference to a 'Urania' whose approval she desires to uphold. Although it appears that she herself would not have intended or desired her manuscripts being printed, after her death, seven of her devotional poems were included in a collection *Poems upon Divine and Moral Subjects* (1719; reissued 1734 as *A Collection of Select Original Poems and Translations*).

The verses of Anne Wharton (1659–1685) offer another example of texts that had extensive circulation in manuscript in their authors' lifetimes and continued being read in print for further decades after their deaths. Wharton, the niece of the Earl of Rochester, had several significant commercial as well as social literary figures as her manuscript readers for her miscellaneous verse, including Aphra Behn, Rochester himself, Edmund Waller and Bishop Burnet. After her death, selected poems identified as being by her appeared extensively in miscellany collections well into the eighteenth century (a format for publication that will be discussed further in a later section of this essay). Perhaps because she wrote not only elegies on Rochester and songs to Cupid, but also paraphrases of the lamentations of Jeremiah, Wharton's poetry appears in diverse groups of printed volumes throughout the next 40 years, including ones edited by Behn, Nahum

Tate, Edward Young's *The Idea of Christian Love* (1688), Charles Gilden's *Miscellany Poems* (1692), Francis Saunders's *A Collection of Poems by Several Hands* (1693), Gilden's *A New Miscellany of Original Poems on Several Occasions* (1701), *A Collection of Poems: Viz The Temple of Death* (1701; 2nd edn 1702), and *The Poetical Works of Philip, late Duke of Wharton* (1731). Her verses, however, were not collected into a volume of their own until 1997, *The Surviving Works of Anne Wharton*, edited by Germaine Greer and Susan Hastings.

In these examples, women authors, whether of prose or verse, had in mind primarily a readership composed of self, family and close friends, readers who knew the author, shared her religious and social beliefs, and needed no glosses or guides to reading. It is notable that in the case of Bury and Mollineux, it was their husbands along with other family members who produced the printed versions posthumously, editing, translating and enclosing them in a framework for readers who never knew the writers in person. In the most elementary sense, this is an important way in which an early modern poet's verses could move from manuscript to print – as memorial volumes dedicated to their talents by loving family members and their contents shaped by them to represent the deceased poet. Mollineux's volume was immediately successful in early modern publishing terms, and sustained its author's name and reputation for several generations of Quaker readers after her death, with six editions in England and an estimated four more in Philadelphia by 1783. As her relatives observed, both her life and her verses were intended in these printed versions to serve as inspirational models for her readers.

At the opposite end of the social spectrum, grieving aristocratic fathers also compiled and had printed the collected verse of their daughters in volumes. The most well known of these is Anne Killigrew (1660–85), a maid of honour in the court of Mary of Modena, the Duchess of York, celebrated after her death by John Dryden for her skills in poetry and painting. She, too, is hailed as an exemplar in this volume, first by her father in the preface and by Dryden in his Ode. Likewise, Viscount Molesworth gathered together the manuscripts of his daughter Mary Monck (c.1678–1715), along with those of several of her primary readers and correspondents with whom she exchanged verses, and published them indiscriminately together in *Marinda* (1716). In his dedication of the volume to the Princess of Wales, he makes it clear to Monck's new, secondary readership that as impressive as his daughter's poetic talents are, the reader should remember that they were merely 'the Product of the leisure Hours of a Young

Gentlewoman . . . without omitting the daily Care due to a large Family'. Thus, in all of these instances, although all the poets did have their works printed, did reach audiences outside their acquaintance, and did achieve a larger readership than while they were alive and writing, their poetry as well as their presence in the printed volumes were controlled and shaped by loving editors for the benefit of these reading strangers.[11]

A related means of getting into print would be the 'pirating' of manuscript verses of a living author, either by well-intended friends and relatives or by unscrupulous booksellers. Perhaps two of the most celebrated women poets in the seventeenth century, Katherine Philips (1632–64) and Anne Bradstreet (1617–72), were apparently surprised and aghast to read their own verses collected in single-author printed volumes. In each instance, the women expressed shocked concern over the corrupt, inaccurate versions of their manuscript texts in the printed format, which left them open, they felt, to critical censure from hostile, strange readers. The earlier of these two, Bradstreet had family members to thank for the surprise of *The Tenth Muse* (1650). In a poem subsequently included in the posthumous second edition, she comments on the initial experience. Addressing 'her book' in the guise of a wayward child, Bradstreet in 'The Author to her Book', laments wryly that 'after birth did'st by my side remain,/Till snatcht from thence by friends, less wise than true'. Their well-intentioned literary kidnapping,

> . . . expos'd to publick view,
> Made thee in rags, halting to th'press to trudg,
> Where errors were not lessened (all may judg).[12]

Bradstreet died before finishing a final, correct version for the press, and again a posthumous volume was carefully prepared by friends and family.

In Katherine Philips's situation, it apparently was not family or friends who sought out the printer for her collected verse. Although she had had individual poems published, for example, a prefatory poem in William Cartwright's *Comedies* (1651) and a poem welcoming Catherine of Braganza in 1662, Philips famously excoriated the mangled 1664 version of her poetry printed by Richard Marriott, to the end that he issued a public, printed apology and withdrew the book from sale.[13] At the time of her death from smallpox, on the advice of friends, she was preparing a 'true' version of her collected verse for publication, one which was subsequently edited by her friend Charles Cottrell in 1667, including her letter to her friends which, in his words, clearly shows 'how little she desired the fame of being in print, and how much she was troubled to be so exposed'.[14]

A final example of 'pirated' verse would be the complicated publishing history of Jane Barker (1652–1732), who accused the printer Benjamin Crayle of publishing 50 of her poems without her consent in *Poetical Recreations* (1688). As her biographer Kathryn King has noted, it is rather difficult to assess exactly how surprised or outraged Barker was about the print appearance of her poetry, given her close association with the other contributors in the volume, students at St John's College, Cambridge (many of whom were friends of her brother and with whom she exchanged verses), and the fact that 8 poems to or about her are identified as having been written by the publisher Crayle himself.[15] As King points out, Barker, too, followed the pattern of correcting the mistakes made in the printed version of the texts by creating a new manuscript of them, on which she stated that previously they had been printed 'without her consent' and are 'now corrected by her own hand'.[16] As we shall see, the revised manuscript texts would find their way into print again decades later, but in a very different format.

Barker's publication history also raises the issue for us of the ways in which literary history has tended to segregate thinking about poets from thinking about prose writers, in particular fiction writers, as if they are separate species, with separate publishing agendas. We thus often lose sight of how many men and women wrote in a variety of genres during their literary careers. We also tend to forget how often in the later part of the seventeenth century, with the explosion of new hybrid genres mixing romance, travel narrative, curiosity tales, confessions and drama, prose texts very often include the writer's verses, whether as part of an imaginary epistolary exchange between characters, functioning as some part of the narrative scheme, or merely to heighten the emotional response of the reader.

In Delarivière Manley's *The New Atlantis* (1709), for example, there is a substantial verse interlude that appears as part of a discussion of the funeral sermons of rich and powerful people, which also sheds light on the writing habits of print poets as opposed to social ones. Commenting on the funeral procession of 'the richest widow in Atlantis', the character Lady Intelligence offers the other female characters, 'the draft of an essay, wrote by an obscure poet, upon [the husband's] death. I'll quickly ransack my satchel for it.'[17] Lady Intelligence identifies the elegy as being by 'a certain poet, who had formerly wrote some things with success but, either shrunk in his genius or grown very lazy, procured another brother of Parnassus to write this elegy for him and promised to divide the profit'. However, the payment turning out to be larger than expected, the 'lazy poet' (identified by the editor Rosalind Ballaster as possibly the playwright Mary Pix) 'defrauded the poor labourer of his hire' (Ballaster suggests this is Manley herself); 'justly incensed against the treachery of his friend, he resolves to own and print this piece in the next miscellanea'. A lengthy elegy in dialogue between Astrea, Aminta, Delia [Manley] and Melissa follows, invoking the shades of Afra [Aphra Behn] and Orinda [Katherine Philips], suggesting that Delia surpasses them both, by intertwining lines in praise of Manley's poetry from Mary Pix's dedicatory poem in Manley's play, *The Royal Mischief*, where Manley is described by Pix as 'Like Sappho charming, like Afra eloquent/Like chaste Orinda sweetly innocent'.[18]

Manley was not unique in including verse in her print fictions to highlight a point or to bring in new characters. We find verse mixed with romance in Eliza Haywood's fictions; Haywood (*c*.1693–1756), who belonged to the next generation of commercial women writers, also wrote in a variety of genres. She incorporated verses into her fictions to heighten the dramatic intensity of a scene and to reveal the inner feelings of the characters, verses apparently written specifically for the characters rather than recycled from her dramas.[19] For example, in *The Injur'd Husband* (1723), Beauclair overhears his lost love Montamour singing in a convent garden, announcing her decision to renounce 'Sense-alluring Bait/Of gay Deceit, in tender Raptures drest!' which causes him, 'with trembling Limbs and aching Heart . . . to fear all his Endeavours to bring her to a Reconciliation would be in vain'. As he despairs in the grotto, fortunately her next song encourages him to throw himself at her feet and beg forgiveness, which after many pages she grants him (76–7). Likewise, verse serves as an important element in revealing the tragic heroine's emotional disorder in *Lasselia* (1724). 'Writ by a Woman in Love to Madness and one who had abandon'd all things for her Passion', the poem 'The Impossibility; or the Combat of the Senses' is supposedly recovered among the papers of the object of her adoration, the married man de L'Amye, after their deaths (120). As with the poetry in *The Injur'd Husband*, this piece does not appear in Haywood's collected verse and thus appears to exist primarily as a means of heightening the fiction reader's sense of the emotional and spiritual peril of the female character who writes them in her response to her lover – 'Each Look, each Word, each Touch, each melting Kiss,/ Gives raging Extasy! – distracting Bliss!' (121) – not to mention arousing the feelings of the reader him or herself.

Barker also incorporated verse into her prose narratives, but uses them in a very different fashion and tone. These pieces, unlike those of Haywood, bear an interesting relationship to poems Barker lamented being printed in *Poetical Recreations* some three decades earlier. As her editor Carol Shiner Wilson has explored, Barker continued to circulate and collect verse in manuscript, but she also actively sought a publisher for her later prose fictions, most notably *A Patch-Work Screen for the Ladies* (1723) and *The Lining of the Patch-Work Screen* (1726). These works all contain significant amounts of Barker's poetry. For example, in 'Leaf III, The History of Lysander', from *A Patch-Work Screen for the Ladies*, Barker interweaves part of Katherine Phillips's song 'If with some pleasure we our griefs betray' with couplets from Horace, several of Barker's own poems revised from their original appearance in *Poetical Recreations* and a new song, 'It was on a Day'. All of Barker's 'novels' contain interpolated verse, so that in effect, in publishing her fictions, she was also publishing her poetry – characters are constantly bursting into verse, and readers thus are presented with both Barker the novelist and Barker the poet in one printed package.[20] King argues that like her collected verse, her early fictions *Bosvil and Galesia* and *Exilius* (1714) were intended for a small, private and largely female readership; by 1723 and the appearance of *A Patch-Work Screen for the Ladies*, she was writing for 'a large, impersonal reading public whose members Barker could no longer rely upon to share her values, prejudices, angers, and identifications'.[21] Thus, it seems of particular interest that Barker chose to 'repackage' her poetry in these later volumes, not as part of a freestanding volume of verse, but instead wrapping them within a larger prose narrative and in the company of other poets.

This same combination of poetic inspiration embedded within a prose frame is also a feature of a very different type of women's writing for a very different type of audience – women's devotional publications, in particular, prophetic works, pamphlets and broadsides. Anna Trapnel's *The Cry of a Stone* (1654) is a good earlier example of the ways in which poetry serves to animate spiritual expression and to illustrate the centrality of interpolated verse in popular religious culture. While the later Quakers tended to discourage the publication of verse by members, it nevertheless features prominently in the religious expression of many of the central women figures in the 1670s and 1680s.

Dorothy White's (1630–85) extensive pamphlet publications mingle exhortation and prophecy, but verse signals celebration:

> So our Beloved is become our Life,
> We are his Virgins, and his Married Wife:
> Who are to him bound all in one Band,
> Who are rejoicing in the Holy Land.[22]

She includes long poems in *A Trumpet of the Lord of Hosts Blown Unto the City of London* (1662) and *Call from God out of Egypt* (1662), where she revels 'in the Love and Fulness of his Power/In us, is shining in this glorious hour' (7). In a different tone, Anne Whitehead's verses look inward, commenting on her early religious awakening and were published by her friend Mary Stout in *Piety Promoted by Faithfulness, Manifested by Several Testimonies concerning that true Servant of God ANN WHITEHEAD* (1680). Anne Docwra (1624–1710), no friend of Ann Whitehead's, also included verse, 'The Mystery of Profession great' in her tract rebuking authorities, *A Looking-Glass for the Recorder and Justices of the Peace and Grand Juries for the Town and County of Cambridge* (1682), as had Mary Adams (f. 1676) who had issued a *Warning to the Inhabitants of England and London in Particular* (1676), which concludes

> What Sins were found in Sodom and Gomorrah,
> Also the Great Cruelty of Pharaoh
> That is not found in this Wicked Generation?
> Therefore repent with speed, lest it prove your Damnation.[23]

Whether in attempting to express a transcendent spiritual moment, to move the reader to a fresh sense of their own sins and lament the current state of the nation, or to confirm the joy of spiritual union, many of these women from middle- and labouring-class backgrounds found verse indispensable to their projects. We rarely think of them as 'poets', but it is clear that poetry was an essential part of their spiritual practice. Unlike social authors requiring a shared frame of reference, for such evangelical poets printed pamphlet publication was clearly the best medium for reaching their desired audience, not only those fellow travellers in the spirit but also those unknown strangers of every social class, needing to see the light and change their ways.

But what of those women who identified themselves primarily as poets, and who envisioned an audience of readers only reached through print, those unseen, unknown individuals perhaps even willing to pay money to read their verses? It is useful to consider what might motivate one to seek a print readership in contrast to the one available for manuscript texts. The model of authorship espoused by Samuel Johnson and Virginia Woolf – money dignifies intellectual and artistic labour – is certainly present by the end of the seventeenth century, but there are still other print venues where authors could see their poems in a printed format but not expect nor desire to receive any compensation for it.

A number of single verses by women appeared in print because they were intended to commemorate significant public events and to address public figures. Clearly, the broadside and pamphlet forms of publication offered the cheapest and widest initial readership for such poetry as well as the best means of reaching a public figure and a public readership. Rachel Jevon (1627–*c.*62) was one of many other poets, famous and amateur, male and female, who celebrated the return of Charles II in 1660. In the subscription under the title of the English version of her Latin ode *Exultationis Carmen* (1660), she hides neither her gender nor her loyalties: 'By Rachel Jevon. Presented with her own hand, Aug. 16th. To the most Pious and most Serene Kings, The Unworthiest of his Majesties Hand-Maids with all Humility Offers this Congratulatory Poem.' Katherine Philips may not have approved of printing a collection of her verse, but she did see it as appropriate for 'To the Queen's Majesty on her Happy Arrival' to appear as a broadside in 1662. Ephelia, more of whom later, likewise used the broadside to publish her 'A Poem Presented to his Sacred Majesty on the Discovery of the Plot' (1678) and an address to the Duke of Monmouth, 'Advice to His Grace' (*c.*1681), both of which she would use in her later collected volume.

In addition to broadsides and small pamphlets dealing with significant public, political events, the process which offered the social author easiest access to the professional's media by the end of the seventeenth century was through submissions to periodicals and miscellanies, rather than compiling complete volumes of verse. John Dunton's *Athenian Mercury* is perhaps the best known of this new type of popular periodical entertainment for readers, which began appearing at the end of the seventeenth century, but it had numerous competitors, all clamouring for contributions. Peter Motteux's *Gentleman's Journal* (1692–94) beseeched readers to consider sending in their friend's poetic efforts as well as their own; the response by women readers was so supportive that the December 1693 issue was even re-titled *The Lady's Journal*.[24] In the pages of the *Gentleman's Journal*, one can follow the contributions of 'Urania', Elizabeth Dalton, 'Salopia',

'A Young Lady', 'Orithya' and Mary B, none of whom that we know of ever published a volume of verse or sought financial remuneration for their poetic labours.

There were several advantages for a woman writer of having a single poem appearing in periodical publications. To begin with, she would not need to be present in London to deal with a printer or bookseller, or in any way have to oversee its preparation or marketing. Thus, Elizabeth Singer Rowe (1674–1737) could, while living far from London in Frome or while at boarding school, be an active participant in Dunton's Athenian Society publications.[25] Kathryn King has recently described Rowe as, 'one of the earliest women writers to capitalize on the possibilities of the periodical press',[26] and her literary career is certainly one of the better documented in this fashion, but she was hardly unique among female poets to seize this inviting format for publication. Starting in as early as 1691 when she was 17, and a decade before she married and moved to London, Rowe's steady contributions to the *Athenian Mercury* (1691–97) had by 1694 earned her the sobriquet 'The Pindarical Lady' from Dunton.

Periodical publication also permitted a social and psychological distance as well as a geographical one, all within the comfortable conventions of social author that were being adapted for commercial publication. Publications such as Motteux's and Dunton's invited the reader not only to purchase the periodical but also to participate in creating its contents, what J. Paul Hunter in his study of the context of the early novel has called Dunton's sense of 'participatory journalism'.[27] In addition to the opportunity for 'all ingenious and curious Enquirers into Speculations, Divine, Moral and Natural, &c' to pose and answer questions in these diverse fields, Athenian-style periodicals, instead of passive consumption of its pages, urged readers to send their own poetic 'riddles' or enigma poems, to dust off their efforts at translating, and to respond in verse to the contents of the issue.

In the case of the *Athenian Mercury*, Dunton, to use modern marketing terms, spun off a secondary publication when he selected poems printed in it for a separate volume of verse, *Poems on Several Occasions* (1696). By doing so, he was tapping into a growing market for anthologies and collections of short pieces. In addition to the periodical papers, the early eighteenth century was also an excellent time for marketing compilation volumes of verse by numerous authors, male and female, such as John Dryden's series of miscellanies and Aphra Behn's *Miscellany, being a collection of Poems by several Hands together with Reflection on Morality, or Seneca Unmasqued* (1685). *Lycidas,* or the Lover in Fashion . . . Together with a Miscellany of new Poems by several hands (1688), Gildon's A New Collection of Poems on Several Occasions (1701), Poems on Several Occasions (1703), Miscellany Poems (1713), Jacob's Poetical Register (1719), Hammond's A New Miscellany (1720), Ramsay's Tea-Table Miscellany (1723), Savage's Miscellaneous Poems (1726), and A New Miscellany . . . Written Chiefly by Persons of Quality (1726?) all contained verse by women.[28]

There was also a lively market for songbooks, such as the Playfair series, containing not only the musical scores but also the lyrics.[29] In the miscellanies and the songbooks, one can catch glimpses of women poets, who never did gather their verses together in volumes, as well as those such as Aphra Behn who published and recycled their poems in a variety of formats, from songs in their plays to inclusion in miscellanies and songbooks. In the songbooks, some poems are identified as being by a specific author, for example 'AB' or Aphra Behn who leads Day's list of women with verse in songbooks, with some 15 different songs to her credit.[30] Popular songbooks also introduced English readers to women outside the borders of England. Alan Ramsay's Scots Songs (1719, 2nd edn), Evergreen (1724; 1761) and Tea-Table Miscellany (1723; multiple editions through 1775) indicate a measure of the English taste for 'native' Scottish verse: Ramsay asserts in the Dedication of Evergreen that 'their Poetry is the product of their own country, not pilfered and spoiled in the Transportation from abroad: Their Images are native, and their Landskips domestick, copied from those Fields and Meadows we every Day behold' (p. vii). In his volumes, Ramsay included 'Hardyknute', a ballad widely attributed in eighteenth-century and early nineteenth-century collections to Elizabeth Halket Wardlaw (1677–1727), which had first been circulated in manuscript before being printed in Edinburgh in 1719. Ramsay also extended the readership of the songs by Lady Grissel Bailie (1665–1746), including the frequently reprinted 'Were ne my Hearts light I wad Dye' that also appears in William Thomson's Scottish song collection, Orpheus Caledonius (1733, 2nd edn).

Songbooks and verse miscellanies, therefore, can be seen as a type of publishing middle ground, where the circulated manuscripts of women poets could be posthumously preserved in print, where living social poets could contribute a small piece or two with little expense or effort, and where commercial writers such as Aphra Behn, Mary Pix, Susanna Centlivre and Delarivière Manley could reprint songs from their plays, poetic dedications and miscellaneous occasional verse. They served as the initial print venue for women poets who later would collect their pieces and publish single-author volumes of verse, perhaps most well known of whom were Anne Finch, Countess of Winchilsea, and Lady Mary Wortley Montagu. As Barbara Benedict has observed in her study of the creation of the early modern reader as consumer, this type of publication acts to bridge the formerly aristocratic court culture of the lyric with middle-class reading tastes, making the boundaries between 'private' manuscript texts and 'public' printed ones less hard and fast.[31]

The type of volume, however, we most associate with the label of 'being a poet' is a collection of an individual's works. There are several important examples of this practice among late seventeenth- and early eighteenth-century women writers. Some of these are by women who clearly see their volumes as representing them as writers, claiming their audience through their poetic merits, but not needing or anticipating financial reward. These would include the volumes by Elizabeth Singer Rowe, Mary, Lady Chudleigh, Anne Finch and Lady Mary Wortley Montagu. Another group of women producing volumes of verse of their own, however, clearly had commercial interests at heart, such as Aphra Behn, Elizabeth Thomas and Mary Barber.

Perhaps one of the most enigmatic and ambiguous volumes of verse published by a female poet during this period is that of 'Ephelia' (f. 1679), whose book *Female Poems on Several Occasions* (1679; 2nd edn enlarged 1682) has been variously attributed to 'Joan Philips', who apparently had some acquaintance with Aphra Behn, who may or may not be the 'Joan' in Behn's *Sir Patient Fancy* (1678), and who strongly appears to have been associated with Mary, Duchess of Richmond and Lennox, to whom the volume is dedicated and who appears as 'Eugenia' in the verses.[32] This volume may include a piece by another poet (an epilogue which speaks of the author in the third person, but is not attributed), but the contents and the arrangement present instead a poetic narrative of Ephelia's complicated, unhappy love life: she loves 'J.G.' also known as Strephon, but he travels to Tangiers where he falls in love with a 'dusky' beauty; meanwhile Ephelia is courted by Cloris, but then rejected for Marina. Its contents suggest that Ephelia, like Jane Barker, was part of a lively literary coterie, but the prefatory material to Mary, Duchess of Richmond and Lennox, suggests that through the publication of these seemingly social, occasional verses, Ephelia may have been seeking financial patronage as well.

In organizing her verse in this apparently autobiographical narrative fashion, Ephelia may have been following the pattern set by the romance fiction of Manley and Barker, or she could be attempting what later generations of women poets would describe as their goal: to produce a volume of verse in which, as Mary, Lady Chudleigh (1656–1710), would announce, the unknown reader would 'find a Picture of my Mind, my sentiments all laid open to their View'. Rather than telling the story of her life or an imagined heroine's adventures to strangers, Chudleigh hopes her verse will instead serve to guide them in dealing with emotional turmoil in their own lives. In her poems, the imagined reader will

> sometimes see me cheerful, pleas'd, sedate and quiet; at other times griev'd, complaining, struggling with my Passions . . . till I have rallied my scatter'd Forces, got new Strength, and by making an unweary'd Resistance, gain'd the better of my Afflictions, and restor'd my Mind to its former Tranquility.[33]

Chudleigh's first publication had been the anonymous *The Ladies Defense* (1701); by 1703 and the publication of *Poems on Several Occasions* (reprinted repeatedly through 1750) Chudleigh had had a successful career as a social author in her country home outside of Exeter, and had attracted the attention of John Dryden, Mary Astell, John Norris and Elizabeth Thomas. There is no indication that Chudleigh received, or desired to receive, any financial remuneration for her artistic labours. In her final publication, *Essays Upon Several Subjects in Prose and Verse* (1710), she acknowledges the authorship of *The Ladies Defense*, but laments that its second appearance as part of the second edition of her collected poems produced by Bernard Lintot was so badly mangled; the initial publication, she records,

> 'twas written with no other Design, but that innocent one of diverting some of my Friends; who, when they read it, were pleas'd to tell me they lik'd it, and desir'd me to Print it, which I should never have had the Vanity to have done, but in a Compliment to them. (248)

For whatever reason drew her into print originally, her observations on the problems of ensuring that her verse was correctly printed make a familiar echo of those voiced nearly 50 years earlier by Philips and Bradstreet.

Even though she lived for most of her life away from that publishing centre, Chudleigh had London relatives and London literary connections, including John Dryden who personally carried her verses from the countryside to London and Lintot. These personal connections provided her access not only to the latest printed books of verse but also to London publishers. Likewise, Anne Finch, Countess of Winchilsea (1661–1720), and her manuscripts had a well-established literary audience with publishing connections of their own, including Nicholas Rowe, Elizabeth Rowe, Jonathan Swift, Alexander Pope, and Matthew Prior, before she moved her verses into print. She also had experimented with periodical publication: before her volume of verse appeared in print in 1713, she had published 'The Spleen' and three other poems in Charles Gildon's *New Collection of Poems on Several Occasions* (1701), as well as her poem 'Life's Progress', appearing in Manley's *The New Atlantis* (1709). Charles Hinnant has characterized Finch's entry into print through the hospitable medium of periodical publication and miscellany collections as intended to

> preserve her privacy and yet present a construction of the self. These poems were not to be thought of as anonymous or authorless, yet the true identity of their author was intended to be recognized only by members of her circle.[34]

Like Chudleigh, there is no indication that Finch benefited financially from her move from manuscript to print; the move signals, however, her willingness to engage with a new audience, an audience of strangers who would value her work sufficiently to pay for it.

Turning now to the last group, women poets who wrote commercially, we see again the ways in which different genres produce different types of textual publication and different readerships.[35] The playwrights Behn, Pix, Trotter and Manley wrote in a variety of commercial genres, but it is clear that they did so in order to have more opportunities to collect payment for their writings. Getting one's manuscripts into print in this milieu meant usually being present in London and being willing and able to negotiate financial matters with publishers and theatre managers. Like other struggling commercial or 'Grub Street' writers, these women were able to see their poetry as commodities as well as a picture of their minds. Behn has left a good example of authorial negotiation in her exchange with Jacob Tonson over *Poems Upon Several Occasions* (1684): 'I shou'd really have thought 'em worth thirty pounds; and I hope will find it worth £25', she opens. Clearly skilled in the art of making a sale, Behn continues that, 'you can not think wt a preety thinge ye Island will be ... and if that pleases, I will do the 2nd voyage, wch will compose a little book as big as a novel by itself'. She concludes 'Pray speake to yor brother to advance the price to one 5lbs more . . . I vow I wou'd not aske it if I did not really believe it worth more.'[36]

Along with Barker, another interesting study of a woman who apprenticed in social authorship but turned to print for purely financial reasons is found in the career of Elizabeth Thomas (1675–1731). Initially, her manuscript readers included Pope, Chudleigh and Astell; she declared that during that time, she had rejected a bookseller's offer of £30 for 'a Manuscript Folio of my Poems &c', but by the early 1720s she was in desperate financial straits.[37] In 1722 she published her *Miscellany Poems* and gained lasting literary notoriety by selling Curll, supposedly for ten guineas, private letters between Alexander Pope and her former lover, Henry Cromwell, which Curll published in *Miscellanea* (1726). Even these measures did not mean that converting manuscript to print meant converting it into money: she was imprisoned for debt in 1727.

As a final example, the volume of verse by Mary Barber (*c*.1690–1757) provides us with food for thought concerning how a woman social author could construct a poetic persona that would carry her into print and into financial recompense without compromising her social status. Her husband was an Irish woollen draper and she had four children; nevertheless her primary audience included some of Dublin's most discerning readers, including Jonathan Swift, Dr Delaney, Constantia Grierson and Laetitia Pilkington, as well as her family. In the preface to *Poems on Several Occasions* (1734), Barber explains how her manuscripts moved from personal exchanges into public commodities. She begins with the declaration that she is aware that 'a Woman steps out of her Province whenever she presumes to write for the Press', but that the contents of the volume began as a means 'chiefly to form the Minds of my Children'.

She notes that the exception to this was an act of compassionate charity, a published poetic petition on behalf of a poor army widow, *The Widows Address* (Dublin: 1725). She omits to mention her publication of *A Tale being an Addition to Mr. Gay's Fables* (London: 1728). Travelling to England in an unsuccessful attempt to secure 'a Favour which some Persons of Great Worth and Eminence had requested for me of the Lord Carteret', Barber found that her manuscript verses appealed to her English friends and she was 'encouraged to print them by several Persons of Quality and Distinction, who generously offer'd to solicit a Subscription for me . . . the Prospect of some Advantage to my Family, drew me into a Resolution of publishing the following Poems'. Thus, like Barker and Thomas, she is represented as being persuaded to move from manuscript to print more by her awareness of a market for women's verse and the possibility of financial recompense for poetry than any desire for reaching a vast, unknown anonymous readership.

The 14-page long subscription list at the front of the volume (published by Samuel Richardson) indicates that indeed by the 1730s there were individuals willing to pay for reading a woman's poetry in print and owning a handsome folio volume for their libraries. The list reveals the wide range of types of readers who wished to possess Barber's volume: starting with the Duke and Duchess of Argyle, Dr Arbuthnot, the Duke and Duchess of Chandos, the list documents the interest also of a Mrs Clayton who bought seven copies, Robert Nugent, esquire, who bought eight, the Earl and Countess of Pembroke, the Earl and Countess of Thomond (each of whom subscribed for five copies, as did Sir Robert Walpole), and concludes with the entirely unknown Mrs Yates, who only needed one.[38]

In the final verse of the volume, 'To a Lady, who commanded me to send her an Account in Verse, how I succeeded in my Subscription', Barber humorously recounts the excuses people offered for NOT subscribing to her volume. 'Albino' has spent all his money supporting fashionable Italian singers, Olivia has gambled away all her gold, while Servilla

> . . . cries, *I hate a Wit*;
> Women should to their Fate submit,
> Should in the Needle take Delight;
> 'Tis out of *Character* to write. (276)

Those most resistant to paying to read her verse are other women, but Barber suggests that perhaps there are ulterior motives behind their refusals:

> Thus Sylvia, of the haughty Tribe:
> She never ask'd me to subscribe,
> Nor ever wrote a Line of me,
> I was no Theme for Poetry!
> She rightly judg'd; I have no *Taste* –
> For *Womens Poetry*, at least. (276–7)

Clearly, Barber was quite aware of not only the commercial possibilities of publishing her verse in a volume of its own, but also of the dangers of moving from a companionable, supportive social readership of friends and family into the gaze of the censorious, impersonal paying audience.

After 1660, women poets' manuscripts had more ways of moving into print than ever before. Not only did evangelical women writers have pamphlet space and broadsides in which to print their verses incorporated into their prophecies but also women engaged with political issues and public events and used this less expensive print format to reach that larger, unknown and faceless readership. From the more affluent reader's point of view, there was an expanding variety of textual products to be purchased and enjoyed, indicated by the growing popularity of songbooks and periodical publications. This meant that instead of poets having to solicit publishers and book-sellers to take their materials, booksellers sought them out, using appeals to their readers to contribute to the volumes' contents. Such publications offered women poets a welcoming format that acted as a continuation of the familiar social exchanges of manuscript transmission.

From the poet's point of view, while there were more genres in which to publish and more formats in which to print, the financial rewards for converting manuscript to print remained slight. Most of the commercial 'poets' of this period were also essayists, translators, dramatists and editors; they ran coffee houses and shops when writing didn't pay enough. As the personal histories of these commercial women poets demonstrate, 1660–1750 was still a very hard time to make a living by writing poetry, for both men and women. However, with the new theatre companies forming in London requiring more plays, new genres becoming established in the literary market place, and new periodicals looking for weekly contributions, women writers in the provinces as well as London had greater opportunities and more options to move into print than ever before, whether they wrote verse as part of their spiritual message, as a member of a social culture dedicated to the muse, or simply as a way to pay the rent.

Notes

1. Helen Wilcox, ' "First Fruits of a Woman's Wit''': Authorial Self-construction of English Renaissance Women Poets', in Barbara Smith and Ursula Appelt (eds), *Write or Be Written: Early Modern Women Poets and Cultural Constraints* (Aldershot: Ashgate Press, 2001), pp. 199–222 (200).
2. Margo Hendricks, 'Feminist Historiography', in Anita Pacheco (ed.), *A Companion to Early Modern Women's Writing* (Oxford: Blackwell, 2002), pp. 361–76 (374).
3. Jane Stevenson and Peter Davidson, (eds), *Early Modern Women Poets: an Anthology* (Oxford: Oxford University Press, 2001), p. xxix.

4. Ibid., p. xlii. See Elaine Hobby's influential *Virtue of Necessity: English Women's Writing 1649–88* (London: Virago Press, 1988) and recent anthologies by Suzanne Trill, Kate Chedgzoy and Melanie Osborne (eds), *Lay by Your Needles Ladies, Take the Pen: Writing Women in England, 1500–1700* (London: Arnold, 1997), and Paul Salzman (ed.), *Early Modern Women's Writing 1560–1700* (Oxford: Oxford University Press, 2000).
5. See Margaret Ferguson, 'Renaissance Concepts of the "Woman Writer" ', in Helen Wilcox (ed.), *Women and Literature in Britain 1500–1700* (Cambridge: Cambridge University Press, 1991), pp. 143–68, and Peter Beal, *In Praise of Scribes* (Oxford: Clarendon Press, 1998).
6. Elizabeth Bury, *An Account of the Life and Death of Mrs. Elizabeth Bury* (London: 1720), pp. 1–5.
7. Ruth Perry, *The Celebrated Mary Astell: an Early English Feminist* (Chicago: University of Chicago Press, 1986), Appendix D.
8. John Locke, *The Correspondence of John Locke*, ed. E. S. de Beer (Oxford: Clarendon Press, 1978): 2: 762 n. 1.
9. Stevenson and Davidson, *Early Modern Women Poets*, p. 413.
10. Quoted in Roger Lonsdale (ed.), *Eighteenth-Century Women Poets* (Oxford: Oxford University Press, 1989), p. 53.
11. See Margaret J. M. Ezell, 'The Posthumous Publication of Women's Manuscripts and the History of Authorship', in George L. Justice and Nathan Tinker (eds), *Women's Writing and the Circulation of Ideas: Manuscript Publication in England, 1550–1800* (Cambridge: Cambridge University Press, 2002), pp. 121–36.
12. Stevenson and Davidson, *Early Modern Women Poets*, p. 236.
13. Elizabeth Hageman, 'Katherine Philips, *Poems*', in Pacheco, *Companion to Early Modern Women's Writings*, pp. 189–202 (189). See also Nathan Tinker, 'John Grismond: Printer of the Unauthorized Edition of Katherine Philips's *Poems* (1664)', *English Language Notes* 34 (1996) pp. 3–35.
14. Hageman, 'Katherine Philips', p. 191.
15. Kathryn R. King, *Jane Barker, Exile: a Literary Career 1675–1725* (Oxford: Oxford University Press, 2000), pp. 35–7.
16. King, *Jane Barker*, p. 32.
17. Delarivière Manley, *The New Atlantis*, ed. Rosalind Ballaster (New York: New York University Press, 1992), pp. 48, 276 n. 110.
18. Manley, *New Atlantis*, p. 276, nn. 111, 117.
19. See Jerry Beasley's notes to Eliza Haywood, *The Injur'd Husband and Lasselia* (Louisville: University of Kentucky Press, 1999), pp. 155 nn. 79 and 82; 158 n. 23.
20. As with *Poetical Recreations*, the publication history of Barker's fictions that include her poetry is complex, especially that of her first, *Love's Intrigues* (1713). See King's account for further explanation.
21. King, *Jane Barker*, p. 193.
22. Dorothy White, *An Epistle of Love and Consolation unto Israel, from the pouring forth of the Spirit, and holy anointing of the Father* (1661), p. 13.
23. Stevenson and Davidson, *Early Modern Women Poets*, pp. 430–1.
24. Margaret J. M. Ezell, 'The *Gentleman's Journal* and the Commercialization of Restoration Coterie Literary Practices', *Modern Philology* 89 (1992), pp. 323–40.

25. For a thorough analysis of Elizabeth Singer Rowe's literary career away from London, see Sarah Prescott, 'Provincial Networks, Dissenting Connections, and Noble Friends: Elizabeth Singer Rowe and Female Authorship in Early Eighteenth-Century England', *Eighteenth Century Life* 25 (2001), pp. 28–42.

26. Kathryn R. King, 'Elizabeth Singer Rowe's Tactical Use of Print and Manuscript', in Justice and Tinker, *Women's Writing and the Circulation of Ideas*, pp. 158–81 (161).

27. J. Paul Hunter, *Before Novels: the Cultural Contexts of Eighteenth-Century English Fiction* (New York: Norton, 1990), p. 12.

28. Anne Russell has documented that Behn's miscellany stands out as 'the first woman to compile and publish a poetic miscellany, and her miscellanies include more works by women than are found in other print collections of the period'. '"Public" and "Private" in Aphra Behn's Miscellanies: Women Writers, Print and Manuscript', in Smith and Appelt, *Write or Be Written*, pp. 29–48 (30).

29. See Frank Kidson, 'John Playford and 17th Century Music Publishing', *Musical Quarterly* 4 (1918), pp. 516–34, and Willa McClung Evans, *Henry Lawes: Musician and Friend of Poets* (London: Oxford University Press, 1941).

30. Charles H. Hinnant, *The Poetry of Anne Finch: an Essay in Interpretation* (Newark: Delaware, 1994), p. 19.

31. Barbara Benedict, *Making the Modern Reader: Cultural Mediation in Early Modern Literary Anthologies* (Princeton: Princeton University Press, 1996), pp. 85–6.

32. Concerning the controversy about her identity, see Maureen E. Mulvihill's edition of *Poems by Ephelia (c.1679)* and Germaine Greer's review of that edition 'How to Invent a Poet', Rev. of *Poems by Ephelia (c.1679)*, ed. Maureen E. Mulvihill, *TLS* 25 (1993), pp. 7–8.

33. Mary, Lady Chudleigh, *The Poems and Prose of Mary, Lady Chudleigh*, ed. Margaret J. M. Ezell (Oxford: Oxford University Press, 1993), p. 44.

34. Charles H. Hinnant, *The Poetry of Anne Finch: an Essay in Interpretation* (Newark: Delaware, 1994), p. 19. See also Barbara McGovern, *Anne Finch and Her Poetry: a Critical Biography* (Athens, Georgia: The University of Georgia Press, 1992). Another example would be Elizabeth Singer Rowe's 1696 *Poems on Several Occasions*, where Elizabeth Johnson explains in the preface that 'they were actually Writ by a YOUNG LADY . . . whose NAME had been prefix'd, had not her own Modesty absolutely forbidden it' (Preface A5r).

35. See McDowell, *Women of Grub Street*; Cheryl Turner, *Living the Pen: Women Writers in the Eighteenth Century* (London: Routledge, 1992); Catherine Gallagher, *Nobody's Story: the Vanishing Acts of Women Writers in the Marketplace, 1670–1820* (Los Angeles: University of California Press, 1994); Julie Aipperspach Anderson, unpublished dissertation, 'Performances of Authorship: Context of Authorship and Audience in the Plays of Delarivier Manley, Catherine Trotter, and Mary Pix' (Texas A&M University, 2002).

36. Quoted in Kathleen Lynch, *Jacob Tonson, Kit-Cat Publisher* (Knoxville: University of Tennessee Press, 1971), pp. 99–100.

37. Lonsdale, *Eighteenth-Century Women Poets*, p. 33.

38. Mary Barber, *Poems on Several Occasions* (London: 1734), pp. xxxi–xliv.

13
Women in the Literary Market Place: Pimping in Grub Street

Germaine Greer

As the trade press gathered momentum in the last decade of the seventeenth century it showed itself only too ready to grant access to women, especially young women, who were marketed in terms that were equivocal to say the least. When decent women do not make themselves public, the women who choose to expose themselves, whether at court or in the streets, on the stage or in print, are necessarily objects of prurient interest. Male hacks occasionally tried to attract new readership by impersonating women, both actual and invented, both alive and dead. Jobbing booksellers solicited material by women and, when it was not forthcoming in sufficient quantity, fabricated it. Occasionally they acquired stolen papers and printed writing that was never meant to be public. Chief among the literary pimps who preyed on indiscreet and vulnerable women with literary ambitions was Charles Gildon (1665–1724). His struggles to stave off destitution would force him to abuse and falsify the work and reputation of many men (even Shakespeare) whose oeuvre has for the most part been reconstituted by careful modern scholarship. The literary women abused by Gildon, who include Aphra Behn, Katherine Philips, Anne Wharton, Jane Wiseman, Catherine Trotter, Anne Finch and Delarivière Manley, have not been so fortunate.

The facts about his life that Gildon alleges in 1698 in the appendix to his redaction of Langbaine's *Account of the English Dramatic Poets* are by and large accurate.[1] He was the son and heir of Richard Gildon, a Catholic gentleman, originally of Motcombe in Dorset, who wasted most of his substance before his death in 1674.[2] At the age of 12 Charles's Catholic relatives, many of whom were active in the English mission, sent him to Douai to study for the priesthood. After seven years at Douai, he returned to England. At his majority in 1686 he inherited what was left of his father's property which did not last long, partly because in 1688 he contracted an unsuitable marriage. Defoe, who had collaborated with him on *The London Mercury* felt sorrier for his wife than for him.

> G[ildon] writes Satyr, rails at Blasphemy,
> And the next Page, lampoons the Deity;
> Exposes his Darinda's Vicious Life,
> But keeps six whores and starves his modest wife;
> Sets up for a reformer of the town,
> Himself a first Rate Rake below lampoon . . . [3]

Who Gildon's Darinda might be and what lampoons he might have written about her is not yet known.

In 1696 Gildon was to claim intimate acquaintance with Aphra Behn, who died in April 1689.[4] It seems most unlikely that Gildon set up in London much before his majority in 1686; even his marriage in 1688 does not seem to have taken place in London. Janet Todd believes that Gildon and Tom Brown met Behn at the same time, before the publication of Behn's *Miscellany* of 1685, which includes five works by 'Mr. T. B.' whom we know to be Tom Brown because one of them 'On Flowers in a Lady's Bosom' turns up in his *Collected Works*. The inclusion of Brown's poems in her *Miscellany* is not itself conclusive evidence that Behn knew him. The fact that Behn and Brown both contributed commendatory verses for Creech's translation of Lucretius published in 1683 is not in itself firm evidence that at this stage they both knew Creech let alone that they knew each other.[5] And there is no evidence whatever that either of them was then acquainted with Gildon. There is no record of any literary activity on Gildon's part before 1691 which is also the time when he can first be positively associated with Brown.[6] Gildon briefly joined with Brown and William Pate in the publication of a rival to John Dunton's *Athenian Mercury* in 1692, before being bought off by Dunton and set to write *The History of the Athenian Society* instead. Brown is certainly one of the architects of the Behn legend as peddled by Gildon, as may be seen from the exchange of letters between the dead Aphra Behn and the 'famous Virgin Actress', Anne Bracegirdle, in Brown's famous *Letters From the Dead to the Living* published in 1703, in which Behn is represented not only as flamboyantly and unrepentantly promiscuous but as a corrupter of youth.[7] To assume that Brown actually knew Behn is to do him too much credit and Behn too little. Brown's biographer suspects that

Brown is the author of one of the more repulsively misogynistic dialogues in Gildon's second publication, *Nuncio Infernalis* (February
1692) for which D'Urfey wrote a preface introducing Gildon to the
literary world, his 'modesty . . . being such that he would not venture
into the world alone'.[8] It is high time that scholars dared to think the
unthinkable, that Charles Gildon never met Aphra Behn, that he
merely commandeered a large part of her literary property years after
her death and used it to his own advantage.

While it is gratifying to imagine Behn in the last years of her life as
the centre of an actual literary coterie which included younger writers
such as Creech, Brown and Gildon, the possibility is remote. In October
1687, Behn wrote in a letter to Waller's daughter-in-law, 'I am very ill,
and have been dying this twelve-month . . . I write this with a lame
hand scarce able to hold a pen'.[9] In those 12 months she had written
two plays, several pindaric odes and a third and last part of *Letters
between a Nobleman and his Sister*. Before her death in April 1689 she
was to produce *Lycidus*, *Oroonoko*, *The Fair Jilt*, *The Lucky Mistake* and
The History of the Nun, besides translations from the French of de
Bonnecorse's *La Montre*, *Agnés de Castro* and Fontenelle's *Histoire des
oracles* and *Entretiens de la pluralité des mondes* and the *Maximes* of De
La Rochefoucauld. It is hard to reconcile Behn's own account of her
sufferings in the last years of her life with the description written by
Gildon in 1696.

> Her Muse was never subject to the curse of bringing forth with Pain:
> for she always writ with the greatest ease in the world, and that in
> the midst of company and discourse of other matters. I saw her
> myself write Oroonoko and keep her turn in discoursing with sev-
> eral present in the room.[10]

What we might interpret as haste and pressure Gildon presents as facility, following the time-honoured convention of praising women for
what in men would be despised. For his part Gildon published nothing
whatsoever in Behn's lifetime and had scant claim to qualify as a
member of any literary salon before the 1690s. Nothing in any of the
miscellanies Behn edited is by Gildon or addressed to him. Among
dozens of dedicatory and occasional verses written to her, not one is
by Gildon.

In the years after Behn's death the Whig propaganda machine set
about furthering the Old Cause by publishing and republishing literary
remains (most of them spurious) of the most glamorous opponents of

creeping absolutism. In 1692 Gildon collected material for a miscellany to be published by Peter Buck; at the head of the list of authors on the title–page of *Miscellany Poems on Several Occasions* stands 'The late Duke of Buckingham'. George Villiers, second Duke of Buckingham (1628–87) was the most brilliant and resourceful upholder of the rights of Parliament against Charles II; he was known to have been a gifted poet but almost nothing can be securely attributed to him. Gildon could produce nothing by Buckingham beyond his (genuine) epitaph 'On my Lord Fairfax' which had been printed three times already and identified him securely with the Whig cause, and the 'Epitaph on Felton' which was equally well known but not by Buckingham.[11] Further down the title–page listing we find 'Mrs. Behn'; what is printed as by her are three poems, including one that was apparently left incomplete at her death, which scholars accept as genuine.[12] The grounds for this acceptance seem to be no more than a misplaced confidence in Gildon, who could hardly be expected to deal more scrupulously with Behn than he had with the Duke of Buckingham. Until we have better evidence, the case for all three poems being authentic Behn must be regarded as open.

The volume also includes a poem written by Anne Wharton in 1683, dissuading Gilbert Burnet from withdrawing from public life.[13] Desperate to cobble a connection with Buckingham Gildon endowed it with a new title, 'Upon the D. of Buckingham's Retirement' and the attribution, 'By Madame Wharton, Jan 1683'.[14] Anne Wharton had been dead seven years; in the year of her death a caveat had been entered in the Stationers' Register preventing anyone from publishing her works. If the embargoed copy or part of it had come into Gildon's hands, it is disappointing that he simply gleaned from it a poem which he could attach to the blazing notoriety of Buckingham. The ascription to 'Madame Wharton' is deliberately ambiguous; in July 1692 Lucy Loftus, who was pretty notorious herself, became 'Madame Wharton' when she became the second wife of the Honourable Thomas Wharton. Confusion about the authorship of the poems of Wharton's first wife Anne has persisted to this day.

At the same time as he was gathering material for *Miscellany Poems on Several Occasions* Gildon was putting together for John Dunton an extraordinary compilation called *The Post Boy Robb'd of his Mail*.[15] The pretext is that a number of gentlemen have waylaid the post and stolen the mail. They meet together to read through the letters at random, commenting on each. The publisher, John Dunton, was later to confess that he was ashamed of his part in this venture, though just why he might have felt so ashamed is hard for today's reader to determine.[16] What was printed had to appear to be genuine letters, so we would not necessarily assume that the plausible names and addresses of the writers and recipients of the letters are actual, except that some of them are historical personages and others can be traced. Many of the putative writers are women, some of them deeply compromised. An actual Madam Price may have fled to Maidstone to avoid C. Smithson (Letter VIII). It is possible that the 'E. Johnson' really was a woman of the town whose keeper had abandoned her, as in Letter IX, 'From a Whore to a Young Spark that was forsaking her'. Madame Justed of Bishopsgate Street just might have been being courted by G. Colts of Salisbury (Letter XIII). It is repulsive to think that Gildon's readers may have recognized the desperate 'E. R.' who wrote to the Templar Mr Richards from Pomfret, begging him to procure an abortion for her (Letter XXIII). Though we have lost the key to the identities of the people mentioned, there can be no doubt that some of them were private individuals who would have been deeply embarrassed by their exposure in print. The intention was to print several volumes, amounting to 500 letters in all, but Dunton seems to have lost his stomach for the enterprise. He was never to be involved in anything like it again but Gildon kept trying to make money out of printing private papers both real and fake until the end of his life. In 1706 his printing of a (genuine) letter of the Electress Sophia to the Archbishop of Canterbury almost cost him his life.[17]

In 1693 a literary prodigy appeared in Grub Street. She was Catherine Trotter, rosy-faced, bright-eyed and a poet at 14 years old. She made a clamorous debut with 'Verses sent to Mr Bevil Higgons, On his sickness and recovery from the Smallpox'. Bevil Higgons was 23, and not long returned from the court of the exiled Stuarts at St Germain. He had contributed several poems to *Examen Poeticum*, the third part of Dryden's *Miscellany*. The young Miss Trotter waxed lyrical and unknowingly equivocal about the charms of his person.

> . . . beauty does, like light, itself reveal;
> No place can either's glorious beams conceal.
>   Thine, as destructive flames, too fatal shin'd,
> And left no peace in either sex's mind.
> The men with envy burn'd, and ev'n the fair,
> When with their own, thy matchless charms compare,
> Doubt, if they should or love, or envy most,
> A finer form than they themselves can boast:
> Repine not, lovely youth, if that be lost.[18]

Miss Trotter had already attracted the attention of Samuel Briscoe, a bookseller who kept the shop opposite Will's coffee house. He was quick to cash in, asking Tom Brown to compile for him a collection of *Letters of Love and Gallantry and Several other Subjects. All Written by Ladies* (1693). The selling point of the volume was a series of sprightly letters written to a gentleman by a 14-year-old virgin signing herself 'Olinda' and giving details of her successful defence of her virtue against various would-be seducers. Olinda, the Wits were given to understand, was none other than Miss Trotter. Brown may have acquired this literary property from Miss Trotter or fabricated it and attributed it to Miss Trotter, or combined the two. Once in possession of a handful of genuine letters, Brown would have found nothing easier than to concoct more in the same style. In 1702 he was to publish the epistolary *Adventures of Lindamira a Lady of Quality* as revised and corrected, that is, written by himself. Once she was in print Trotter had no option but to exploit her own notoriety as far as she could. *Letters of Love and Gallantry* was Briscoe's most successful, perhaps his only successful, publication.

In the Appendix to his rifacimento of Langbaine Gildon describes 'Mrs Catherine Trother' as 'admirable for two things rarely found together, *Wit* and *Beauty*; and with these a *Penetration* very uncommon in the Sex'.

> She discovers in her Conversation, a *Fineness* and *Nicety* of *Reasoning* on the highest *Metaphysical Subjects*; nor is she less entertaining on the more Gay and Conversible.[19]

This is meant to imply a certain degree of familiarity existing between Gildon and the teenaged author, an implication which is much more to his advantage than hers. Trotter's first work for the theatre was her blank verse tragedy *Agnes de Castro* which was played at the Theatre Royal in Drury Lane in December 1695. The play is a dramatization of a novella by Aphra Behn, published both separately and as part of *Three Histories* by William Canning in 1688. By 1695 Gildon had begun collaborating with Samuel Briscoe on an expanded edition of Behn's novellas; it may have been they who suggested to the deserving Miss Trotter that she dramatize *Agnes de Castro*, and Briscoe was certainly one of the three publishers who issued Trotter's play early in 1696. Trotter's authorship was well known, but she decided that the printed play should appear without her name so that she could 'shun that of Poetress', tacitly dissociating herself from her notorious predecessor. In true Grub Street fashion, though Trotter quotes verse and dialogue verbatim from Behn's novella, she does not acknowledge her indebtedness.[20]

In 1694 Gildon began a collaboration with Benjamin Bragg, producing for him a volume of *Miscellaneous Letters and Essays On several subjects. Philiosophical, Moral, Historical, Critical, Amorous, &c. in Prose and Verse . . . By several Gentlemen and Ladies*. Gildon himself is the only writer to be identified (six times) by his own name. The ladies appear under coterie names. 'Cloe' writes 'to Urania, against Womens being Learn'd' and Urania replies with 'An Answer to the foregoing Letter in Defence of Women's being learn'd'. Cloe has allowed herself to be convinced by 'Lysander', who cites Halifax's *Advice to a Daughter* of which Urania has no very high opinion. Lysander is also opposed by 'Viridomar' who is the author of seven letters to Urania in which he declares that he wishes a 'settl'd Correspondence' with her whether she 'be a real or counterfeit Woman'. 'The Ingenious and Honourable Theocrine' writes to 'Theopompus; shewing Her the faithfullest of Lovers, and most Pious of Children'. 'Theocrine' is the widow of 'Poliarchus' under which name Sir Charles Cottrell would appear in *Letters from Orinda to Poliarchus* which Bernard Lintott would publish in 1705. It may very well be that to Gildon's contemporaries the ladies and gentlemen who used these names were well known, but historians of women's writing have no way of knowing if all or none or some of them were counterfeit women. Cloe, Urania and Theocrine are probably of the same ilk as the insubstantial Ephelia, but history has yet to decide what ilk that is. That women writers of the 1690s are both notorious and mysterious is largely due to the unscrupulous activities of Gildon and the booksellers and printers who collaborated with him.

In 1694 Gildon ventured once more to exploit the reputation of the notorious dead, with *Chorus Poetarum: Poems on several occasions. By the Duke of Buckingham, the late lord Rochester, Sir John Denham, Sir Geo. Etheridge, Andrew Marvel, Esq., the famous Spencer, Madam Behn and several other Eminent Poets of this Age*, published by Benjamin Bragg as 'never before printed'. The use of Buckingham's name was justified only by the inclusion of a 16-line paraphrase of Horace 'On Fortune' which had been printed in the third edition of *The Rehearsal* in 1675.[21] Though Gildon was clearly as anxious to exploit the name of 'Madam Behn' as he had been in 1692, this time he had nothing to hand. This may also have been the case in 1692 but this time we know the attribution to Behn to be false. Under the title 'By Madam Behn' Gildon printed a version of Sappho's πηαινεται μοι which had already been printed in Nahum Tate's miscellany of 1685 as by William Bowles. The point of the deliberate misattribution can be guessed from Bowles's version of Sappho's account of the female lover's liquefaction at the sight of the male beloved.

O then I feel my life decay
My ravished Soul then flies away;
Then faintness does my limbs surprise,
And darkness swims before my eyes.

Then my tongue fails, and from my brow
The liquid drops in silence flow;
Then wandring fires run thro my blood,
Then cold binds up the languid flood;
All pale and breathless then I lie,
I sigh, I tremble, and I die.[22]

The association of such passionate writing with Behn, who was known to her enemies as Sappho, was irresistible. When reprinted anonymously in *State Poems* 1703 Bowles's poem was titled 'On Madam Behn'; when Briscoe published an edition of Buckingham's plays in 1715 he or his editor, who may have been Gildon, included Bowles's poem as 'Sapho addrest to his Grace the Duke of Buckingham, in the year 1681. Translated by Madam Behn'. In *Chorus Poetarum* Gildon also reprinted an elegy on Buckingham first published in broadside in 1687.[23] In Briscoe's Buckingham the elegy follows Bowles's poem, and is described as 'Written by Madam Behn, in the year 1687'. To this day, scholars who should know better are involving Behn in the generation of these two texts which have nothing to do with her.

Chorus Poetarum did not sell, and was reissued twice with cancellans title–pages giving false dates and revised lists of the celebrated dead. The second of these includes 'Madam Philips'. There is no poem by Orinda or even attributed to her in the miscellany. At or around this time Gildon finally came into possession of genuine Behn papers, principally her play *The Younger Brother* which he prepared for performance at the Theatre Royal by partially rewriting it, removing all disparaging reference to Whigs. 'An unknown Hand' (almost certainly his own) provided a Prologue which exploited Behn's memory almost more than decency allowed.

Oh! then be kind to a poor Orphan-Play,
Whose Parent, while she liv'd oblig'd you all; . . .

Who cou'd, like her, our softer Passions move,
The Life of Humour, and the Soul of Love?[24]

Gildon was later to lament that he had not taken sufficient liberties with Behn's text,

> which he introduc'd by the Importunacy of a Friend of hers and his, on the Stage . . . out of the Respect to her Memory, and a deference, which was too nice, to her Judgment, he durst not make any alterations in it, but what were absolutely necessary, and those only in the first and second Act, which reflected on the *Whigs*; when if he had altered the jejune Stile of the three last Acts, betwixt Prince *Frederick* and *Mirtilla*, which was too heavy, in all Probability it would have been more to the Advantage of his Purse . . . [25]

If we believe Gildon, a friend of Behn's, and not Gildon himself, came into possession of the play text after her death and gave it to him to prepare for the stage. When *The Younger Brother* was published in 1696 as the work of the 'late Ingenious Mrs A. Behn', Gildon dedicated it in obsequious terms to Christopher Codrington, a leading Whig and fellow habitué of Will's.[26] He also affixed his name to two songs that appear in the play. The reader may not make her own assessment of the nature of Gildon's interference with Behn's work, for the original text has not survived, which is the more galling because the play deals with real people who were in Surinam at the same time as Behn. When the play was printed, Gildon included 'some accounts' of the life of Aphra Behn which, though they include only information that could have been gleaned from published sources (and not all of that), are the basis of all the expanded biographical notices published subsequently. The author had by now become Gildon's subject, which he would embroider at will.

In 1690 William Canning, publisher of Behn's three novellas, *Oroonoko*, *The Fair Jilt* and *Agnes de Castro*, as well has her translation of Bonnecorse's *La Montre*, was arrested for publishing a Jacobite broadside, imprisoned, tortured and effectively put out of business. In 1696 Briscoe took his opportunity and hastily reprinted all four Canning titles in a single-volume edition called *Histories and Novels*. The selling point of the edition was 18 pages of 'The Life and Memoirs of Mrs Behn. Written by One of the Fair Sex' who was 'a Gentlewoman of her Acquaintance'. As the 'Life and Memoirs' is an amplification of the biographical notice that Gildon had written for the printing of *The Younger Brother* it seems likely that the gentlewoman is none but he. In the course of printing Briscoe decided to add *The Lucky Mistake*, originally printed by Richard Bentley in 1689. By 1696 Bentley was ailing and no more likely than Canning to defend his right. He died the following year. In a second afterthought Briscoe added 16 pages of invented 'Love-letters by Mrs. A. Behn'. They may have been written for him by Gildon or Brown, or any of the other Grub Street pasticheurs. He then sold part of the edition to Richard Wellington who reissued it under his own imprint with a cancellans title–page.

Paul Dottin includes in his incomplete list of titles associated with Gildon *Poetical Remains of Mrs Behn*, published in octavo by A. Bettesworth in 1698.[27] This would appear to be a reissue of two reissues bound together, which first appeared in 1697 as *Poems upon Several occasions; with a voyage to the Island of love*. Also *The Lover in Fashion, being an Account from Lycidus to Lysander of his Voyage from the Island of Love. By Mrs A. Behn*. Those historians who believe that Behn earned a living by her pen would do well to consider the significance of the fact that unsold copies of Tonson's 1684 edition of *Poems on Several Occasions* existed in sufficient quantities 13 years after the original publication to justify a reissue. The reissue was put together by the original publisher of *Lycidus*, Francis Saunders, who had unsold sheets remaining from the single edition of 1688. The combined re-issue also remained unsold, which explains how Saunders came to sell off part of his reissue to Bettesworth the next year. As Dottin gives no grounds for his association of Gildon with this enterprise, we may assume that it has come about because he assumes that Gildon was exercising some kind of literary executorship. In fact the copies would not have been a part of Behn's literary estate, which is a concept that did not yet exist in law. Not only were the copies printed by Tonson his to sell, the copyright also was his to dispose of as he wished. As far as we can ascertain Aphra Behn made no will and appointed neither executors nor trustees; it follows that at no time was Gildon acting in the interest of Aphra Behn or her heirs. In packaging Behn he was simply trying to make money. It was to prove no easier for him than it did for Tonson and Saunders.

In 1698 Briscoe published an enlarged 'third' edition of *Histories and Novels*, and this time Gildon clearly emerges as the editor, writing his own dedication of the publication to his college friend Simon Scroop of Danby in place of Behn's original dedication to the now disgraced Lord Maitland and signing it with his full name. He also expanded 'The Life and Memoirs' from 18 to 60 pages, and gave it a new, titillating title, 'The History of the Life and Memoirs of Mrs. Behn. Never before printed. By One of the Fair Sex. Intermixed with Pleasant Love-Letters that passed betwixt her and Minheer Van Bruin, a Dutch merchant; with her Character of the Country and Lover; And her Love-letters to a Gentleman in England'. Three new novellas were added to the original four, 'Memoirs of the Court of the King of Bantam', 'The Nun, or the Perjured beauty' and 'The Adventure of the Black Lady'. Briscoe attempted to ward off scepticism about the genuineness of these in an 'Advertisement to the Reader':

> The stile of the Court of the King of *Bantam* being so very different from Mrs. *Behn*'s usual way of Writing it may perhaps call its being genuine in Question; to obviate which Objection, I must inform the Reader, That it was a Trial of Skill, upon a Wager, to shew that she was able to write in the Style of the celebrated *Scarron*, in imitation of whom 'tis writ, tho' the Story be true. I need not say anything of the other Two, they evidently confessing their admirable Author.[28]

If Behn was ever interested in imitating Scarron, this is the first that was heard of it. The person who was steeped in Scarron at this time was Gildon's friend, Tom Brown, who was working on an English edition of Scarron, which was published in 1700.[29]

To assume that the three new novellas are authentic works of Aphra Behn is to place far too much confidence in Briscoe and Gildon. In the last years of her life, when she was chronically ill and in severe pain, Behn was forced to work desperately hard for very meagre returns. It is literally unthinkable that she would have had three polished novellas sitting by the while unsold; all told Briscoe and Gildon would come across five more, making a total of *eight* finished works unsold at the time of her death. Four of the five were printed for Briscoe by William Only in 1698, but they remained unissued for the time being, perhaps because Briscoe had run up debts to all his suppliers and was unable to trade.[30] A 'fourth' edition of *Histories and Novels* was published in 1699 by Richard Wellington who reissued part of his printing in 1700 with a cancellans title–page.[31] By this time Briscoe had managed to put together *Histories, Novels and Translations, Written by the most Ingenious Mrs Behn. The Second Volume.* This consisted of Behn's versions of Fontenelle originally published in 1688 bound up with the four new novellas printed by Only in 1698, *The Unfortunate Bride, or The blind Lady a Beauty, The Unfortunate Happy Lady, The Wandring Beauty* and *The Unhappy Mistake*, plus one more, *The Dumb Virgin: or, The Force of imagination: A Novel*. None of these has a better claim to be authentic Behn than the three that appeared in print for the first time in 1698. The later history of this literary property (in common with all Gildon's literary properties) is confused. Wellington published *Histories and Novels* again in 1705; his heir published another edition in 1718; in 1718, Briscoe surfaces as one of six publishers of part of the edition while the edition of 1722 is said on the title–page to be 'Published by Mr. Charles Gildon'. The same is said of the edition of 1735. Our Charles Gildon having died blind and destitute in 1724, it is not clear who this Charles Gildon might be; the title–page of the edition of 1752 describes it too as 'Published by Mr. Charles Gildon'. One explanation could be that Gildon retained the copyright and left it to a son. What seems clear is that Behniana appeared to the world to be Charles Gildon's literary property.

When Jane Wiseman appeared on the London scene with the verse tragedy that she had written in her spare time while working as a domestic in the household of the recorder of either Oxford or Cambridge, there was some competition in Grub Street to see who could most usefully exploit her.[32] In 1701 Abel Boyer bounced into print with *Letters of Wit, Politicks and Morality* . . . which included some by 'Mrs W—n under the Name of Daphne'. The section in which she appears 'Original Letters of Love and Gallantry by several Gentlemen and Ladies' is a kind of epistolary *roman-à-clef* involving Captain Ayloffe, Susanna Centlivre, referred to as 'Mrs. C—l' and sporting the sobriquet 'Astraea', 'Mrs. T—r', 'Mr. B—y', 'Mr. B—', 'Dr. G—' and 'Mr. F—r'. As Daphne, Wiseman is apparently uncertain whether she should confer her favours on Damon (George Farquhar) or Amintor (Captain Ayloffe) neither of whom is in the least reticent about his intentions to love her and leave her.

At some point Wiseman encountered Gildon who was only too happy to help her bring her play upon the stage. When *Antiochus the Great: Or the Fatal Relapse. A Tragedy* was performed at Lincoln's Inn Fields a Prologue and Epilogue were supplied by a nameless friend. When the play was printed a musical dialogue in Act III was credited to Gildon. Wiseman described her play as 'the first fruits of a Muse, not yet debas'd to the Low Imployment of Scandal or Private Reflection'.

> The Reception it met with in the World, was not kind enough to make me Vain, nor yet so ill to discourage my Proceeding. The Language they are unwilling to believe my own: and have chose one of our best Poets for my Assistant, one I had not the Happiness to know, 'till after the Play was finished.[33]

This statement hardly dispels the possibility that the Poet in question did not 'correct', that is, largely rewrite Wiseman's play (as he had 'corrected' *The Younger Brother*, say). Though Wiseman's play remained in the repertoire, being revived in 1711, 1712 and 1721, she appears indeed to have been discouraged from pursuing a literary career. Instead, she married a vintner called Holt and together they ran a tavern in Westminster. History does not record whether they let Gildon run a long tab. The 'Mrs Holt' who published *A Fairy Tale . . . With Other Poems* in 1717 is assumed to be the same person, but nothing beyond the surname suggests the identification. 'Mrs Holt' addresses herself to minor gentry for the most part, and seems more likely to have been an upper servant or poor relation (or both) than running a tavern in Westminster.

Also in 1701 Gildon compiled, once more for Peter Buck, *A New Miscellany of Original Poems on Several Occasions, Written by the E[arl] of D[orset], Sir Charles Sidley, Sir Fleetw. Shepheard, Mr Wolesely, Mr Granvill, Mr Dryden, Mr Stepney, Mr Rowe and Several other eminent hands*, with nothing to identify the compiler beyond a signature at the foot of the dedicatory epistle. Though no women are mentioned on the title–page, works by three women, Aphra Behn, Anne Wharton and Anne Finch, are to be found in this miscellany. Aphra Behn's 'Desire. A Pindarick', first published in *Lycidus* in 1688 and reissued in 1697, is reprinted without attribution.[34] If it is true that Gildon's contemporaries were curious to know more of such a notorious poetess, we can only wonder why Gildon failed to mention that this poem about female sexual desire was by her. The only possibility is that he did not know it for Behn's work, which rather undermines both his claim to have been a close friend and the assumption by modern scholars that he was some kind of literary executor.

In any case Gildon was not interested in rendering female poets their due. He was apparently still in possession of papers connected to Anne Wharton, from which he gleaned her most original poem, 'Thoughts occasioned by her Retirement into the Countrey', which he set about rewriting as 'The Retirement', for inclusion at the end of his miscellany, without attribution.[35] Her amorous song 'Spight of thy Godhead, Pow'rful Love' also appears, and once more the attribution is 'Mrs Wharton' rather than the late Mrs Wharton, in a deliberate equivocation.

The Behn poem may have been simply a makeweight. *A New Miscellany of Original Poems on Several Occasions* appears to be based on a collection of works deriving from the circle of Charles, Earl of

Winchilsea. It opens with a translation of the first Edilium of Bion, attributed simply to the 'Earl of Winchilsea', followed by three poems by Nicholas Rowe, one of which is addressed to Richard Thornhill, the Finches' neighbour at Godmersham, and a poem dedicated to Rowe by William Shippen, who was later to provide a commendatory poem for Anne Finch's *Miscellany Poems on Several Occasions*. Rowe's friendship with Shippen and Thornhill, both fervent Jacobites, ended some time before the huge success in 1701 of his play *Tamerlane* which represented the tyrannical warlord of history as a conciliatory figure with marked affinities with William III. For Grub Street in general, and for a failed rival playwright in particular, the urge to publish, at the very moment of Rowe's emergence as unofficial Whig dramaturge, convincing evidence of his past association with the lunatic fringe of Jacobitism must have been irresistible. A shortened and emended version of Rowe's 'Epistle to Flavia', by whom is meant Thornhill's sister, Mary Thornhill, introduces four of Ardelia's most important poems, her masterpiece, 'The Spleen', her 'Pastoral between Menalcas and Damon', 'An Epistle from Alexander to Haphaestion' and 'To Death', all printed for the first time without attribution.[36] Though the Honourable Heneage Finch and his wife were of the class that cannot seek to enrich itself by its own efforts, there is some evidence from Ardelia's manuscripts that the couple had hopes of publication and they certainly needed any income to be derived from it. The virtual pirating of some of her most ambitious work may well have been perceived by Ardelia as a calamity.

Gildon, who was in effect a dependent of the Whigs, may have had cause to regret his association with a publication that was intended to embarrass them. When *A New Miscellany of Original Poems on Several Occasions* was reissued with a cancellans title–page his signature at the end of the dedicatory epistle had been removed.

In November 1701 Bernard Lintott paid Gildon an advance of £5 7s 6d to put together another miscellany called *Examen Miscellaneum*.[37] Once more Gildon produced unpublished material by Anne Wharton, in this case the full text of her 'Elegy on the Earl of Rochester', which is otherwise known only from two manuscript copies, and attributed it to 'the Honourable Mrs. Wharton'. In *Examen Miscellaneum* it is followed by 'On the forgoing Elegy by Mr. J. How' and 'On the same Elegy. By Mr Waller'. It is no easy matter to decide whether Gildon was in possession of the now lost copy of Anne Wharton's plays and poems and simply mined it for odds and ends to plump out his various miscellanies, or whether good copies of her poems wandered occasionally into his ken. He was not the only anthologist to print material by her. The person who compiled *A Collection of Poems by Several Hands* for Francis Saunders in 1693 brought seven new poems into print. If that person was Gildon, the case could be regarded as proven.

In 1705 Gildon decided to turn to profit a number of personal letters that had come into his possession, by finding makeweight material and printing them as part of a two-volume set. Three-quarters of the 1692 *Post-Boy Robb'd of his Mail* made up the first volume of a so-called second edition, and bound in with it was a second volume including *inter alia* eight love letters written by Elizabeth Broadhurst to her protector, Charles Granville, with a ninth inviting Paul D—y, MP to visit her.[38] Before the letters stands a cover letter directed 'to Mrs Broadhurst at Mr Bevill's in Red-Lion-Street' by 'Strephon', that is, Granville, saying that he is returning her letters as she bade him (Letter XV). As the recipient of the letters Charles Granville was in law their owner, until he returned them to the writer at her request; the cover letter would have protected Gildon in the event that any action against their printing was attempted. It seems unlikely in the extreme that Broadhurst would have sought publication herself. The most likely person to have furnished Gildon with the letters remains Granville. Both men were habitués of Will's coffee house in Covent Garden. If Broadhurst was to be embarrassed by the exposing of her passion for Granville and the easiness of the transfer of her affections, her new protector would have been even more embarrassed to have it made public that she was Granville's 'cast whore'. Amid the new material that Gildon rustled up is a series of letters by 'Honetto', otherwise 'W. B.', another habitué of Will's, as well as an exchange of letters between 'Belvidera' and 'Lysander', names that appear elsewhere amid Gildoniana, and four letters written by 'Artemisa' to one of the nine gentlemen 'concern'd in the frolick'.

By 1709 Gildon was working mostly for Edmund Curll. At the beginning of 1714 Curll suggested that he write a memoir of Delarivière Manley, incorporating 'a severe Invective upon some part of her Conduct'.[39] Curll was probably driven by his own bitter resentment of his rival, Manley's employer, John Barber, whom he knew to be publishing pro-Jacobite material at the same time as he enjoyed the monopoly of printing for the Whig Corporation of London. Not daring to antagonize a man as powerful as Barber, Curll hit upon attacking his vulnerable dependent whom he assumed, as many afterwards have done, to be his mistress. Gildon was the obvious choice; not only was he an in-house hack, he had known Manley in her heyday when she was the toast of the town. In 1698 he had been eager to convey the impression that she was his friend:

> I think Mr. Pope's Observation on this Subject is justly her due; for, upon reading her Two tragedies, it will appear, that
> > She wakes the soul by tender strokes of art,
> > Raises the Genius and improves the Heart.
> her Friendship being as sincere as her Conversation is entertaining.

When Gildon's book was advertised, a distraught Manley came with her sister to Curll's printing house in Fleet Street to see the manuscript and begged Curll in floods of tears not to issue the book. It is not clear whether there was a manuscript to see; what is clear is that Manley was terrified of what Gildon, with his 'venal quill' and his scant regard for truth, would find to say about her. Curll saw his opportunity and offered to withdraw Gildon's book if she would supply him with another in time for it to appear under the same title, and so she was blackmailed into writing *The Adventures of Rivella* in absolute secrecy and delivering it to Curll free of charge within days.[40]

For Curll in 1716 Gildon edited a tiny chapbook called *Irish Tales*, purporting to have been written by a 'Sarah Butler' who is not known from any other source. If an author is to be Irish, the surname Butler is a good one to adopt, being the family name of the Dukes of Ormonde. As Gildon's preface is written in exactly the same style as the tales, it seems reasonable to suppose that his claim that the fair author had entrusted her work to him on her deathbed is false, and that 'Sarah Butler' is another of his pseudonyms.

In 1718 blind and destitute and reduced to living in a printer's shop on Ludgate Hill Gildon returned to the kind of publishing that he had found most lucrative, and brought out a third edition of *The Post-Boy Robbed of his Mail*. This time the centre piece was a series of letters by 'Stremunia', subtitled 'The Lover's Sighs'. Backscheider is of the opinion that these were fictional.

> *The Lover's Sighs* points firmly to the epistolary fiction of Richardson; its themes and narrative strategies have evolved in a number of ways from *Five Love Letters from a Nun to a Cavalier* and Gildon's own early material.[41]

Gildon's contemporaries were not deceived and prepared to take action on behalf of the lady whose privacy had been breached. In a panic,

Gildon dictated a letter to the ailing Addison seeking protection from 'some persons', who were 'displeased' on account of the letters 'of the love of Straminia [*sic*]'.[42] As far as we can tell, Addison did not reply. It could conceivably be objected that Gildon promoted women writers, acting out of chivalry and in their best interests. Before such a case can be sensibly made, the extent of his misappropriations and misrepresentations must be understood. There is no scope here to explain how misogynist Gildon and his cronies were, or illustrate their cynical way of discussing the women who were grist to their mill.[43] Neither is it easy now to imagine how Gildon's pushing himself into the limelight alongside young women writers, getting his name into their published works and boasting of intimacy with them, must have worked against their interest. The effect of the packaging of Behn by Gildon and Briscoe has been permanently to distort our perspective so that good literary historians say foolish things, such as that Behn's name on a title–page was a guarantee of commercial success. The transformation of a hard-working woman into a triumphant sex goddess who scribbled facile tales while entertaining her many admirers has obscured Behn's true originality, belying both the self-consciousness of her art and the bitterness of her struggle. As the case of Rochester has shown, where literary prestige is concerned less is more; it is high time Gildon's rubbish was weeded out of the oeuvre of Aphra Behn.

Notes

1. [Charles Gildon], *The Lives and Characters of the English Dramatic Poets . . . First begun by Mr Langbain, improv'd and continued down to this Time, by a Careful Hand* [1699], pp. 174–6.
2. In 1654 Richard Gildon had been admitted to Gray's Inn; by 1664 according to *Dorset Hearth Tax Assessments 1662–1664*, ed. C. A. Meekings (Dorchester: Dorset Natural History and Archaeological Society, 1951), he was sharing a single hearth in Gillingham with a 'Widd[ow] Haylock'.
3. Daniel Defoe, 'More Reformation', broadside, July 1703.
4. See 'An Account of the Life of the Incomparable Mrs. Behn', in [Charles Gildon], *The Younger Brother, or the Amorous Jilt. A Comedy. Acted in the Theatre Royal, By His Majesty's Servants. Written by the late Ingenious Mrs. Behn. With some Account of her Life* (1696), Sig. A4ʳ.
5. *T. Lucretius Caro. The Epicurean Philosopher, His Six Books De Natura Rerum Done into English Verse. With Notes* (Oxford, 1683). As commendatory poems were important in introducing unfamiliar authors or texts, they often separately commissioned and paid for by publishers.
6. Benjamin Boyce, *Tom Brown of Facetious Memory: Grub Street in the Age of Dryden* (Cambridge, MA: Harvard University Press, 1939), p. 38). Both

dialogues appeared in Brown's *Works* of 1702 as by Brown, but then the editor of those was Charles Gildon.

7. Tom Brown, *A Continuation or Second Part of the Letters from the Living by Mr Tho. Brown, Capt Aylott, Mr Henry Barker etc.*, n.p. 1703, 'From Worthy Mrs. Behn the Poetess to the famous Virgin Actress' and 'The Virgin's Answer to Mrs. Behn'.

8. Charles Gildon, *Nuncius Infernalis: or a New Account from below. In 2 Dialogies. The First (From the Elizium Fields) of Friendship. The second (from Hell of Cuckoldom) being the Sessions of Cuckolds. . . . With a preface by Mr Durfey* (1692), p. ix.

9. Aphra Behn to Abigail Waller, Pierpont Morgan Library MS.

10. [Charles Gildon], 'An Account of the Life of the Incomparable Mrs. Behn'.

11. *Miscellany Poems upon Several Occasions: Consisting of Original Poems by The late Duke of Buckingham, Mr Cowley, Mr Milton, Mr Prior, Mrs Behn, Mr. Tho. Brown, &c . . .* (1692).

12. For example, M. A. O'Donnell, *Aphra Behn: an Annotated Bibliography of Primary and Secondary Sources* (New York and London: Garland Publishing Inc., 1986), pp. 271–2.

13. *The Surviving Works of Anne Wharton*, ed. G. Greer and Susan Hastings (Stump Cross: Stump Cross Books, 1997), Poem 17, pp. 177–9.

14. *Miscellany Poems upon Several Occasions* (1692), p. 54.

15. *The Post Boy Robb'd of his Mail. Or the Pacquet Broke Open. Consisting of Five Hundred Letters to Persons of Several Qualities and Conditions. With Observations upon each Letter. Publish'd by a Gentleman concern'd in the Frolick* (1692).

16. John Dunton, *Life and Errors* (1705), p. 241.

17. Paul Dottin, *Robinson Crusoe Examin'd and Criticis'd or a new edition of Charles Gildon's famous pamphlet now published with an introduction and explanatory notes together with an essay on Gildon's life* (London and Paris: J. M. Dent and Sons Ltd, 1923), pp. 22–6.

18. 'Verses sent to Mr Bevil Higgons, On his sickness and recovery from the Smallpox, in the Year 1693', 'Poems on Several Occasions', *Works of Catherine [Trotter] Cockburn*, edited by Thomas Birch (London: 1751).

19. [Charles Gildon], *The Lives and Characters of the English Dramatic Poets . . . First begun by Mr Langbaine, improv'd and continued down to this Time, by a Careful Hand* [1698], p. 179.

20. [Catherine Trotter], *Agnes de Castro. A Tragedy. As it is Acted at the Theatre Royal, by His Majesty's Servants. Written by a Young Lady* (1696).

21. Buckingham's poem is an expanded version of Horace, *Odes*, Book III, Ode 29, ll. 49–56.

22. *Poems by Several Hands, and on Several Occasions. Collected by N. Tate . . .* (1685), p. 85.

23. For a full discussion of this text, see M. A. O'Donnell, *Aphra Behn: an Annotated Bibliography of Primary and Secondary Sources* (New York and London: Garland Publishing Inc., 1986), pp. 310–11, 316–19.

24. *The Younger Brother, or the Amorous Jilt.* Sig. x1^{v-r}.

25. [Charles Gildon], *The Lives and Characters of the English Dramatic Poets . . . First begun by Mr Langbain, improv'd and continued down to this Time, by a Careful Hand* (n.d.), p. 175.

26. Todd assumes that this dedication is prompted by Codrington's connection with Behn through the long-dead George Marten who bought property in Barbadoes from Codrington's father 50 years before. It seems more likely that the dedication was made in his own interest, as a servant of the Whigs, than in Behn's.
27. Dottin, *Robinson Crusoe Examin'd and Criticis'd*, p. 49.
28. *The Histories and Novels Written by the late Ingenious Mrs. Behn. Entire in One Volume* (1698), Sig. A5^v.
29. *The Whole Comical Works of Monsr Scarron Containing I. His Comical Romance. II. All his Novels and Histories. III. His Select Letters, Characters, &c . . . Translated by Mr. Tho. Brown, Mr. Savage and others.*
30. Germaine Greer, 'Honest Sam Briscoe', in *A Genius for Letters: Booksellers and Bookselling from the 16th to the 20th Century*, ed. Robin Myers and Michael Harris (Delaware: Oak Knoll Press, n.d.), pp. 35–41.
31. M. A. O'Donnell, *Aphra Behn: an Annotated Bibliography of Primary and Secondary Sources* (New York and London: Garland Publishing Inc., 1986), pp. 174–80.
32. Giles Jacob, *Poetical Register, or Lives and Characters of the English Dramatic Poets* (1723), Vol. 2.
33. *Antiochus the Great. A Tragedy. As it is now acted at the New-Theatre in Lincoln's-Inn-Fields. By His Majesty's Servants. Written by Mrs. Jane Wiseman* (1702).
34. *A New Miscellany of Original Poems on Several Occasions, Written by the E[arl] of D[orset], Sir Charles Sidley, Sir Fleetw. Shepheard, Mr Wolesely, Mr Granvill, Mr Dryden, Mr Stepney, Mr Rowe and Several other eminent hands* (1701).
35. See *The Surviving Works of Anne Wharton*, pp. 166–8, 318–20.
36. The original of the 'Epistle to Flavia' is to be seen on ff. 203–204^v of MS 81 of the Harrowby MSS at Sandon Hall.
37. *Examen Miscellaneum consisting of verse and prose. By the most Honourable the Marquis of Normanby. The Late Lord Rochester. Mr Waller. Mrs Wharton. Mr. Wolesely. With Satires and fables and translations from Anacreon. In prose Above an Hundred Original maxims and Reflections . . .* (1701). Lintot's payment is recorded in John Nichols, *Literary Anecdotes of the 18th Century* (1812), pp. viii, 293.
38. *Post-Boy Robb'd of his Mail: or, the Pacquet Broke Open. Consisting of letters of Love and Gallantry and all Miscellaneous Subjects: in which are discover'd the Vertues, Vices, Follies, Humours and Intrigues of Mankind. With remarks on each Letter.*
39. R. Straus, *The Unspeakable Curll* (London: Chapman & Hall, 1927) pp. 44–7.
40. [Delarivière Manley], *The Adventures of Rivella; Or, The History of the Author of the Atalantis. With Secret memoirs and Characters of several considerable Persons her Cotemporaries . . . Done into English from the French* (1714).
41. *The Plays of Charles Gildon*, edited with an introduction by Paula R. Backscheider (New York and London: Garland Publishng, 1979), p. xxxiv.
42. Letter of 12 February 1719, Charles Gildon to Joseph Addison, BL MS Egerton 1971, ff. 33–4.
43. A glance at *Nuncio Infernalis*, Gildon's second publication (February 1692), should suffice.

Part III
Poetic Practice

14
Classical and Biblical Models: the Female Poetic Tradition

Claudia Thomas Kairoff

Toward the end of the eighteenth century, Samuel Johnson remarked that 'Classical quotation is the parole of literary men all over the world'.[1] He spoke in the aftermath of a well-documented rise of middling readers, literate men and women who had not received a classical education but who nevertheless enjoyed enough income and leisure to devour newspapers, periodicals, novels, conduct books and other genres published for their amusement and instruction. Johnson's statement reflects his conservative perspective, but it also suggests that despite the century's progress in constructing a 'common reader' (another Johnsonian phrase), 'literature' was still perceived as the domain of men who had received a classical education. Such an education began in elite homes, under private tutors, and was completed at public schools and universities. Such an education was denied the vast majority of men, but was never available to women of even the highest class.

Since a man's parole was, in the word's principal contemporary sense, his gentlemanly word of honour, Johnson's phrase doubly confirms women's exclusion. Women were denied the password (the word's secondary sense) that confirmed membership in the world of letters. Johnson, for example, made his observation during a conversation with John Wilkes, whose radical principles he despised (and who considered classical quotations pedantic), but with whom he could converse amicably about classical literature. As educated gentlemen, Johnson and Wilkes had their learning as a common resource when alternative conversational topics would have been awkward. Throughout the early modern period, women were uncomfortably aware of learning's functions. Women could not usually hold the kind of erudite conversation in which Johnson engaged Wilkes. Writers such as

Aphra Behn and Anne Finch complained of self-consciousness due to their lack of classical learning. Critics intimidated women by stigmatizing their lack of familiarity with Greek or Latin models. Conversely, when women engaged in translation, the results were scrutinized for evidence of presupposed feminine incompetence. Women writers, partly in consequence, were often more confident working in genres such as the familiar letter, the spiritual autobiography, drama and the novel, which did not require classical references. Or, like Behn and Finch, they preferred translating romances, plays and poems from the languages customarily taught ladies, French and Italian.

Women poets arguably faced the most severe challenge in this environment. Poetry had historically been a genteel art. Epic poetry, after all, occupied second place in Aristotle's hierarchy of artistic value. William Shakespeare evidently cared little for the fate of his plays, but arranged for the publication of *Venus and Adonis* (1593) and *Lucrece* (1594) to establish his literary reputation. Among his contemporaries, gentlemen and ladies circulated their poems in manuscript, an elegant pastime that permitted display of virtuosity and coded exchange of information and opinions while guarding privacy. As Margaret Ezell has documented, the late seventeenth and early eighteenth centuries encompassed a long transition for writers from a manuscript to a print culture.[2] The very writers most likely to view themselves as participants in an elite art form might now choose to reach a wider audience. That audience could be limited by subscription or the choice of an expensive format, or it could be quite general. But whether in manuscript or print, poems had to meet accepted literary criteria in order to satisfy critical expectations of either a private or a public audience. Among those criteria, by the mid-seventeenth century, was apt use of classical models for theme, style and even turns of phrase. A few families, such as Elizabeth Tollet's, maintained the Renaissance tradition of endowing daughters with a classical education. But by the Restoration, most women with pretensions to literature had to overcome insufficient, often nonexistent, classical training to pay their respects to the Parnassian Muses.

An alternative model, more comfortable for women, was the Bible. The Reformation had established individual Bible study as desirable for both men and women. In Western Europe, the Bible held supreme authority (Johnson, for example, regarded study of his Greek testament as the highest form of reading).[3] Available to all, if only through pastoral readings at church services, the Bible was less exclusive but more authoritative than classical texts. As Ezell has observed, women throughout the early modern period spoke both publicly and in extensively disseminated manuscripts on religious matters, especially during the Civil War.[4] Biblical patterns and references were thus sanctioned for women writers in a way that classical models were not. Women poets made extensive use of biblical allusions both when engaging in straightforward polemic and, as Carol Barash has demonstrated, when cloaking seditious political sentiments in poems addressed to discerning coterie readers.[5] Biblical imagery enabled Anne Finch to protest women's limitations and Elizabeth Rowe to express quasi-erotic longing without impropriety. In the mid-eighteenth century, Elizabeth Carter and her friend Catherine Talbot could write as confident mentors to other women based on their spiritual rather than secular priorities. Carter wrote as one of the rare women proficient in a range of classical and modern languages, but the Bible was the source of her authority. She railed against sceptics such as Lord Bolingbroke, whose learning and travels had led him to embrace a deistic philosophy. In this view, she was closer than Bolingbroke to the values shared by most contemporaries, and her writings met with general acclaim.

Both classical and biblical references infused women's poetic analyses of their culture. For example, Carol Barash has definitively analyzed political references in women's poetry from the Interregnum to the Hanoverian settlement. She traces the beginning of a female royalist poetic tradition to the claims of earlier, dissenting women writers who claimed divine sanction for their religious and political prophecies. The radical women's dispensation created a precedent for later women to communicate their loyalty to Charles I and his sons, and then to James II's daughters, in language borrowed from both biblical and classical sources. Aphra Behn, despite her lack of classical training, adapted to the literary norm by updating and revising others' translations or by writing original poems in classical genres. A clever example is her 'Ovid to Julia', a thinly disguised comment on Lord Mulgrave's attempted seduction in 1682 of the Duke of York's younger daughter, the future Queen Anne.[6] Mulgrave evidently rewarded Behn for the poem, perhaps because it both literally disavows any ambition beyond love and subjects the bereft lover to gentle mockery, further reducing the threat of his pretensions.

Aside from its political function, 'Ovid to Julia' is a witty complement to the Roman poet's heroic epistles in which a discarded mistress pleads with her lost lover. In Behn's poem, Ovid himself addresses the supposed historical paramour for whom he suffered exile, Augustus Caesar's married daughter. Perhaps Behn hints that Ovid's preoccupation with deserted heroines had its roots in sympathy, or was a sort of literary revenge for his own predicament. The poem thus served her literary as well as political purposes. Behn opened her 90-line epistle with a feminine rhyme worthy of Butler or Byron: 'Fair Royal Maid, permit a Youth undone/To tell you how he drew his Ruin on' (1–2). Making Ovid/ Mulgrave the cast-off lover, hopelessly pleading with his lost Julia/ Anne, Behn feminizes her speaker, further lessening his potential for treason. Through a mixture of flattery (41–50), amusing puns ('Ovid' claims his female admirers 'languish'd for the Author of their flame', 32), paradox ('Ovid' feels 'A soft Ambition', 49), and invidious comparison of his pursuit to the Earl of Monmouth's genuinely dangerous activities (60–70), Behn explains away the courtship that had resulted in Mulgrave's banishment from court. The poem ends on a bathetic note, as 'Ovid' accepts his fate although 'Julia's' scorn is more terrible to him than the rigours of warfare, battle scars, accusations of cowardice, even intimations of political disloyalty (79–88). Behn deserved Mulgrave's payment, for the poem indeed renders him, if not a buffoon, an unlikely usurper: a desirable outcome in that volatile era.

Barash concludes *English Women's Poetry* with the poems of Anne Finch, who gradually but deliberately muted the political dimensions of her poetry after the Glorious Revolution deprived contemporary royalist women of their cherished ideal, Mary of Modena. In the course of her writing career and as hope for a Stuart successor to Anne faded, Finch represented herself and other women as seeking solace in a garden figured as a sort of fallen or substitute Eden.[7] Barash discerns in such poems as 'The Petition for an Absolute Retreat'[8] Finch's portrait of the female poet representing 'a politically oppositional community of privately pro-Stuart women'.[9] 'The Petition for an Absolute Retreat' warrants even closer attention than Barash's study permits, as the poem is replete with images that would remain associated with political conservatism throughout the century, here ostensibly drawn purely from classical and biblical texts.[10] The poem's opening stanza, for example, concludes with the poet's plea that she might, before she dies, enjoy the bliss of retreat into 'unshaken Liberty'.[11] 'Liberty' was a contested concept when Finch's *Miscellany Poems* were published in 1713. Continuation of the Stuart line, through the return of the 'Old Pretender' after Anne's imminent death, was widely associated with fear of 'popery and slavery'. In Finch's poem, however, pro-Stuart sentiment is associated with freedom from 'enslavement' to imported goods and the pursuit of wealth, associated popularly with the anti-Stuart Whig party. Finch delineates an ideal both edenic and arcadian, the myth of an isolated garden whose trees supply grapes, figs, peaches, cherries and strawberries in every season, without the effort of harvest. She contrasts this local bounty with such fare as truffles, morels and ortolans, representing the imported delicacies and foreign cuisine satirized by opponents of Whig mercantilism. Finch's orchard, despite its improbably conflated harvest, bears British fruits and is therefore ideologically preferable. Finch closes her poem with several examples drawn from biblical and classical annals, illustrating the wisdom of contentment with poverty and friendship. Her final allusion to Sertorius may be a veiled reference to William or his avatar Marlborough, both accused of 'wild Ambition' for their continental adventures.[12] Finch's wish to be freed from 'all roving Thoughts', all contention, all pursuit of goods[13] is therefore as much a political creed as a Christian reworking of the classical retreat ideal.

As women withdrew from explicit political discourse after the deaths of Anne (1713) and Mary of Modena (1718), Barash argues, they devoted themselves to what today would be termed gender politics, especially in their demands for inclusion in the national literary arena.[14] Nevertheless, she maintains, their writing displayed characteristics that had evolved during the past fifty years: a posture of authority toward readers conceived as a community and expressions of their political 'otherness'. These characteristics indeed appear in many of the poems written by women during the first half of the eighteenth century. Even when women acquired classical training, they might refrain from alluding to such knowledge in verse. Mary Barber celebrated Constantia Grierson in 1734, for example, as mistress of Latin and Greek and many of the liberal disciplines.[15] Not least among Grierson's virtues, in Barber's estimate, was reluctance to display the learning she chiefly used to correct copy and compose dedications for works printed in her husband's shop. Barber included five poems by Grierson in her collection, all graceful occasional poems that could have been written by a person with no classical training at all. The only evidence of Grierson's learning in the volume is Barber's testimony, reiterated in verses praising her friend for valuing motherhood above scholarship: despite her learning, Grierson 'Left Men to take assuming Airs from thence,/And seem'd unconscious of superior Sense' ('Occasion'd by seeing some Verses . . . by Mrs. . . . . Grierson', 5–6). In a tribute 'Upon [Barber's] Son's speaking Latin in School', Grierson claimed that Apollo himself had deprived Barber of classical languages. Envious of the result should she 'unfold her Mind/In Language understood by all Mankind', the god denied Barber the language that ensured Virgil and Ovid 'matchless fame' (37–9). Both Barber and Grierson understood the prestige and potential fame associated with 'the parole of literary men', but Grierson contented herself with occasional verses in English to members of her circle rather than 'take assuming Airs' by composing in Latin.

Lady Mary Wortley Montagu, the best-known example of such reticence, wrote wittily to men and women who shared her Whig affiliation, castigating the shenanigans of courtiers and Opposition writers. A self-taught reader of Latin, Lady Mary participated in the vogue for Horatian imitations through manuscript epistles denouncing Pope and Bolingbroke and odes lambasting Walpole's enemies. She satirized women who exposed themselves to public censure for indecorum while confiding her personal responses to the seemingly inescapable sexual advances of courtiers. She also composed at least two poems, imitations of Horatian odes, ostensibly reflecting personal responses to advancing age.[16] Lady Mary evidently suffered much interior conflict over her literary ambition. Her desire to share her opinions and talent were countered by strong determination to maintain her status by refraining from print. For Lady Mary, the fashion for classical imitation may have provided an additional veil between private thoughts and emotions and their expression to her readers. Posing as classical satirist, Lady Mary inveighed against her contemporaries in scornful tones.

It might be argued, however, that Lady Mary's confident tone was partly that of the satirical persona she often affected, and partly due to the fact that her verse was literally to be read 'in confidence': that is, she shared manuscript copies of her poems with selected friends but did not intend them for publication. Her sense of 'otherness', moreover, derived literally from self-exile after 1739, when she left England in hopes of establishing a ménage with Francesco Algarotti. At the same time, she frequently copied her poems into letters to highly placed correspondents, where she must have known they would circulate among acquaintances. She may have felt that she reached her most significant readership through that process. Likewise, she was well aware that many poems were published from copies taken from those circulating manuscripts. She refused to admit authorship but probably took ambivalent pride in knowing that her perspective on social and political affairs influenced the public sphere. Did she, like Katherine Philips, envision herself a guardian of national ideals or principles? Or, like Finch, excluded from what might have been a viable role in national affairs? When women poets no longer viewed themselves as direct influences on or participants in state affairs, how did they extend or modify the roles identified by Barash as characteristic of female poets? To pursue this question, not just for Lady Mary but for all women poets whose careers took place mainly in the first half of the eighteenth century, we will turn to a less familiar but accomplished poet, Elizabeth Tollet.

Elizabeth Tollet is typical of many early women poets in that biographical facts are sparse. A contemporary described her as small and 'crooked . . . but a sharp wit'.[17] Newton is said to have encouraged Mr Tollet to educate his misshapen but brilliant daughter. A brief biography prefacing her posthumous volume lists music, drawing, Latin, Italian, French, history, poetry and mathematics as the subjects in which she was schooled, without detailing how or by whom she was tutored. Unlike Aphra Behn – whose shadowy figure can be traced through her publications, some correspondence and references by contemporaries – or Lady Mary, more of whose correspondence and manuscripts survive, Tollet left no manuscripts or letters that have been discovered and figures rarely in the writings of others. As Deborah Wyrick remarked in her *Dictionary of Literary Biography* essay, we can glean Tollet's life and personality only through her published poems.[18] Wyrick astutely observes that Tollet's youthful residence within the walls of the Tower of London, where her father had a house from 1701 to 1714 as extra commissioner of the navy, probably inspired her interest in Anne Boleyn and Lady Jane Grey, as well as in other imprisoned women such as Hypatia and Mary, Queen of Scots. Following Wyrick, we can draw further conclusions about Tollet, as well as about women poets in the first half of the eighteenth century, by observing her use of classical and biblical references in the two volumes that preserve most of her writings.

Tollet's first *Poems on Several Occasions* appeared anonymously in 1724, and was forgotten until Roger Lonsdale identified it as hers in his anthology of *Eighteenth-Century Verse*.[19] This 84-page collection contained, with five exceptions, poems republished in the expanded 1755 volume of the same title.[20] Since the first volume was published anonymously and the second posthumously, Tollet apparently fits Ezell's description of social authorship: she did not publish her writings to gain reputation or profit.[21] The first volume may have been an attempt to forestall unauthorized publication of widely circulated manuscript poems; one poem is addressed 'To a Person who printed and mangled some Verses of Mine' (51). The second volume may have been a memorial tribute by her family. The 1724 collection suggests a lively circle of acquaintance that enjoyed debating and bantering about the merits of authors ('On a Lady saying, Spenser wrote broad Scotch'), exchanging books ('To a Lady lending me Heliodorus just before her Marriage'), and recording their responses to literary events such as the death of Anne Finch, the publication of Congreve's works and of Pope's Homer, and a poem by Lady Mary Wortley Montagu in *Hammond's Miscellany*.

While Tollet's 1724 volume is not untypical in its range from cavalier to devotional verse, its representative verse forms such as the heroic epistle popularized by Pope, and its biblical and classical references, it is unusual in its number of translations from and poems in Latin. Since Tollet's family extended the number of Latin poems and translations in the 1755 volume, they clearly did not agree with Lady Mary that a woman should 'conceal whatever Learning she attains, with as much solicitude as she would hide crookedness or lameness'.[22] Perhaps Tollet's crookedness made her education acceptable, as her learning was not destined to intimidate a spouse. Some prominent women poets had translated Latin poems before, but these were usually taken from French translations or were refinements of previous English translations, as in the case of Aphra Behn and Lady Mary Chudleigh.[23] Tollet evidently enjoyed a thorough education in Latin writers such as Horace and Cicero, with an emphasis on philosophical, religious and other meditative compositions. John Andronica believes that she may have had a clerical tutor, or that such texts were chosen as appropriate for a young woman's reading.[24] Tollet developed a facility in Latin prosody that enriched her English poems, as the study of classical writings had benefited privileged male poets for centuries. Tollet thus anticipates such fluent classicists as Elizabeth Carter, while her choice of classical models will test our assumptions about the community of women poets.

Both of Tollet's volumes commence with an early translation – Michael Londry observes that she must have been under 19 – of Ovid's 'Apollo and Daphne' (1724, 3). Tollet indicates her choice of the *Metamorphoses* episode with a subtitle, the first line of the Latin original. Perhaps this indicated to her readers that the poem was not a new version of an English translation, but her translation from Ovid's Latin. Daphne's wish to be transformed into a laurel rather than endure Apollo's assault was an unimpeachable choice for a young, unmarried gentlewoman. The poem recently had been associated with John Dryden, whose version of the *Metamorphoses* figured prominently in Jacob Tonson's *Examen Poeticum* (1693), a third edition of which appeared in

1716.[25] Tollet may have undertaken a stylistic refinement of Dryden's version, for she pared his 163-line episode down to 130 lines. She also eliminated some suggestive passages. When Dryden's Apollo beholds Daphne, 'He praises all he sees, and for the rest/Believes the Beauties yet unseen are best' (676–7). Tollet eliminates that reflection, as well as Dryden's Apollo's admiration for Daphne's 'panting Breast' (675). Dryden draws out the climax: 'She urg'd by fear, her feet did swiftly move,/But he more swiftly, who was urg'd by Love' (728–9). Tollet's concise description of the race's conclusion ('He borrows Speed from Hope, and She from Fear' (96)) conveys the split second in which Daphne acknowledges imminent rape and determines to preserve her chastity at all costs. Dryden's couplet is witty, intimating the predictable triumph of a lover that shortly declines into the almost comical spectacle of Apollo hopelessly trying to embrace and kiss a tree. But Tollet's emphasis is upon Daphne's panic and the desperation that inspires her to seek transmutation rather than endure the 'Shame' unwittingly invited by her beauty (105–6). A tour de force, Tollet's translation establishes her as both a refined gentlewoman and a competitor in the man's world of classical translation.

Both of Tollet's editions open with the same series of classical translations, a sign that she and her family took pride in her unusual literary prowess. Like many women poets of the century's first half, she generally chose topics amenable to Christian application, particularly those enjoining contentment with human vicissitude and within narrow boundaries. While a number of contemporary women chose to translate Epictetus – working from Latin and English translations as well as Greek[26] – Tollet concentrated on brief poems by Horace and Claudian about the wisdom of moderation. In an era when women were often confined to their families' or husbands' estates for much of the year and rarely commanded their own travel schedules, learning to accept pain, boredom and disappointment was perhaps as much the point of women's education as were the acquisition of dancing, drawing and music. At any rate, the themes of Tollet's Latin translations are typical of women's verse, tending to verify Barash's description of a tradition in which women urged their readers to seek consolation in retirement and in hopes of a future life, due to the lack of options for them in civic venues.

But in addition to (or despite) that tradition, Tollet's classical training gave her an anomalous entrée into the masculine literary world characterized by Johnson. Her poem 'On Mr. Congreve's Plays and Poems', for example, pays due homage to his comedies and tragedies, but concludes with a detailed tribute to his skill as translator: 'When he translates, still faithful to the Sense,/He copies, and improves each Excellence' (36–7). She mentions Virgil, Horace and Pindar, praising the discourse on Pindaric that Congreve had published with an ode to Queen Anne in 1702. Few women would have been in a position to define Congreve's excellence as a translator. But Tollet often employed her classical knowledge to produce brilliantly feminized versions of such classical themes as the choice of life. Her 'The Portrait' is a sparkling refutation of the fashions celebrated in *The Rape of the Lock* as young women's ideal. In that poem, Tollet eschews such luxuries as a coach and six, brocade gowns, diamond earrings, visits to spa towns and all-night card parties. Instead, she embraces a Horatian medium, a 'lazy Life' spent paying and receiving visits from likeminded friends engaged in talk of books, rather than of gossip or politics, over their tea. Tollet's ease with Horace allows her to describe the golden mean in brisk hudibrastics.

Judging from those poems that can be dated in the posthumous edition, Tollet continued throughout her life to compose Latin poems in honour of learned addressees such as the virtuoso John Woodward. Perhaps she had made Woodward's acquaintance through Newton and his Royal Society circle. From the inclusion of these occasional poems, we can at least deduce that Tollet's family was proud of her facility in Latin, in an era when classically trained women seemed if anything more anomalous than they had been in the previous century, when the Renaissance tradition of educating aristocratic women lingered as a model for the elite. The second volume also retains 'Hypatia', a plea for female education whose stern tone echoed writings by Chudleigh, Finch, Astell and others earlier in the century, when the English people's 'divorce' from James II and 'remarriage' to William III raised the possibility of analogous advances in individual women's rights. While most women poets substantiated their arguments for female education with biblical examples, Tollet chose a classical model, a young 'pagan' scholar stoned to death by Christian monks in late fourth-century Alexandria. This rather daring manoeuvre had its precedent in works such as *Oroonoko*, which exposed the hypocrisy of professed Christian merchants, while softening her seeming attack on Christianity by identifying Hypatia's persecutors as monks, associated in post-Reformation England with superstition and cruelty.

'Hypatia' may by 1755 have seemed as outdated as Mary Astell's proposal for female monasteries. Tollet's family nevertheless reissued the poem and included several Horatian translations in addition to those in the first volume. Other female contemporaries, such as Mary Leapor and Mary Jones, wrote a substantial amount of Horatian satire in the Popeian vein. Their poems are replete with allusions that all but quote their Twickenham model. Jones, 13 years younger than Tollet, acquiesced in the publication of her writings in 1750.[27] Jones lived with her brother, the choral director at Christ Church Cathedral, Oxford, but she visited and corresponded with highly placed friends. Her sprightly poems, often Horatian essays and epistles, reflect both familiarity with fashionable life and her anomalous perspective. Jones's poems usually echo several of Pope's; 'Of Patience', for example, alludes to the 'Epistle to Lord Cobham', 'Epistle to Lord Bathurst' and *Essay on Man*. The result, however, is no mere pastiche. Jones often distills her observations and wide reading into philosophical passages recommending contemporary wisdom:

> To me it seems, howe'er our lot may fall,
> That pain and pleasure's dealt alike to all;
> That every station has its proper ill,
> In what we fancy, or in what we feel . . .
> Thus wisely deals th'impartial hand of heav'n,
> To check our pride, and keep the balance even.
> ('Of Patience', 135–42)

Jones assumed Pope's authoritative tone in order to counsel, here, Lord Masham suffering from gout. In other poems, she advised Miss Lovelace after her brother's death or Lady Bowyer when she advised Jones to publish. To advert once more to Barash's criteria, Jones wrote confidently to her circle while mindful that 'the world and I are no such cordial friends' ('Epistle to Lady Bowyer', 23). Her persona was modelled on at least two authorities, Horace and Pope, and often on Swift as well. Her favourite, Pope, clearly suggested to Jones her guise of the righteous but debonair outsider. Tollet, however, is among the few women who could, in effect, compete with Pope in the genre of classical imitation.

Margaret Ezell has observed that, besides the fact that they often chose manuscript rather than print circulation, early modern women writers sometimes remain obscure because their religious topics are unappealing to current scholars.[28] Women poets' writings are replete with religious allusions. The religio-political nature of the Civil War guaranteed that religious imagery characterized women's political poems.

In poems such as 'Friendship's Mystery' and 'Friendship',[29] Katherine Philips describes her courtly friendship for 'Lucasia' in language reminiscent of Roman Catholic mysteries such as visions and miracles. Her 'The World' (Philips, Vol. 1, p. 72) and 'The Soul' (Philips, Vol. 1, p. 73) echo the prophetic cry, 'All is vanity'. Among many religious poems, Lady Mary Chudleigh wrote 'On the Vanities of this Life: A Pindarick Ode' (Chudleigh, 59). In 'The Elevation' (Chudleigh, 78), she imaginatively describes her spirit's flight to heaven.

Perhaps Chudleigh's most remarkable poem, 'The Song of the Three Children Paraphras'd' is a 2,065-line Pindaric Ode updating the apocryphal story of three young men cast into a furnace for failing to worship an image of King Nebuchadnezzar (Chudleigh, 167–241). In an introductory preface, Chudleigh explains that her subject, praise of the created world, recommends itself to a woman's poetic treatment because although women are rarely 'skill'd in Physics' (172), even learned men find the universe mysterious. Her vast poem commands every portion of the universe, each of the elements and all created beings to join in praise of God, using current theories to describe such phenomena as clouds and earthquakes. While the original version, in the book of Daniel, simply names phenomena and invokes praise, Chudleigh greatly expands these invocations to include descriptions of natural cycles and events as the intervening centuries have defined them. She also includes the history of the creation itself as recent natural philosophers had reconciled it with Genesis. Chudleigh's poem recapitulates not only Genesis but also the New Testament, particularly Revelation, as if to confirm the wisdom of the ancient text: succeeding events and discoveries have rendered the natural world and sacred history even more wondrous. Even clouds, for example, evoke amazement due to their intricate cycles:

> Ye Exhalations that from Earth arise,
> Whose minute Parts cannot be seen,
> Till they're assembled in the lower Skies;
> Where being condens'd, they fall again
> In gentle Dews, or Show'rs of Rain. (196–200)

Christians should study such phenomena, Chudleigh implies, to appreciate their creator. Near her conclusion, she offers more conventional advice, instructing the clergy to preach charity, humility, abstemiousness and sincerity (1,499–1,766). Having restored the ancient prophetic song to contemporary relevance, Chudleigh undertakes the equally prophetic task of instructing the Church in its duties. Although her preface excuses this gesture as mere encouragement of the clergy, Chudleigh's addition of this section emphasizes her authority as a knowledgeable as well as a devout Christian writer.

Anne Finch's best-known poems, as we have seen, resonate with biblical imagery. Elizabeth Singer Rowe, however, was perhaps Tollet's most influential predecessor. From her early publications under the pseudonym 'Philomela' through numerous editions after her death in 1737, Rowe achieved prominence for her devotional poetry and prose. Rowe's vivid and inspiring verse moved her contemporaries, particularly the young Elizabeth Carter, who later invoked Rowe as her poetic foremother in 'On the Death of Mrs. Rowe'. Carter and her friend Catherine Talbot were among mid-century poets whose writings on the transitory nature of life and the consequent urgency of spiritual development won them praise as exemplary literary women. Their careers were made possible by Rowe's; in an era when women writers were often slandered, her Christian verse was deemed unimpeachable if perhaps enthusiastic. Virginia Woolf urged women to strew flowers on the grave of Aphra Behn for winning them the right to speak their minds. She might have asked them to honour Rowe, also, for winning them the right to publish without risking their reputations.

Rowe is usually associated with the fervent, nearly mystical poems she wrote to accompany devotional meditation.[30] Many of the biblical texts she imitates (from Exodus, the prophets, the Canticle of Canticles) feature direct addresses to God, rapturous expressions admired by her contemporaries. A 20-line imitation of Canticle 2.8–9 exemplifies her style:

> Is it his face? Or are my eager eyes
> Deluded by some vision's bright disguise?
> 'Tis he himself! I know his lovely face. (3–5)

Some critics have concluded that Rowe, heartbroken by the death of her husband after just five years of marriage, sought in such verse to ease her hopeless longing for Thomas. Indeed, Madeleine Forrell Marshall contends, Pope constructed 'Eloisa to Abelard' partly to correct what he believed to be Rowe's elegiac confusion of divine and erotic longing.[31] Marshall convincingly defends Rowe from Pope's and other similar imputations, recalling the long tradition of devotional conventions from which Rowe drew.[32] She argues, moreover, that misconstructions of Rowe's verse are misogynistic, reflecting failure to appreciate Rowe's spirited adaptation of traditional images of the soul as a passive or 'feminine' receiver of God's grace. Read in this way, Rowe's poems demonstrate her ability to transmute private experience of love and grief into expressions of the far more emphatic, because divinely directed, devotional versions of those human passions.

Rowe set an important precedent for women poets with her epic, *The History of Joseph: A Poem* (1736). The poem, in ten books of up to 272 lines each, narrates briskly the momentous events of Joseph's life. Rowe makes Joseph's resistance to Potiphar's wife the chief episode. The instructional popularity of this story is easily attested by such examples as Henry Fielding's choice of the same episode as his inspiration for *Joseph Andrews* (1741). Fielding, of course, found rich humour as well as integrity in Joseph's resistance to his 'Potiphar's wife', Lady Booby. Fielding insisted in his preface that his work was in a new genre, the 'comic epic-poem in prose', while Rowe's serious epic contained no satire. Instead, she grants Potiphar's wife a name, Sabrina, and dramatizes both her failure to resist, and his heroic triumph over, adulterous temptation. While in the Bible, Potiphar is described as a eunuch, suggesting a motive for his wife's attraction to Joseph, Rowe's Sabrina resembles the heroine of a Restoration tragedy, inexplicably seized with desire. Her maid, attempting to beguile her, instead inflames her passion with the tale of Semiramis' doomed love. When her nurse's resort to an infernal oracle fails to procure Joseph's consent, Sabrina goes mad (assisted by fiends, 6.177), and accuses him of attempted rape. Joseph's subsequent imprisonment is ameliorated by the angel Gabriel, whose visit is observed by guards and fellow prisoners. Thus convinced of his innocence, they eventually win his freedom. Sabrina, meanwhile, dies in torment after confessing her guilt. In the Bible, Potiphar's wife simply disappears, while Joseph languishes in prison for two years. Rowe's Joseph languishes, but for an indeterminate length of time: his temporary 'death' and release contrast neatly with her descent to the 'dark uncomfortable coasts' of hell (8.35). Unlike Fielding, Rowe finds nothing humorous in Sabrina's obsession or Joseph's plight. Her epic is less ambiguous than is the Bible itself, crafting from its sprawling material a didactic saga appropriate for the same youthful readership of both sexes that devoured the era's popular fiction.

At about the same time Rowe published *The History of Joseph*, Mary Jones also rendered a biblical story in heroic couplets. 'The Story of Jacob and Rachel attempted' is a rarity among the satires in her collected writings: a 192-line didactic narrative. The poem is dedicated to her young friend Charlot Clayton; the choice of story, that of Joseph's parents, may even have been inspired by Rowe's epic. Jones's invocation prepares the reader for an exemplary courtship plot:

> So may some chosen Youth hereafter view
> All *Rachel*'s Graces bloom in thee anew,
> And love, like *Jacob*, tenderly and true. (5–7)

Jones proceeds to interpret the story as a rather conventional love story, in which the 'Fame and Charms' (36) of Rachel lead Jacob, with Isaac's blessing, to seek his cousin's hand in marriage. Jones's version omits many biblical details, such as the messy circumstances of Jacob's ménage: Leah's seven children before Rachel's first conception and the competition between the two wives, who grant Jacob the sexual use of their maids rather than endure a lapse in childbearing. Jacob's personality in the Bible is somewhat that of a cunning trickster. Laban's substitution of Leah appears, in context, a case of 'the biter bit'. Rachel, also, is a complex personality, blaming her husband for her barrenness and later stealing her father's household gods. Leah seems pathetic, continually bearing sons, hoping that each will win her Jacob's affection. Jones flattens all these characterizations and telescopes the turbulent years between Jacob's marriage and the birth of Rachel's second son, Benjamin. Jones wrote sophisticated satire and certainly could have included more of the complex details in Genesis. Her penchant for crude Swiftian humour suggests that she did not omit the sexual politics of Jacob's household because of prudery. Instead, she seems to have designed her biblical love story for the same audience to which Rowe addressed *The History of Joseph*. Each writer seems to have found the Bible a potentially rich source of didactic but entertaining poems. By aligning the ancient plots and characters with those of contemporary entertainment, they produced works that were not intended for a scholarly but for a youthful audience, the audience that would in time be drawn to the writings of successors such as Hannah More.

Tollet seems to have composed for a more sophisticated audience than did Rowe and Jones in their biblical narratives. Nevertheless, like them, she adapted scriptural sources rather boldly to suit her purposes. Tollet's impulse, throughout her poetry, was to demonstrate that classical philosophy and modern science supported, rather than undermined, biblical truths. Chudleigh had taken a similar position in her 'Song of the Three Children'. For example, Chudleigh incorporated Thomas Burnet's *The Sacred Theory of the Earth*, a recent account of the origin of mountains following Noah's flood, into her elaboration of the young men's hymn. Tollet adverted to many recent scientific advances in 'The Microcosm, asserting the Dignity of Man'. Her stated goal was to rebut a recent poem called 'The Universe' that accused humanity of 'Self-Love and Arrogance'. Tollet begins her 261-line poem by recounting the Genesis story of Adam's creation from dust. She marvels at the life principle, at the intricacy of human physiology (33–55), especially fascinating to scientists following William Harvey, who had in the previous century discovered the circulation of the blood. More important than the 'circulating Spirits', however, is the mysterious gift of reason: 'Pleasure or Pain their Action may bestow,/ But 'tis the Mind determines Bliss or Woe' (61–3). The rest of Tollet's poem celebrates not only reason but also humankind's historic progress in using reason to augment our physical abilities, from using the hand to sheer sheep, break oxen to the plough (77–80) and gather useful herbs (132–43) to inventing the microscope and telescope to gather more precise knowledge of the world (144–181). Newton's protégée clearly saw no impiety in the pursuit of such knowledge. The biblical God who gave Adam the power of speech so that he might praise his Maker (64–73) enabled his study of the natural world for the same purpose. Just as Newton once remarked that the First Cause was undoubtedly 'very well skilled in Mechanicks and Geometry',[33] Tollet invites her reader to observe the precise architecture of a beehive 'and the great Geometer adore' (137).

Besides continuing to translate classical verse and to write in a variety of styles on occasional topics, Tollet concentrated her mature creativity on translating the Psalms, 32 of which appeared in the 1755 volume. Henry Dell thought highly enough of these poems that he included 26, as well as 2 hymns she composed on psalm verses, in his *Select Collection of the Psalms of David . . . by the most eminent English poets* (1756).[34] Psalm 29 exemplifies Tollet's approach.[35] The King James Version of the psalm orders the world's princes to praise and worship God. The Book of Common Prayer simply commands the mighty to 'bring young rams unto the Lord'. Both Tollet and the Roman Catholic version of the same psalm command these rulers more specifically to bring animal sacrifices to the temple. The psalm invokes the voice of God, heard throughout the earth and capable of destroying as well as creating. The psalm concludes by assuring the Israelites that the Lord will give them strength and peace. Tollet rewrites the 11-verse biblical passage as a 34-line poem in heroic couplets. She interprets its opening lines as a demand that the powerful bow and worship the God whose authority they merely represent. Tollet defines the Old Testament's metaphors, such as the thunder imagery that represents 'the voice of the Lord':

His Sov'reign Voice restrains the swelling Floods;
He rolls his Thunder thro' the sable Clouds:
His Pow'r to Bounds confines the raging Sea;
And Nature's Laws his dreaded Voice obey. (11–14)

Tollet's is Newton's God, the God who established the natural laws that Newton observed and theorized. While the psalmist insists that thunder is the voice of God, Tollet suggests that God gives commands, after which the clouds part, the lightning flashes and the thunder roars. Her version speaks to a different sensibility, to a generation more knowledgeable about natural phenomena such as storms. The psalmist's God reigns as king, but Tollet characterizes the deity with added authority: 'The Lord, for ever King, tho' Tempests rave,/ Enthron'd resides above the roaring Wave' (31–2). While the Book of Common Prayer also features a God who 'sitteth above the water-flood' and 'remaineth a King for ever', Tollet's imagery emphasizes his sovereignty as well as his imperviousness to mortal vicissitude. Her God is removed from the elements, enthroned beyond them, appropriate for the contemporary understanding of God as the being who created the universe but does not necessarily interfere with his creation.

Tollet did not, most likely, speak to particular political exigencies in her psalm translations. Until dated manuscripts or records are discovered, we cannot assume a civic function such as we might assign to the work of a contemporary like Eliza Haywood. Tollet did seek, however, to give contemporary readers a version of these sacred poems adjusted to modern refinements of taste and knowledge. If the hallmarks of women's poetry were, as Carol Barash has suggested, authoritative speech from a position of alterity to a community of readers, then Tollet's psalms certainly maintain those traditions. Under the guise of King David, she exhorted readers of her manuscript poems – most likely fellow Anglicans – to obey God, as conceived according to recent natural philosophy.

An exceptional woman, Tollet was reared in privilege and counted Sir Isaac Newton among her acquaintances. Her classical education was rare; perhaps even more precious was her family's pride in her literary accomplishments. Given her facility with contemporary verse forms and her lively interest in music and literature as well as in classical writings, modern science and religion, Tollet's current obscurity is unfortunate. Her poems, records of an unusually vital mind, suggest that while women's immediate purposes for writing and their cultural situation changed, certain trends persisted among female poets from the Interregnum throughout the first half of the eighteenth century. In her use of classical and biblical models, Elizabeth Tollet hearkens back to writers such as Lady Mary Chudleigh and anticipates successors such as Elizabeth Carter. All these writers may have been emulating 'a man's tongue' and communicating in a man's world, but each succeeded in transmitting her opinions, and her membership in a female poetic tradition, to a community well beyond whatever she imagined as she wrote for her coterie, her subscribers, or the 'Common Reader' of Restoration and eighteenth-century England.

Notes

1. Samuel Johnson to John Wilkes, 8 May 1781, recorded by James Boswell, in *Boswell's Life of Johnson, Together with Boswell's Journal of a Tour to the Hebrides and Johnson's Diary of a Journey into North Wales*, ed. George Birkbeck Hill, rev. L. F. Powell, 6 vols (Oxford: Clarendon Press, 1934), 4:102.
2. Margaret J. M. Ezell, *Social Authorship and the Advent of Print* (Baltimore: Johns Hopkins University Press, 1999).
3. Robert DeMaria, Jr., *Samuel Johnson and the Life of Reading* (Baltimore: Johns Hopkins University Press, 1997), pp. 65–71.
4. Margaret J. M. Ezell, *The Patriarch's Wife: Literary Evidence and the History of the Family* (Chapel Hill: University of North Carolina Press, 1987).
5. Carol Barash, *English Women's Poetry, 1649–1714* (Oxford: Clarendon Press, 1996).
6. Aphra Behn, *The Works of Aphra Behn*, ed. Janet Todd, 6 vols (Columbus: Ohio State University Press, 1992), Vol. 1, pp. 182–4. All Behn poems will be cited by line number in this edition.
7. Barash, *English Women's Poetry, 1649–1714*, p. 279.
8. Ibid., pp. 278–82.
9. Ibid., p. 282.
10. Anne Finch, *Selected Poems of Anne Finch, Countess of Winchilsea*, ed. Katharine Rogers (New York: Frederick Ungar, 1979), p. 59.
11. Ibid., p. 7.
12. Ibid., pp. 250–5.
13. Ibid., pp. 258–61.
14. Barash, *English Women's Poetry, 1649–1714*, p. 289.
15. Mary Barber, *Poems on Several Occasions* (London: C. Rivington, 1734), pp. xxvi–xxx. All quotations of Barber's and Grierson's poems will be cited by line number in this edition.

16. For Lady Mary Wortley Montagu's poems, see *Essays and Poems and Simplicity, a Comedy*, eds Robert Halsband and Isobel Grundy (Oxford: Oxford University Press, 1977). The odes reflecting on advancing age are 'The 5th Ode of Horace Imitated' (302) and 'The Fourth Ode of the First Book of Horace, Imitated' (310).

17. Jocelyn Harris and Joyce Fullard, 'Elizabeth Tollet', in Janet Todd (ed.), *A Dictionary of British and American Women Writers 1660–1800* (Totowa, NJ: Rowman and Littlefield, 1987), p. 304. Michael Londry generously permitted me to read the proofs of his forthcoming *New Dictionary of National Biography* entry for Tollet, which I will cite within the text as 'Londry'. His extensive research has uncovered new facts about Tollet's life that should assist future studies. I would like to thank Mr Londry and Dr Isobel Grundy for their gracious help with this essay.

18. Deborah Baker Wyrick, 'Elizabeth Tollet', *Eighteenth-Century British Poets, First Series*, in John Sitter (ed.) *Dictionary of Literary Biography* (Detroit: Bruccoli Clark Layman, 1990), 95:329.

19. [Elizabeth Tollet], *Poems on Several Occasions. With Anne Boleyn to King Henry VIII. An Epistle* (London: John Clarke, 1724). Roger Lonsdale (ed.), *The New Oxford Book of Eighteenth-Century Verse* (Oxford: Oxford University Press, 1984), p. 842, n. 116.

20. Elizabeth Tollet, *Poems on Several Occasions. With Anne Boleyn to King Henry VIII. An Epistle*, 2nd edn (London: T. Lowndes, 1756). All quotations of Tollet will be cited by page or line number in this edition unless otherwise specified.

21. Ezell, *Social Authorship*, pp. 45–60.

22. Lady Mary Wortley Montagu, *Complete Letters*, ed. Robert Halsband, 3 vols (Oxford: Oxford University Press, 1965–67), Vol. 3, p. 24.

23. Janet Todd, in *The Secret Life of Aphra Behn* (New Brunswick, NJ: Rutgers University Press, 1996), pp. 200–21 and *passim*, cites Behn's acknowledgement of her exclusion from classical languages. Margaret J. M. Ezell remarks in the introduction to *The Poems and Prose of Mary, Lady Chudleigh* (New York: Oxford University Press, 1993) that Chudleigh relied on English translations for her classical knowledge (p. xxvii). Further references to Chudleigh's verse will be cited by page or line number in this edition.

24. I am indebted to John Andronica, my colleague in the Classics Department of Wake Forest University, for his analysis of Tollet's Latin poems and translations as well as for his deductions concerning her education.

25. John Dryden, *The Works of John Dryden*, 20 vols, gen. ed. H. T. Swedenberg, Jr. (Berkeley: University of California Press, 1956–96), Vol. 4, pp. 394–8. All quotations of Dryden will be cited by line number in this edition.

26. Isobel Grundy notes that besides Lady Mary and Elizabeth Carter, Mary Astell and Mary, Lady Chudleigh, were also drawn to Epictetus' stoic doctrines. See Grundy, *Lady Mary Wortley Montagu* (Oxford: Oxford University Press, 1999), pp. 36–7.

27. Mary Jones, *Miscellanies in Prose and Verse* (Oxford: Dodsley et al., 1750). All quotations of Jones will be cited by page or line number in this edition.

28. Ezell, *Patriarch's Wife*, p. 84.

29. Katherine Philips, *The Collected Works of Katherine Philips, The Matchless Orinda*, 3 vols, ed. Patrick Thomas (Stump Cross: Stump Cross Books,

1990), Vol. 1, pp. 17, 57. Further references to Philips's poems will be cited by page number in this edition.

30. Madeleine Forell Marshall (ed.), *The Poetry of Elizabeth Singer Rowe (1674–1737)* (Lewiston, NY: Edwin Mellen Press, 1987). Quotations of Rowe's verse will be cited by line number in this edition. I am indebted to Marshall's informed reading of Rowe's devotional poems.

31. Marshall, *Poetry of Elizabeth Singer Rowe*, pp. 24–8.

32. Ibid., pp. 64–6.

33. Isaac Newton to Richard Bentley in a letter dated 10 December 1692, in *Newton*, eds I. Bernard Cohen and Richard S. Westfall (New York: Norton, 1995), p. 332.

34. [Henry Dell (ed.)], *A Select Collection of the Psalms of David, as imitated or paraphrased by the most eminent English poets* (London: 1756).

35. Lacking records of Tollet's source, I consulted the *Holy Bible. Authorized* (Edinburgh: 1715–16), the King James translation, *The Book of Common Prayer . . . Together with the . . . Psalms of David* (Cambridge: Baskerville, 1761), and *The Holy Bible, Translated from the Latin Vulgate* (1609; rpt New York: Douay Bible House, 1953), the Roman Catholic translation. Unless she worked from the Book of Common Prayer texts, Tollet may have translated the Psalms from a Latin testament.

15
Political Verse and Satire: Monarchy, Party and Female Political Agency

Kathryn R. King

The period from the Restoration to the mid-eighteenth century was the great age of political writing in Britain. The once widely held view that women declined public themes in favour of small, intimate, private concerns has been challenged in recent years by literary histories that emphasize the political origins and meaning of women's writing in the seventeenth century, including groundbreaking accounts by Carol Barash and Paula McDowell.[1] We now know that women produced nearly every form of political writing that circulated during the period: pamphlets and treatises, topical ballads, partisan dramas, squibs and satirical broadsides, ceremonial odes, royal elegies and panegyrics. They declared themselves Tories, Whigs and Jacobites; Anglicans, Catholics and dissenters. They lent their pens to a range of widely differing political interests, from the 'good old cause' of godly republicanism to the Jacobite cause of a Stuart restoration. They stated opinions on affairs of state, smeared political enemies, displayed loyalty, entered into religious controversy, shaped public opinion and explored the questions of allegiance, integrity and national memory that troubled nearly all thoughtful members of the political nation during this uncertain time. In addition, they used political verse to chart their own complicated relation as women to the public order.

The body of political verse produced by women during this period is so rich, wide ranging and various that I have had to omit a number of important strands from this account. I do not discuss sexual politics in the current feminist sense or the repressed meanings Fredric Jameson had in mind when he referred to the political unconscious of texts. These and other 'politics' will have to await treatment in a longer study. So will topical verse satire and indeed manuscript verse more generally, including that intriguing corpus of work by 'a Lady' as well as male appropriations of the female voice such as the widely circulated 'Jenny Cromwell's Complaint against Sodomy'. I focus instead upon 'high' literary forms, especially royal panegyrics, odes and elegies. State poems, with their self-consciously elevated manner, seldom give us writers at their brightest or most memorable, but they usefully reveal important shifts in thinking about rulership, subjects and female political agency. As will be seen, such verse enabled women of varying political persuasions to enter into the debate over the succession that dominated the national political consciousness until well into the 1720s, when the Protestant succession at last came to seem assured. This chapter begins with the leading figures in the seventeenth-century Stuart tradition and their Jacobite successors, turns to the Whiggish counter-tradition that developed in the 1690s, and finally considers partisan writing during the Age of Anne and George I. In addition to tracing general patterns of development and identifying a shared body of poetic tropes, motifs and forms, this account identifies some distinctive features of the work of individual women writers and, insofar as possible within brief compass, directs attention to some complexities of manner and matter discoverable in their verse.

Katherine Philips, royalism and the politics of clemency

Katherine Philips (1632–64), the 'matchless Orinda', was arguably Britain's first female poet of the state. Such an assessment sits oddly with Philips's present reputation as the private poet par excellence, lyricist of female friendships and feminine microcosms of 'retir'd life'; or with the earlier idealized image of 'Orinda' as exemplar of the chaste, virtuous, self-effacing and apolitical woman writer. But Philips's royalist orientation has long been recognized, and Andrew Shifflet has recently called attention to her Republican sympathies.[2] Philips is emerging a more complicated figure, politically speaking, than has been suspected, and some of her best poems reveal a subtlety of political awareness that warrants close study.

The complications begin with the biography. Born and bred Presbyterian in a family of future parliamentarians, Philips married a Cromwellian who sat in the interregnum Parliament and on a court that had condemned to death a prominent royalist. By temperament, however, Philips had Stuart sympathies and desires for notice at court. She cultivated an important ally in Sir Charles Cotterell, the king's

Master of Ceremonies, and sought patronage from the Duchess of York. The theme of royal clemency that looms so large in her post-Restoration royal panegyrics doubtless represents a considered response to the public debate over the possibilities and limits of monarchical forgiveness in the post-Civil War state;[3] but it grows out of enlightened self-interest as well and shows her willingness to use her poetic talents in the service of her husband's political career. (An earlier impolitic outburst against one of her husband's political adversaries left her mortified that she may have damaged his prospects.)[4] In short, Philips was thoroughly embroiled in politics herself, a circumstance which may help explain why she wrote some of the more thoughtful poems on affairs of state to be produced in the late fifties and early sixties.

The printed volumes of 1664 and 1667 begin with a group of 11 poems written to or about a member of the royal family, most dating from around 1660. The return of Charles Stuart in 1660 released an outpouring of euphoric verse. Philips's poems, however, sound a dark, contrite note. One stresses the infirmities of 'gasping' England, an 'exhausted land' which (in a pun) is 'growne old with woes'; Charles, in another pun, is a 'soveraigne remedy' who will soon bring comfort and healing to the ailing body politic ('On the numerous accesse of the English to waite upon the King in Holland').[5] Another, speaking for the erring country, 'banish'd' from the Stuart presence by 'Our crimes', offers the wishful hope that 'our stormes are ceast' and 'Our faults forgiven' ('The Princess royall's Returne into England').[6] Another praises the king's merciful nature: revenge gives 'no pleasure' to Charles who, 'like a God', 'spar'd their bloud who gap'd for his' ('Arion on a Dolphin to his Majestie').[7] References to royal forgiveness belong to a poetry of self-interested diplomacy that seeks to construct, through images of Stuart clemency, an England in which the errors of parliamentarians (and their wives) might be set aside.

A poem on the coronation of Charles II exemplifies the ambiguities of her royal panegyrics. Despite the title – 'On the faire weather at the Coronacon' – the 18-line poem emphasizes the terrible thunderstorm that followed the ceremony, the coronation itself being no more than a 'bright Parenthesis' that occupies only 3 lines in the poem's centre. This unusual conceit, apparently the poet's invention,[8] suggests an equivocal interpretation of the occasion and, by extension, of the events of recent history. On the one hand, comparison of the brief moment of sunshine to the parting of the Red Sea seems to indicate divine approval of Stuart rule; on the other, the coronation is threatened by 'invading raines' and is said to be 'snatch'd from stormes'. The effect is to situate the fragile joyfulness of the Restoration in the context of continuing political crisis. This strangely sombre coronation poem captures not so much the jubilation of the occasion as its anxieties and thus manages to celebrate the new king while acknowledging the uncertainties of the moment.[9]

When Philips arranged her poems on affairs of state, she placed at their head what may have been her earliest poem on a public theme, 'Upon the double murther of K. Charles', an answer to a libel on Charles I that dates from the early 1650s when Philips may still have been in her teens.[10] In addition to exhibiting strong sympathy for the executed king and contempt for the regicides ('No bounds will hold those who at scepters flye'), the poem shows Philips facing down patriarchal injunctions against public female speech by casting herself in the role of defender of the father/king. The speaker begins by disclaiming interest in political matters –

> I thinke not on the state, nor am concern'd
> Which way soever that great Helme is turn'd,

– but then uses the patriarchal analogy between kingdom and family to construct a sustained simile justifying her 'breach of nature's lawes'. She is like a son who owes the father silent obedience but who, in the face of terrible danger to the king/father, is 'force[d]' to speak out:

> But as that sonne whose father's danger nigh
> Did force his native dumbnesse, and untye
> The fettred organs: so here is a cause
> That will excuse the breach of nature's lawes.
> Silence were now a Sin.[11]

Often cited to illustrate the transgressive nature of female political utterance at this time, the passage shows as well the skill with which Philips is able to bend hostile thinking to her own purposes, to turn patriarchal ideology against itself. It is also one of the first of many instances of a woman poet stepping forward to defend, champion, or counsel a beloved monarch.

The Jacobite tradition: Behn, Barker and Finch

Scholarly emphasis on the royalist or Tory affiliations of women poets in this period sometimes gives the impression of an almost inevitable link between female poetics and conservative politics. The example of Lucy Hutchinson (1620–post-1675), an important but understudied republican poet now receiving recognition as the author of a politically allusive epic, reminds us otherwise.[12] That said, the women who aspired to notice as state poets in the several decades after Philips's death were indeed Stuart loyalists who shared (in differing ways) their precursor's courtly orientation. Aphra Behn, a Tory propagandist for most of her writing life, never ceased seeking notice from the Stuarts. Jane Barker sought royal patronage at the court-in-exile at St Germain, where she produced a volume of Jacobite and Catholic verse for presentation to the young Prince of Wales, the future 'Old Pretender'.[13] Anne Finch served as maid of honour to Mary of Modena and, much later, wrote an elegy for James II, who died in exile, in which the speaker claims to give voice to England's silenced sorrows. Barker and Finch refused to accept the legitimacy of the Revolution of 1688–89 and, at no small cost to themselves, remained faithful to the House of Stuart. Barker fled to France (where she wrote under the name 'Fidelia') and, after returning home, engaged in Jacobite conspiracy. Finch and her nonjuring husband retired to the countryside. Whether Behn would have ended up a Jacobite as well is unclear since she died shortly after William and Mary took the throne, but we can feel confident that the poet who 'Ador'd' James as a 'thing Divine' would not have shunned the label. All three adhered to a Jacobite ideology of political absolutism, and each developed in her state poems a worshipful stance toward sacred monarchy that goes well beyond the mild royalism exhibited by the more centrist and conciliatory Katherine Philips.

To move from Philips to Aphra Behn (*c.*1640–89) is to descend into the rough-and-tumble world of party politics. Behn emerged as a public writer during the Exclusion Crisis (1678–81), commonly seen as the beginning of party politics in England, and she inhabited a literary environment at once more politicized and more professionalized than anything imaginable by Philips who, in the early sixties, wrote as a genteel amateur on behalf of national unity and healing. Behn made a name for herself as the author of anti-Whig plays designed to consolidate support for the Stuarts, turned out 'Tory Farce, or Doggerell', composed extravagant panegyrics on members of the royal family, and, in the final months of her life, wrote two remarkable odes that probe with painful honesty the cost of her Stuart loyalties in the post-Revolutionary world. Behn lived by the pen, or tried to, in an era when literature was partisan politics by another name.

Behn's royal odes respond to moments of national crisis that punctuated the short and unhappy reign of James II (1685–88) including, most disastrously for the Stuarts, the birth of a Catholic heir, an event that strained James's relation to the political nation to the breaking point and called forth Behn's most lavish efforts on behalf of the Stuart line. Her ode on the death of Charles II illustrates the recurrent features and tendencies of her state poems. The dramatized first-person speaker, exclamatory hyperbole (*'So Great a King! So much a God!'*), baroque conceits (Charles's temporary revival from the effects of a stroke is likened to Christ's resurrection and ascension), prophetic stance and Catholic diction and imagery all subserve her central theme: the divinity of kings. As Janet Todd points out, the poem is finally less concerned with the death of Charles than with the 'orderly and desired transfer of legitimate political power' from Charles to James, and Behn uses all the resources of royal panegyric to mobilize support for the Stuart line during this perilous time.[14] The deathbed scene between Charles and James imagined in the poem's centre, for example, invokes the traditional association between monarchy and the sun to suggest the inexhaustible renewal of Stuart rule. The 'Sacred Lights' in Charles's eyes may fade, but they are translated to the heavens ('every Beam above informs a Star'), to reappear in the eyes of James, 'the Sacred Promis'd Prince', and thence to beam out over the entire 'Globe'. 'Long may You Shine', she writes to James,

> . . . and spread Your Beams as far,
> As from the Morning to the Ev'ning Star;
> 'Till Your *Convincing Rays*, Your Foes o're come,
> And for Your *Glorious Magnitude* the scanted Globe want room.[15]

The theatrical, even operatic expression of loyalty to James is meant to project a magnificence that legitimates kings, but the very excesses of Behn's figurations suggests how shaky the whole concept of political absolutism had become by this time.

Behn lived to see the 'Wond'rous Change', as she ironically calls the Revolution of 1688–89, and to deplore the shift in power that left her 'Useless and Forlorn'. The 'Pindaric Poem to The Reverend Doctor Burnet' from which these phrases are taken explores with great subtlety the ambiguities of her public position as a Stuart propagandist after the expulsion of James II. Read by some as a tactful dismissal of Burnet's request that she write on behalf of the new regime, by others as a shrewd piece of negotiation with the new powers, the poem projects the difficulties of reconciling political loyalty and literary professionalism. A sense of self-division underlies Behn's rueful self-portrait as an 'Excluded Prophet'. 'My Muse', she writes, would 'fain' move easily with the 'fair prosperous Gale' and 'full driving Tide' upon 'the thriving Course'; yet another part of herself is rendered stubbornly immobile by a 'Loyalty' that binds her 'with Pious Force' to the ousted James II. While others prosper, she is left stranded on the deserted shore, a latter-day Moses who has lived too long to enter the promised land:

> The Brieze that wafts the Crowding Nations o're,
>> Leaves me unpity'd far behind
>> On the Forsaken Barren Shore,
> To sigh with Echo, and the Murmuring Wind;
> While all the Inviting Prospect I survey,
> With Melancholy eyes I view the Plains,
> Where all I see is Ravishing and Gay,
> And all I hear is Mirth in loudest Strains;
> Thus while the Chosen Seed possess the Promis'd Land,
>> I like the Excluded Prophet stand,
>> The Fruitful Happy Soul can only see,
>> But am forbid by Fates Decree
> To share the Triumph of the joyful Victory.[16]

Even if the poem hints that Behn is capable of compromise, as has been suggested, it offers compelling testimony all the same to a professional author's struggle to find an acceptable political stance while maintaining a degree of personal integrity: 'Let me be Just', the speaker writes, 'but Just with Honour too'.[17]

On the other side of the channel, Jane Barker (1652–1732), a recent convert to Catholicism, portrayed herself in an autobiographical manuscript poem as 'helpless, friendless, destitute forlorn'.[18] In contrast to Behn, who remained in London and accommodated herself as best she could to the new order, Barker fled to France to live with other Jacobite exiles at St Germain. There she fired off bitter denunciations of 'curssed orange' and hurled imprecations at James's enemies: '[I] wish all cursses Hell cou'd e'er invent,/May light on those who caus'd his banishment'.[19] Although both write in support of royal absolutism, they craft a strikingly different kind of poetry. Behn, who addressed the public in print, uses baroque splendour to engender awe for the Stuart monarchy; Barker, who circulated her verse in manuscript, employs unheroic, homely, even rough effects. Her James is a saintly figure, a holy man, perfect in his Christ-like sufferings, a 'pilgrim' and 'mighty missioner' sent 'by heav'n' to defend the Catholic faith.[20] Behn favours ceremonial odes, Barker syllabic couplets. Her stance is that of a plain-speaking outsider with little use for poetical fictions, figures of speech, or fancy. Typical of the measured simplicity of her style are these lines addressed to the young Prince of Wales:

> Then let's rejoyce, sing, love, and with you smile
> Forgeting friends, estates, or native soyle,
> For having you we'r here in full content,
> Tis they in England suffer banishment.[21]

One of her most poignant poems, 'The Miseries of St. Germains', describes the famine and plague in France, 1694–95, which, according to Carol Shiner Wilson, together claimed more than a million lives.[22] The famished exiles, in Barker's phrase, 'Curss god, themselves, fate, orange, and so dy'.[23] A striking feature of this poem is its unheroic glance back at the military action in Ireland in the early nineties. In Whig verse of the period, as will be seen, the Battle of the Boyne (1690) is a triumphant event, the occasion for pro-William mythologizing and, often, bloody-minded cheering. Barker, on the losing side, focuses on the human cost of the Boyne and other battles. A widow cries for her parents slain at Aughrim, another for her husband killed at Limerick. Soldiers return from the 'unluckey' Boyne dismembered, and the fighting, in her swift summation, is anything but heroic:

> Some with lost armes, and some with leggs of wood,
> Crying they lost those limbs because they stood,
> When others fled, at Boyn's unluckey flood.[24]

At the impoverished court at St Germain Barker saw first-hand the limits of absolutist claims and witnessed only too clearly the day-to-day inadequacies of monarchs. The rough verse she wrote during the decade or so following the Revolution, while faithful to the Jacobite ideals of a disappearing past, addressed itself to a fallen world stripped of its courtly artifice.

Anne Finch (1661–1720) wrote autobiographical verses that express strong identification with the Stuarts and a sense of loss at once national and personal. 'The Fragment' likens the ousting of the Stuarts from court to the expulsion from the Garden of Eden – 'There plac'd too soon the flaming Sword appear'd/Remov'd those Pow'rs, whom justly she rever'd'[25] – and depicts the speaker as participating in the ruin of the royal family, 'thrown' with them 'prostrate to the humble Ground'. The speaker of 'Petition for an Absolute Retreat' compares herself to a 'lonely stubborn Oak' – the oak is the symbol of the House of Stuart – ruined by 'a Storm of Fate' felt throughout 'the *British State*': she too is 'Fall'n, neglected, lost, forgot'.[26] Some of her finest poems, 'Upon the Hurricane' to take just one example, engage deeply and with tough-minded intelligence the public as well as private implications of political upheaval.

Finch's elegy on the death of James II (1701) explores relations among poetry, female utterance and the public realm from a Jacobite perspective.[27] The speaker, identified only as 'a Lady', depicts herself as giving voice to the 'Loyal Grief' of fellow Britons, mourning for the lost – in at least two senses – king, who died in exile in France. She begins with an indirect attack on the mercenary values of Williamite England that serves to distinguish her 'free disinterested Muse' from poets who write for hire: 'none shall pay this Verse,/Bred in a Land not Honour'd with thy [James's] Herse'. In the middle stanzas the personal voice gives way first to that of the national historian intent upon recording truths about James's accomplishments rendered invisible in Whiggish national histories – acts of heroism that are, in her memorable phrase, 'in this Reverse of Sight forgot' – and then to the impersonal elegist, speaking to and for the English nation ('Weep then ye Realms . . . ') and those who served James personally ('Weep ye Attendants . . . '). The final stanza sees a return of the personal voice. In a moving image, the speaker projects the present rupture between king and kingdom into the future, the Day of Judgment, when 'States and Monarchies shall be no more' and the truth can be told of what 'sad Chance or weighty Causes' 'forc'd' an exiled king to 'arise from out a Foreign Tomb'. The poem ends on a note of quiet, personal reflection, a wish for a place of retreat from the turmoils of the state:

> Whilst for my self, like Solitary Men,
>> Devoted only to the Pen,
>> I but a Safe Retreat amidst thee crave
> Below the Ambitious World, and just above my Grave.

The speaker's withdrawal into a 'Safe Retreat' would seem to support a reading of Finch as illustrative of the turn from seventeenth-century political engagement toward 'private', 'authoritatively female' poetic worlds constructed by women in the eighteenth century and beyond.[28] Yet such an approach risks passing over the rich political subtexts of much of Finch's post-Revolution poetry. The final word of this elegy, for example, 'Grave', returns us to the Jacobite themes developed earlier in the poem. James, we recall, lies even now in a 'Foreign Tomb'. The speaker is destined to exist in painful and unnatural separation from her rightful monarch in death as in life, just as he was compelled to die, as he lived, separate from the 'Maternal Bosom' of his native land. At the Day of Judgement 'States and Monarchies shall be no more', but until such time as such dislocations as these dissolve the poet exists in a contingent political realm and will continue to explore the great Jacobite themes of loss, exile and the precariousness of cultural memory.

Whiggish writing under William and Anne

The poetry produced by Stuart loyalists after the Revolution is elegiac verse acutely sensitive to the historical misrepresentations that accompany the shift from one political order to another, disposed to meditate upon its own exclusions. Nothing could be more different than the verse of the next generation of women poets, a self-consciously forward-looking lot who eagerly attached themselves to the new Whig order and advanced a cultural and political agenda that was Protestant, militaristic, triumphalist and intensely nationalistic. These Whiggish women sought, along with such male poets as Joseph Addison and Richard Blackmore, 'to mythologize current events, and to create a body of poetry that would do justice to the momentous political achievements of post-Revolution England', as Abigail Williams has written.[29] They congratulated themselves on being history's winners: for them the Revolution was indeed 'Glorious'. Their icon, hailed as 'the Pindarick Lady' in the national press, was Elizabeth Singer, a fervent Whig who proudly declared her political colours: '*William!* A Name my Lines grow proud to bear!'[30] Elizabeth Singer, the future Mrs Rowe, is known today more for piety than politics, but she made her name as a Williamite poet, as Sarah Prescott has shown, and it was as a panegyrist of 'Great *William*' that she attracted the attention of her earliest male admirers, men associated with John Dunton's Whiggish *Athenian Mercury*.[31] To women she represented, at least in her earliest years, a set of liberating possibilities opened up by shifts in political thinking that accompanied the Revolution. As Carole Pateman has observed, universalist notions that 'men were born free, equal, and rational' had acquired 'wide currency' at the end of the century, raising tantalizing questions about the political position of women in the new order: 'Was there, for example, such a creature as a freeborn Englishwoman?'[32] Some women said, emphatically, yes. Elizabeth Johnson, in her preface to Singer's *Poems on Several Occasions* (1696), uses Whig rhetoric of the liberties of the freeborn Englishman to align Singer with fashionable ideas about resistance to absolutism. In the face of the *'Tyranny* of the *Prouder Sex'*, women can hardly be expected to remain 'so *Compleatly Passive* as to bear *all* without so much as a *Murmur'* (the reference is to the Tory doctrine of passive obedience, which held that even in the face of private misgivings one must passively obey the reigning monarch). Submission to male rule, she urges, would be the destruction of women's 'Fundamental Constitutions' and a violation of the *'Liberties of Freeborn English-Women'*.[33]

The buoyant spirits of these freeborn young Englishwomen are evident in the verse of Sarah Fyge Egerton (1670–1723). Egerton, who began writing in the eighties, published in 1703 a volume of poems dedicated to the great Whig patron the first earl of Halifax. 'The Liberty', one of her best-known poems, breathes that same air of personal and political freedom celebrated in Whig rhetoric of the Williamite period. It begins, boldly, with a rhyme on *fools* and *rules* in a rhetorical question that sets a new tone of female restlessness: 'Shall I be one, of those obsequious Fools,/That square there [*sic*] lives, by Customs scanty Rules'. By the sixth line it declares its contempt for 'Foolish, dull Trifling, Formality'. The speaker, determined to break through restraints that mark out her narrow sphere, will not 'bow' to 'the Idol Custom', be 'chain'd to the nice Order of my Sex', 'ty'd' to 'dull fulsome Rules', or enclosed within 'Manacles' of social expectations. Her 'daring Pen' stands on the side of 'uncheck'd freedom' and 'will bolder Sallies make' – punning with the word 'Sallies' on her first name, Sarah.[34] The spirit of liberty is discernible in Tory verse of the time, as well. In 'To the Ladies', Lady Chudleigh indicts marriage as affording women no protection against men's arbitrary powers. The husband, a 'haughty lord', is free to behave with oriental tyranny, while wives are denied the freedoms and self-determination assumed to be the birthright of an English*man*. Chudleigh's conservative politics do not, however, permit the kind of open defiance Whig women happily claim for themselves and their daring pens; and so, after casting essentially Whiggish aspersions on male domestic tyrants, the speaker retreats to the kind of stoic argument employed by Barker and the Tory Mary Astell: 'Value your selves, and Men despise:/You must be proud, if you'll be wise'.[35] Compare this with the Whiggish treatment of similar themes developed by Singer in her 'A Farewel to Love', in which the disenchanted speaker resolves to range the world 'Uncontroul'd' and envisions her freedom from male control as a heady mix of 'Liberty and Bliss'.[36]

Egerton's 'To the Queen' expresses the complexities of women's relationship to the state at this moment of high feminist expectations. Addressing Queen Anne directly, the speaker declares herself resentful of the restrictions imposed by gender:

> Why are we barr'd, or why I Woman made,
> Whose Sex forbids to Fight, and to Invade,
> Or give my Queen, more than my wish for Aid?

She is eager to take up arms on behalf of her sovereign – 'I shall not tremble, at the Launce, or Sword' – and will fight 'Mankind from Pole to Pole' until 'all the Kingdoms, in one Empire meet'. The final couplet stresses the obligation of 'every Subject', female no less than male, to protect the Queen: 'May every Subject you protect; Profess/As much as I, and dare to act no less'.[37] The identification of the public-spirited female political subject with British military and imperial might is striking, as is Egerton's impatience with the limitations placed upon female citizenship. The mood of female insurgency at the turn of the century, linked in many recent accounts with the empowering presence on the throne of a female monarch, here expresses itself as a kind of frustrated desire for a more meaningful relationship with the monarch and, by extension, the public realm over which she rules.

If Whiggish women register a flawed incorporation into the public order, they also write to promote the Whig cultural agenda, that 'self-consciously modern programme for English poetry' developed in the 1690s and 1700s by 'writers concerned to identify the literary forms and models appropriate to a nation which, with the Glorious Revolution of 1688, has grasped its political liberty and entered into possession of itself'.[38] Singer's early verse illustrates many of the ways women appropriated the poetic practices of the royalist predecessors as part of the larger process of Whig cultural self-definition. In one poem after another she tries out inherited symbols, motifs and forms and gives them a Whiggish cast, as if to claim poetic tradition for a new kind of woman in a new age. 'To Madam S— at the Court', a come-be-with-me lyric in the tradition of Marlow and Raleigh, revises the poem of homoerotic pastoralism associated with such courtly writers as Philips and Behn. 'Come prethee leave the Courts', she invites her Philis, and then, echoing Philips and behind her Donne, urges Philis to disdain 'that mean influence' that controls the 'duller world'. In a decidedly odd stanza that places the female poet and her female beloved beside a mermaid-haunted stream, she declares herself for William:

> Now seated by a lovely Stream,
> Where beauteous Mermaids haunt;
> My Song while *William* is my Theam,
> Shall them and thee inchant.[39]

The effect is to plant a Whig flag in the very centre of royalist poetic territory.

Related strategies are at work in the poems of courtly friendship and platonic love, themes which can be traced back to the court of Henrietta Maria, wife of Charles I, which Singer adapts to her literary friendships with men. Her 'Pindarick, to the Athenian Society' praises the 'matchless men' of Athens (Dunton and his circle) who have shown fashionable vice to be *'Unmanly, sensual and effeminate'*, and lays hyperbolic claim, again with self-conscious boldness, to a new manner of friendship: 'A friendship so exalted and immense,/A *female breast* did ne're before commence'.[40] Elsewhere Singer praises the pure flames of platonic love in such a way as implicitly to discredit the sexual licentiousness of royalist courtly culture: 'No stragling wish, or symptom of desire,/Comes near the Limits of this holy fire' ('Platonick Love').[41] Whigs, as Rachel Weil has observed, 'were eager to establish themselves as the party of sexual order' and 'to show that libertinism and debauchery were characteristic of the old regime'.[42] Her poems of platonic love signal by their fervent purity the moral renewal of the new regime and implicitly propose in the Whiggish writers associated with the *Athenian Mercury* an alternative to debauched and permissive verse that flourished in and around Stuart courts.

'Upon King William's passing the Boyn', a rapturous display of loyalty in which a female speaker addresses the new king during an imagined pause in the fighting at the river Boyne, where William III and his forces met James and the Jacobite troops, appears to be a deliberate reworking of the trope of the female defender of the embattled monarch's body. The poem begins by rehearsing a familiar deferential gesture, the speaker declaring the inadequacy of her 'soft' voice to sing the *'Hero and the King'*; but like Philips, Behn and others before her she manages to find her voice, which expresses itself in martial-minded lines set (oddly) within parentheses:

(Secure, and Threatning as a *Martial God*,
Among the thickest of his Foes he Rode;
And, like an Angry *Torrent* forc't his way
Through all the Horrors that in Ambush lay:)[43]

The appropriation of royalist imagery and language that marks the poem as a whole may underlie the comparison of William to an angry torrent, which recalls royalist uses of river imagery popularized in Denham's 'Cooper's Hill', where the river within its banks signifies monarchical restraint and stability. Here the figure of William-as-torrent expresses the revolutionary virtues of eruption, dynamism, and upheaval. The 'smiling *Naides*' who 'did him Homage as he pass'd' recall the kind of mythological apparatus beloved of courtly writers. (In her coronation ode Behn allows the 'Ravisht' naiades of the Thames three stanzas of their own.) Singer even deploys the idiom of monarchical divinity – William, a *'Martial God'*, possesses 'Sacred Heat' and 'Sacred Blood' – an idiom which at first seems strangely at odds with Whig political principles. This usage is, however, consistent with that found in other Whiggish verse of the time which, as Abigail Williams has shown, coopts royalist traditions of dynastic praise in order to legitimate William's, and later George I's, place in the line of succession.[44]

That the speaker averts her gaze from the scene of *'Death and Horror'* at the Boyne suggests a distaste for warfare and violence. The mildly pacific tendency of this poem is counterbalanced, however, by the zest for military force found elsewhere in Singer's verse and, indeed, in that of other whiggish women poets. Elizabeth Thomas (1677–1731), for example, obviously relishes her portrait of William at Namur, his *'sacred Person'* standing tall amid 'hissing *Bullets*' and 'Hurricane of *Fire* and *Blood*'.[45] Singer concludes 'A Pindarick Poem on Habbakuk' with a fierce call for military triumph that assumes God is a Whig and only too pleased to inflict humiliating punishment upon all who dare oppose her beloved William:

So now, great God, wrapt in avenging *Thunder*,
Meet thine and *William's Foes*, and tread them *groveling* under.[46]

'To Sir Thomas Travel', printed in the *Athenian Mercury*, 18 June 1695, celebrates male military heroism in lines that approvingly equate manliness, honour and bloodshed: Sir Thomas, 'prompted by a Manlier Blood', is urged to pursue 'Bright Honour, wading through a crimson Flood'. The association between femininity and pacifism that has come to seem almost natural in our time was not yet forged in Singer's; and her verse discovers a satisfaction in military force that has less to do with gender as we understand it than with Whig foreign policy.

The rise and fall of partisan rage

Women fed the 'rage of party' during the acrimonious reign of Queen Anne (1702–14). Among the best known of the party writers is playwright, fiction writer and Tory propagandist Delarivière Manley (*c.*1663–1724), sometime editor of the political journal the *Examiner*. Her medium of choice was not verse, however, but prose fiction, especially that scandalous mix of fact and fiction known as the 'secret history', best exemplified by the politically influential *New Atalantis* (1709). Her great political target, Sarah Churchill (1660–1744), first Duchess of Marlborough, is seldom thought of as a poet; but in 1708 Churchill, an ardent Whig, collaborated in a nasty ballad campaign directed against Anne's Tory confidante, the 'Dirty Chamber-Maid' Abigail Masham, smeared as a 'Slut of State' and charged with certain 'dark Deeds at night' with the queen.[47] The popular playwright Susannah Centlivre (1669?–1723), life-long champion of the Protestant succession, became 'outspoken' in her advocacy of the Whig cause, according to her modern biographer, and for the 'next five years service to the Whigs and the House of Hanover was central to her thought'.[48] She welcomed George I as the 'great Deliverer' of England from its Tory and Jacobite enemies in 1714, published party political verses in such Whig anthologies as *Mug House Songs* (1716), and lambasted Catholics at every opportunity, thereby securing the lasting enmity of Alexander Pope and a place in the 1728 *Dunciad*. In 1717, in the aftermath of the Jacobite uprising known as the 'Fifteen', the country was alarmed by rumours of a pro-Stuart invasion led by Swedish forces under the command of Charles XII. Where many Whig propagandists sought to stir up popular fears of a Jacobite invasion as a way of stiffening support for Hanover, Centlivre chose instead to poke fun at the Swedish king, a Jacobite hero (Anne Finch, for example, wrote verses in his praise), in a fascinating piece of anti-Jacobite satire, 'An Epistle to the King of Sweden, From a Lady of Great-Britain' (1717).

Centlivre's epistle to Charles XII, a mock version of the poem of female counsel to kings ('To *Thee* a WOMAN sends with Gen'rous Care,/And Warns thy Rashness timely to beware'), reveals important shifts in attitudes toward the female political subject. At the beginning of Anne's reign, as we saw earlier, the public-spirited speaker of Egerton's 'To the Queen' imagined herself bearing a sword in her monarch's service. Centlivre, not two decades later, replaces the sword with an equally metonymic fan that signals the relegation of women to the private, feminine and amatory sphere coming to stand alongside and apart from the sphere of politics, commerce and war – the public world of men. In the gender-divided world then under ideological construction, women exercised political agency by virtue of their influence: 'At *Flurt* of *Fan*, our armed Legions fly'. Centlivre's 'lovely Toasts', in this new understanding of woman's place in the political nation, mobilize men's energies with no more than a flick of the wrist: 'Each lovely Toast, her Hero's Soul inspires,/Urges the War, and wakes his Martial Fires'. The battlefield, moreover, is an extension of the drawing room. British soldiers, 'well-dress'd *Youths*' in this curiously devirilized imagining of war, go off to battle wearing lace, velvet stockings and snowy shirts. The odd mix of satire and fantasy at work in Centlivre's epistle, which weds the female warning-to-kings poem of the late Stuart era with modish notions about female influence of the early Georgian period, acknowledges and (arguably) protests female exclusion from the public sphere. We are reminded of Sarah Churchill's forthright complaint, in 1714, that she 'should have been the greatest Hero that ever was known in the Parliament Hous, if I had been so happy as to have been a Man'.[49]

During the reign of Anne and in the early years of the Georgian era women contributed significantly to the outpouring of political poetry that is one of the most often noted features of this period. The twenties onward mark a decline in obviously political poetry by men and women alike. Anne Finch in 'A Song on the South Sea, 1720', and Jane Barker in some lines on the South Sea bubble in her novel *A Patch-Work Screen for the Ladies* (1723), joined in the assault on the dangers and corruptions of the Whig financial revolution initiated during the Williamite nineties, for which the 1720 bubble was a convenient symbol, but on the whole the partisanship of earlier years gave way to the search for a unified national voice – one suitable for a Britain that increasingly identified itself with empire, international trade and naval supremacy. The new mood is felt in the volume of light verse published in 1734 by the Irish poet Mary Barber (c.1690–1757). The volume includes its share of poems on public themes, including at least one criticizing English policies in Ireland, but Barber seeks to distance herself from the partisanship of previous decades: the 'Muses are nor *Whig* nor *Tory*' and will not 'be judg'd by *Party* Zeal'.[50]

Public political verse no longer carried its old prestige and, as Christine Gerrard writes, 'the extensive network of Whig literary patronage . . . which had flourished under William III and continued into Anne's reign, dwindled significantly under the first two Hanoverians'.[51] But understandings of gender were changing as well, as Centlivre's vision of fan-flurting women as 'Arbitrators of the *War*' indicates, and one result of the complex of cultural shifts transforming Britain into a commercial empire was that women of middling and upper ranks assumed a role in the emerging modern state as consumers. Fashion and dress become new forms of public spirit. In the epilogue to *The Rival Father* (1730), written for Eliza Haywood, we can see that female political agency has been realigned to serve the needs of an expanding consumer society in which women wield not sword but fan:

There was a Time, old Authors tell us, when
Women were Patriots as well as Men:
In every Action of their Lives, 'tis said,
The Public Good ran always in their Head;
And oft this Zeal has urg'd 'em on so far,
As to embroil their little Hands in War.
But let our Heroines do whate'er they will,
'Tis wiser far for Women to – lie still.
A modern Female wears no Sword upon her,
A Fan's a fitter Weapon for her – Honour.
Many a one receives a Wound and – dies,
From a fair Hand skill'd in Fan-Exercise.

And they serve the 'Country's Good' by . . . shopping:

But yet, what proves the Patriot little less,
Our Ladies show their – Principles in – Dress.
In such Attire ye see 'em still appear,
Their Country's Good's express'd in what they wear.[52]

Several points to emerge in this account of women's political verse deserve underlining. First, the idea advanced first by Barash that women poets were attracted to myths and poetic practices associated with the sacred body of the monarch finds considerable support in the verse written in the first half of the long eighteenth century. The poetic role of monarchical advocate (or defender or counsellor) offered women of Whiggish as well as royalist and Jacobite outlooks a useful vehicle, an enabling fiction that served not only to authorize but in some cases to oblige women to speak out in verse, as Katherine Philips did in one of her earliest political poems. Her verse defence of the doubly murdered Charles I establishes the general pattern: the political ideal of fidelity and obligation to one's monarch trumps the patriarchal social ideal of female silence. Second, the assumption that the female political sensibility in the early modern period was predisposed toward royalist or Tory positions is not borne out by the evidence. In fact there is no consistent link to be found between conservative political principles and female public mindedness or between a Tory frame of reference and feminist assertion. The body of Whiggish verse examined here is sufficient proof that what once appeared to be a natural link between feminism and royalism is in no small part a matter of history, political circumstance and possibly opportunism. Much remains to be learned about the political dimensions of women's poetry during this period, but it is already clear that 'high' politics is integral to their achievement in ways that, just ten or twenty years ago, were almost completely unsuspected.

Notes

1. Carol Barash, *English Women's Poetry, 1649–1714: Politics, Community, and Linguistic Authority* (Oxford: Clarendon Press, 1996); Paula McDowell, *The Women of Grub Street: Press, Politics, and Gender in the London Literary Marketplace 1678–1730* (Oxford: Clarendon Press, 1998).
2. Andrew Shifflett, ' "Subdu'd by You": States of Friendship and Friends of the State in Katherine Philips's Poetry', in Barbara Smith and Ursula Appelt (eds), *Write or be Written: Early Modern Women Poets and Cultural Constraints* (Aldershot: Ashgate, 2001), pp. 177–95.
3. See the chapter on Philips in Andrew Shifflett, *Stoicism, Politics, and Literature in the Age of Milton: War and Peace Reconciled* (Cambridge: Cambridge University Press, 1998).
4. 'Upon the double murther of K. Charles, in answer to a libellous rime made by V. P.', discussed below, fell into the hands of one of her husband's political adversaries, one J. Jones, much to Philips's distress. See 'To the truly competent Judge of Honour, Lucasia, upon a scandalous libell made by J. Jones' and 'To Antenor, on a paper of mine wch J. Jones threatens to publish to his prejudice'.
5. Patrick Thomas (ed.), *The Poems: the Collected Works of Katherine Philips, the Matchless Orinda* (Stump Cross: Stump Cross Books, 1990), p. 70.
6. Ibid., p. 77.
7. Ibid., p. 72.

8. Elizabeth H. Hageman, 'The Matchless Orinda: Katherine Philips', in Katharina M. Wilson (ed.), *Women Writers of the Renaissance and Reformation* (Athens, Georgia, and London: University of Georgia Press, 1987), pp. 566–608 (601).
9. See Philips's 'On the 3d September 1651' for another equivocal image of the fallen Stuart monarchy.
10. Thomas, *Poems*, p. 321.
11. Ibid., p. 69.
12. For the emerging view of Hutchinson, see David Norbrook, 'Lucy Hutchinson's "Elegies" and the Situation of the Republican Woman Writer (with text)', *English Literary Renaissance* 27 (1997), pp. 468–521.
13. Barker's manuscript volume, 'A Collection of Poems Refering to the times', is discussed in my *Jane Barker, Exile: a Literary Career 1675–1725* (Oxford: Clarendon Press, 2000), pp. 101–43.
14. Janet Todd, *The Secret Life of Aphra Behn* (London: André Deutsch, 1996), p. 345.
15. 'A Pindarick on the Death of Our Late Sovereign', in Janet Todd (ed.), *The Works of Aphra Behn: Volume 1* (Columbus: Ohio State University Press, 1992), p. 195.
16. Ibid., p. 309.
17. Virginia Crompton, 'For when the act is done and finish't cleane,/what should the poet doe, but shift the scene? Propaganda, Professionalism and Aphra Behn', in Janet Todd (ed.), *Aphra Behn Studies* (Cambridge: Cambridge University Press, 1996), pp. 130–53 (148–9).
18. 'A dialogue between Fidelia and her little nephew, Martius', in Carol Shiner Wilson (ed.), *The Galesia Trilogy and Selected Manuscript Poems of Jane Barker* (New York and Oxford: Oxford University Press, 1997), p. 317.
19. 'Fidelia weeping for the Kings departure at the Revolution', cited in King, *Jane Barker*, p. 132.
20. Wilson, *Galesia Trilogy*, pp. 312, 313.
21. Ibid., p. 293.
22. Ibid., p. 302.
23. Ibid., p. 303.
24. Ibid., p. 305.
25. Myra Reynolds (ed.), *The Poems of Anne Countess of Winchilsea* (Chicago: University of Chicago Press, 1903), p. 13.
26. Reynolds, *Poems of Anne Countess of Winchilsea*, p. 73.
27. References to 'An Elegy on the Death of K. James' are from the printed version reproduced in Barash, *English Women's Poetry*, pp. 308–13.
28. See Barash, *English Women's Poetry*, Chapter 6.
29. Abigail Williams, 'Whig Literary Culture: Poetry, Politics, and Patronage, 1678–1714', D. Phil. thesis (Oxford: 2000), p. 8.
30. 'Poetical Question' to *Athenian Mercury*, 29 May 1694.
31. Sarah Prescott, *Women, Authorship and Literary Culture, 1690–1740* (Palgrave Macmillan, 2003), Chapter 5.
32. Carole Pateman, 'Women's Writing, Women's Standing: Theory and Politics in the Early Modern Period', in Hilda L. Smith (ed.), *Women Writers and the Early Modern British Political Tradition* (Cambridge: Cambridge University Press, 1998), pp. 365–82 (369).

33. Preface, *Poems on Several Occasions, by Philomela* (London: Dunton, 1696).
34. Sarah Fyge Egerton, *Poems on Several Occasions* (J. Nutt, 1703), pp. 19–21.
35. 'To the Ladies', in Margaret J. M. Ezell (ed.), *The Poems and Prose of Mary, Lady Chudleigh* (New York: Oxford University Press, 1993), p. 84.
36. Madeleine Forell Marshall (ed.), *The Poetry of Elizabeth Singer Rowe (1674–1737)* (Lewiston/Queenston: Edwin Mellen Press, 1987), p. 106.
37. Egerton, *Poems*, pp. 18, 19.
38. David Womersley, 'Introduction', *Augustan Critical Writing* (London: Penguin, 1997), p. xiv.
39. Marshall, *Poetry of Elizabeth Singer Rowe*, pp. 113–15.
40. Ibid., pp. 99–101.
41. Ibid., p. 135.
42. Rachel Weil, *Political Passions: Gender, the Family and Political Argument in England 1680–1714* (Manchester: Manchester University Press, 1999), p. 152.
43. Marshall, *Poetry of Elizabeth Singer Rowe*, p. 111.
44. See Williams, 'Whig Literary Culture', Chapter 2.
45. 'To King William. Occasionally Written on the Reading of a Libel', in Elizabeth Thomas, *Poems on Several Occasions. By a Lady* (London: Thomas Combes, 1726), p. 170.
46. Marshall, *Poetry of Elizabeth Singer Rowe*, p. 138.
47. See Frank H. Ellis (ed.), *Poems on Affairs of State: Augustan Satirical Verse, 1660–1714* (New Haven: Yale University Press, 1975), Vol. 7, pp. 306–16.
48. John Wilson Bowyer, *The Celebrated Mrs. Centlivre* (New York: Greenwood, 1968), p. 144. Centlivre rehearses her history as a partisan writer in 'A Woman's Case' (1720).
49. Frances Harris, *A Passion for Government: the Life of Sarah Duchess of Marlborough* (Oxford: Clarendon Press, 1991), p. 3.
50. 'To a Gentleman, who had abus'd Waller', in Mary Barber, *Poems on Several Occasions* (London: C. Rivington, 1735), p. 81.
51. Christine Gerrard, 'Political Passions', in John Sitter (ed.), *The Cambridge Companion to Eighteenth-Century Poetry* (Cambridge: Cambridge University Press, 2001), p. 42.
52. 'Epilogue', William Hatchett, *The Rival Father: or, the Death of Achilles* (London: 1730).

16
The Labouring-Class Women Poets: 'Hard Labour we most chearfully pursue'

Donna Landry

In the foreground of George Stubbs's painting *The Haymakers* (1785), a woman rests on her rake, hand on hip, bold-faced and provocative. It is not quite a come-hither look she gives, but very nearly. She also appears unabashed by the viewer's gaze, and somehow authoritative in returning it so coolly. What she isn't is meek. She neither courts our approval nor looks demurely downcast. The bold glance could easily signify resistance to rather than compliance with being looked at and represented. She does not hide herself from the painter, the spectator, the imagined appraisal of posterity.

Two of the earliest known English labouring-class women poets, Mary Collier and Mary Leapor, might easily have inspired Stubbs's bold-faced haymaker. This essay will assess the oeuvres of Collier and Leapor in the light of recent scholarship.[1] Rockclimbers ascending Parnasssus, they have got a fragile hold upon the slopes of the eighteenth-century canon.[2] Roger Lonsdale's *Eighteenth-Century Women Poets* (1989) was the major step in getting both poets back within reach of non-eighteenth-century specialist readers. David Fairer and Christine Gerrard's more recent *Eighteenth-Century Poetry: an Annotated Anthology* (1999), which gives the complete texts of Duck's *The Thresher's Labour* and Collier's *The Woman's Labour*, as well as seven poems by Leapor, goes even further.[3]

The emergence of the English working class's consciousness of itself as a class, as Raymond Williams observes, was first made 'evident' in 'the cultural process', including the production of working-class writing.[4] 'A new class is always a source of emergent cultural practice', Williams argues, 'but while it is still, as a class, relatively subordinate, this is always likely to be uneven and is certain to be incomplete'.[5] In working-class writing, then, 'the fundamental problem of emergence is clearly revealed', according to Williams. And this fundamental problem is the dominant culture's tendency to 'incorporate' emergent forms of cultural practice, such as working-class writing. The effect of such incorporation is to defuse any radical content or possible troubling of the mainstream that might result from such writing.

In the case of Collier's and Leapor's verse, to use Williams's terms, the basis of incorporation is already there in their work in 'the effective predominance of received literary forms – an incorporation, so to say, which already conditions and limits the emergence'.[6] If Collier and Leapor struggled to articulate the specificities of their experience in poetic forms previously associated with polite rather than plebeian culture, this should not be viewed as a fault or regrettable aesthetic choice. The artistry of both poets is at least as significant as their testimony of labouring-class experience. As Williams admits,

> What matters, finally, in understanding emergent culture, as distinct from both the dominant and the residual, is that it is never only a matter of immediate practice; indeed it depends crucially on finding new forms or adaptations of form. Again and again what we have to observe is in effect a *pre-emergence*, active and pressing but not yet fully articulated, rather than the evident emergence which could be more confidently named.[7]

By the mid-nineteenth century, working-class writing can be 'more confidently named' because of the existence of working-class movements and labour organizations, especially trades unions. Collier and Leapor articulated a class-inflected version of eighteenth-century verse before the time had come for more confident naming.

Collier, 'the washerwoman of Petersfield', and Leapor, a Northamptonshire kitchen maid, followed in the wake of Stephen Duck, a Wiltshire thresher, who had enjoyed considerable fame when his poems were first published in pirated editions – at least seven editions of *The Thresher's Labour*, his most famous poem, appeared in 1730, with further editions in 1731 and 1733.[8] Duck's *Poems on Several Occasions* (1736) was the first edition of his work to appear with his authority. Having obtained the patronage of local gentlemen, Duck became a protégé of Queen Caroline, which led to social advancement through a number of odd jobs including Yeoman of the Guard and librarian and tour guide for Queen Caroline's Library at 'Merlin's Cave' in Richmond Park. After the queen's death in 1737, public interest in Duck subsided, and in the 1740s his name largely disappeared from the literary periodicals.[9] In 1746 he took Holy Orders, becoming Rector of Byfleet in Surrey in 1752.[10] For reasons that shall forever remain mysterious (he appears to have left no surviving papers), Duck committed suicide in 1756.

Raymond Williams laments in *The Country and the City* that the thresher-poet was not able to perpetuate the innovative strain he had developed in *The Thresher's Labour*. There he had criticized the pastoral mode as inadequate for articulating the experience of agricultural labour, and produced something of a counter-pastoral, but as Williams observes,

> Within a few years Duck was writing, with the worst of them, his imitations from the classics, elevated and hollowed to the shapes of that fashionable culture which was not only a literary stance – the 'high' tradition – but, as always, a social ratification.[11]

Thus Williams allows us to admire *The Thresher's Labour*, but only as an unusual experiment of a kind which Duck was unable to sustain.

More recent criticism has attempted to revise this patronizing view by representing Duck, Collier and other labouring writers as first and foremost *writers*, and only secondarily as spokespeople for the working class. There is a danger of a kind of reverse prejudice creeping in if, in trying to rescue forgotten writers of lower-class backgrounds from what E. P. Thompson called 'the enormous condescension of posterity', we reduce their accomplishments to merely autobiographical testimony or statements of lived experience, denying them any access to the literary culture of their time.[12] As John Goodridge makes clear, a kind of injustice is being done when readers fail to acknowledge 'what (after all) was the central aspiration of Duck and Collier: to write poetry, to be poets'.[13]

'What fully to declare is past my Art', or is it? Mary Collier

What little we know of Mary Collier's life comes from her own hand. 'Some Remarks of the Author's Life drawn by herself' appeared in her collected *Poems* of 1762.[14] Collier tells us that she was born near Midhurst in Sussex 'of poor, but honest Parents' who taught her to read 'when very Young', to her 'great delight', but after her mother's death she 'lost' her 'Education, Never being put to school' (p. iii). As she grew up, she was 'set to such labour as the Country afforded' (p. iii). She looked after her ailing father until his death, at which time she went to Petersfield in Hampshire as a washerwoman, brewer and seasonal labourer (p. iii). She continued such work at Petersfield until, at 63, she became housekeeper at a farm near Alton (p. v). '[T]here I staid till turn'd of Seventy', she writes, 'And then the infirmities of Age rendered me incapable of the labour of that place', so that she had retired to a garret in Alton where she was 'endeavouring to pass the Relict' of her days 'in Piety, Purity, Peace, and an old Maid' (p. v). Collier claims to have been 72 when she wrote the final poem in the collection on the marriage of George III and Queen Charlotte, envisaging their coronation, which took place on 22 September 1761.[15] Collier was thus very likely born in the same year as Alexander Pope and Lady Mary Wortley Montagu, 1689/90 – a good year for poets! We hear no more of her after 1762.

Apart from these bare facts, the 'Remarks' is concerned entirely with Collier's reading and writing. From the first, she says,

> My Recreation was reading, I bought and borrow'd many Books, any foolish History highly delighted me; but as I grew Older I read Speed and Bakers Chronicles, Fox's Acts and Monuments of the Church, Josephus, and others. (*Poems*, p. iii)

A 'great delight' in reading, a propensity for 'any foolish History' – we might think of Arabella in Charlotte Lennox's *The Female Quixote* (1752) as this kind of reader. The pleasures of the foolishly, historically literary are well known to Collier before, along with the new sobriety of adulthood, piety kicks in. Then she reads as a good Anglican churchwoman should. When Duck's poems 'came abroad', she soon got them 'by heart', she reports, and though she fancied he had been 'too Severe on the Female Sex' – so that she wrote *The Woman's Labour* as the next best thing to calling 'an Army of Amazons to vindicate the injured Sex' – she was evidently inspired into verse-making by his example (p. iv).

Collier introduces the question of publication casually, as if she had never aspired to print:

> Therefore I answer'd him to please my own humour, little thinking to make it Public it lay by me several Years and by now and then repeating a few lines to amuse myself and entertain my Company, it got Air. (p. iv)

And so a local reputation for verse-making was born. The generation of *The Three Wise Sentences* from 1 Esdras 3 and 4, which was published as a companion piece to *The Woman's Labour* in 1739, is presented in a still more casual fashion. Collier 'happen'd' to nurse a gentlewoman who asked to be entertained by her verse-making. It is the first of a number of command performances (soon a gentleman is asking her to write something on the 'Subject of the Happy Husband', which resulted in 'The Happy Husband, and the Old Batchelor. A Dialogue', in *Poems*, p. iv). So successful was *The Three Wise Sentences* that the woman's husband could not stop talking about it. Collier's poetry became a matter not only for Petersfield gossip, but a 'Town Talk' – the object of London gossip as well:

> I happen'd to attend a Gentlewoman in a fit of Illness, and she and her Friends persuaded me to makes Verses on the Wise Sentences, which I did on such Nights as I waited on her. I had learn'd to write to assist my memory, and her Spouse transcrib'd it with a promise to keep it private, but he expos'd it to so many, that it soon Became a Town Talk, which made many advise me to have it printed and at length I comply'd to have it done at my own charge, I lost nothing, neither did I gain much, others run away with the profit. (p. iv)

Collier persuades us that she was all but coerced into going public. And that her first literary endeavour was not remunerative, at least for her – was it J. Roberts of Warwick Lane, her London bookseller, who 'run away with the profit'?[16] The price of this edition of *The Woman's Labour* and *The Three Wise Sentences* was six-pence – the same as a day's wage for female labourers, as Collier tells us in *The Woman's Labour*: 'Six-pence or Eight-pence pays us off at last' (line 199).[17]

Against this self-effacement, we should perhaps set the words of the 'Advertisement' to the 'New Edition' of Collier's *Poems* published in Petersfield. On the one hand, Collier is the humblest of the humble and 'without education', yet, on the other hand, she is so possessed of genius that only a lack of 'cultivation' has prevented her from becoming, not just a great poet, but one of the greatest poets of Great Britain – 'had her genius been cultivated, she would have ranked with the greatest poets of this kingdom'.[18]

Manual labour and any hint of 'cultivation' are thus mutually exclusive, in spite of the evidence presented by Collier herself. That she had no formal education, and certainly no opportunity to acquire genteel accomplishments, is clear enough. But by her own testimony, she was nothing if not self-cultivated – indeed she was such an enthusiastic autodidact that she used all the hours available to womankind for reading. We will return to the question of Collier as a nascently national poet later. For now we need only register the double-bind of the self-taught labourer. The unlettered poet warbling native woodnotes wild was also a sign of potential eternally unfulfilled. Collier appears as a muted, not-quite glorious Milton.[19]

Stephen Duck wrote as if he felt himself compelled to be a Poet. The trouble was that, as a farm labourer, he had a hard time making poetry from his own experience, despite a plenitude of English pastoral and georgic poems devoted to rural subjects. On the threshing floor, there was no opportunity for song or music, and nothing pleasing to look at, especially not the expected beauties of pastoral:

> The Eye beholds no pleasant Object here:
> No chearful Sound diverts the list'ning Ear.
> The Shepherd well may tune his Voice to sing,
> Inspir'd by all the Beauties of the Spring:
> No Fountains murmur here, no Lambkins play,
> No Linets warble, and no Fields look gay;
> 'Tis all a dull and melancholy Scene,
> Fit only to provoke the Muses Spleen. (ll. 56–63)[20]

This is a brilliant moment of innovation within the pastoral tradition as well as a plebeian georgic challenge to it. The thing that really gets to Duck about polite, gentlemanly pastoral is the shepherds' fancied leisure. With nothing else to do but watch the sheep, soothed by 'chearful' sounds of birds and fountains, why not sing or tell a story? The noise and dirt of the threshing floor put paid to all that. Readers are invited to be amazed that anyone could make poetry out of the total absence of the necessary features of it, but that is exactly what Duck has done, first by cataloguing what is absent from his prospect, and then by describing what is present, the substance of the poem.

Mary Collier derives a pleasure comparable to Duck's in the 'writing' of her testimony in *The Woman's Labour*, in the sheer literariness of it. She begins by addressing Duck directly – and ironically – as an 'Immortal Bard' and 'Fav'rite of the Nine' before reminding him that he was but 'lately' as 'poor and low' as the poet who addresses him thus. An appeal from one would-be immortal bard to another, then, is Collier's opening shot. But her difference from the poet who has been 'Enrich'd by Peers' and 'advanc'd by CAROLINE' is immediately apparent to her:

Accept these Lines: Alas! what can you have
From her, who ever was, and's still a Slave?
No learning ever was bestow'd on me;
My Life was always spent in Drudgery:
And not alone; alas! with Grief I find,
It is the Portion of poor Woman-kind. (5–10)

The voice is so confident, yet modest. It is bold without stridency, and calm without muffling its palpable hits. The rhyming of nine, as in muses, with Caroline, as in royal promoter, establishes an equation between Duck's being recognized as a poet at all and his conscription by the powerful. The patronage machine is inseparable from the very definition of a poet. We should remember this when we come to read 'On The Marriage of George the Third'.

If the poet has never had any learning 'bestowed' upon her, she has obtained it by other means. Collier's next move is to invite us to think of her, fatigued from manual labour, using the very classical learning she has been denied to work out one of the knottier problems in human history: how to explain female drudgery in general, and women's subordination to men in particular? This fact of life strikes the weary poet as inexplicable, given the divine origins of humanity. The only explanation she can offer is that familiarity bred contempt:

Oft have I thought as on my Bed I lay.
Eas'd from the tiresome Labours of the Day,
Our first Extraction from a Mass refin'd,
Could never be for Slavery design'd;
'Till Time and Custom by degrees destroy'd
That happy State our Sex at first enjoy'd . . .
JOVE once descending from the clouds, did drop
In Show'rs of Gold on lovely *Danae's* Lap;
The sweet-tongu'd Poets, in those generous Days,
Unto our Shrine still offer'd up their Lays:
But now, alas! that Golden Age is past,
We are the Objects of your Scorn at last. (11–16, 25–30)

'Time and Custom' have been the enemies of women. Age has withered and custom staled what was once a harmonious relationship between the sexes. The most recent instance of this is Duck's ridiculing of female farmworkers in order to achieve a literary effect. Goodridge celebrates the 'splendid classicism' of Collier's writing in the above passage while remarking that there is an element of burlesque in it too that makes Duck's own classicism seem rather heavy.[21] When Collier turns to analyzing Duck's poem line by line, she repeats her formulation that Duck was not content to consign women to oblivion:

> But on our abject State you throw your Scorn,
> And Women wrong, your Verses to adorn. (41–2)

According to Goodridge, this observation is 'acutely perceptive', recognizing as it does Duck's 'primarily literary intentions'.[22] Duck's 'concern with style at the expense of content' and his failure to think very much at all about what women do in the hayfield, or anywhere for that matter, does not excuse his male chauvinism, according to Goodridge, but it might help explain how it came to figure so large in *The Thresher's Labour*.[23]

Collier's own best writing in this poem thus subtly out-distances Duck's in literary accomplishment as well as seeming verisimilitude. Like Duck, Collier represents the chief events of the agricultural year, from haymaking in early summer through late summer's harvest, and on into winter, portrayed as a season of perpetual charring where Duck gives us threshing. Collier's central argument is that however hard working men work for their wages, women of the same class face a triple shift – of waged labour, housework and child care. How would the haycocks ever get erected, mocks Collier, if the women raking and turning the hay didn't make them? Duck appears not to have noticed this. He seems to have been as negligent an observer of women's work as many eighteenth-century gentlemen and the landscape painters they employed were of agricultural work generally.[24] However humble and 'low' the male labourer might have been regarded as being, his female counterpart was lower still, and even more badly paid.[25]

Against Duck's criticism of women haymakers as idle chatterers, Collier defends women's right to conversation and gossip:

> Since you have Liberty to speak your Mind,
> And are to talk, as well as we, inclin'd,
> Why should you thus repine, because that we,
> Like you, enjoy that pleasing Liberty?
> What! would you lord it quite, and take away
> The only Privilege our Sex enjoy? (69–74)

Collier has seized her freeborn liberty of speech. 'Against your coming Home' (77), she retorts, women labour twice over. First there is the boiling in the pot of the '*Bacon* and *Dumpling*' (79) that Duck was rather snooty about. Duck implied that men, exhausted with their competitive scything in the field after having turned haymaking into an epic contest, go wearily home, only to be treated indifferently, if not actually nagged, by their wives:

> Our good expecting Wives, who think we stay,
> Got to the Door, soon eye us in the way;
> Then from the Pot the Dumpling's catch'd in haste,
> And homely by its side the Bacon's plac'd.
> (Duck, *Thresher's Labour*, 153–6)

Anyone would think that these good wives begrudged their mates a bite of supper! Or is it that the food can never be served up fast enough? Or that the men would prefer some much less homely fare? From Duck's point of view, food is clearly 'an issue', as we say – a site of conflict. What Collier suggests, however, is that cooking, if it happens to be performed with unseemly haste, is just one task within the never-ending cycle of female housekeeping, along with provisioning, bed-making, pig-feeding, table-setting, clothes-mending – and then there are the children to be attended to! The pleasures of chatting it merrily in the hayfield are the only sociable consolation these women have to look forward to, and the idea of this as their 'only Privilege' is thus highly ironical. English marriage for women, among the poor at least, is a kind of 'Orientalized' slavery, reminiscent of the Ottoman empire: 'For none but *Turks*, that ever I could find,/Have Mutes to serve them' (Collier, *Woman's Labour*, 66–7).

The poem's aesthetic climax occurs as the women pit their strength (and desperate need for a wage) against heaps of washing, pots and pewter to be scoured, beer to be brewed, and a penny-pinching and dishonest mistress to be satisfied. (Presumably those of Collier's employers who applauded her verses, especially those who subscribed to the *Poems*, failed to identify themselves as the originals for this caricature.) The hardest toil provides the most rewarding material, neatly summarized by the line 'Hard Labour we most chearfully pursue' (137). The enormity of the 'Hardships' experienced during living-out charring is, Collier opines, 'What fully to declare is past my Art' (140–1). There is no need to be taken in by the inexpressibility topos. Collier comes as close as anyone has to making her art declare fully the hardships of female labourers in the eighteenth century.

> Heaps of fine Linen we before us view,
> Whereon to lay our Strength and Patience too;
> Cambricks and Muslins, which our Ladies wear,
> Laces and Edgings, costly, fine, and rare,
> Which must be wash'd with utmost Skill and Care;
> With Holland Shirts, Ruffles and Fringes too,
> Fashions which our Fore-fathers never knew. (157–63)

The gap between rich and poor is nowhere more apparent than in clothing, it would seem. The gentry even in country districts are wearing imported ornamental textiles – French, Indian, or Dutch – a luxury unknown to previous generations. These new luxuries demand new skills for their maintenance. Hence the mistress's concern as she arrives to supervise, well after sunrise, and rather careless of the women's comfort: 'And in her Hand, *perhaps*, a Mug of Ale' (171). The mistress admonishes them not to 'her Cambricks nor her ruffles tear':

> And *these* most strictly does of us require,
> *To save her soap, and sparing be of Fire*;
> Tells us her Charge is great, nay furthermore,
> Her Cloaths are fewer than the Time before.
> Now we drive on, resolv'd our Strength to try,
> And what we can, we do most willingly;
> Until with Heat and Work, 'tis often known,
> Not only Sweat, but Blood runs trickling down
> Our Wrists and Fingers; still our Work demands
> The constant Action of our lab'ring Hands. (177–87)

Combined with the seemingly effortless classicism of the epic formulations – 'resolv'd our Strength to try' – the driving rhythm here makes the poetry of strenuous labour splendidly transcend the sordidness of its conditions. Mary Collier forged tensile poetry from what she knew and resented. In this respect she has something in common with another woman poet of the previous century. In two poems about hunting, Margaret Cavendish, Duchess of Newcastle, managed to criticize bloodsports as callous and cruel while simultaneously reproducing in the very textures of her verse the music and rhythmical excitements of hunting:

The *Hornes* kept time, the *Hunters* shout for *Joy*,
And valiant seeme, *poore Wat* for to destroy:
Spurring their *Horses* to a full *Career*,
Swim rivers deep, leap Ditches without feare;
Indanger *Life*, and *Limbes*, so fast will ride,
Onely to see how patiently *Wat* died. (73–8)[26]

Collier's washing contest is similarly a fusion of revulsion and exult-
ation.

The Woman's Labour is undoubtedly Collier's greatest poetic achievement. Her radical remaking of the georgic in a distinctly female and
plebeian form is unmatched by any other poet of the eighteenth century. What then of the claim that, had she been allowed a genteel
education, she would have ranked with the greatest poets of the kingdom? At the close of her *Poems*, Collier might well have made a final
bid for the kind of royal patronage which Duck, whose death she
mourns in 'An Elegy upon Stephen Duck', had enjoyed:

AWAKE, My Muse! once more thyself display,
Since thou hast liv'd to See this happy day,
Great George the Third Adorns the British Throne;
In room of's Royal Grandsire lately Gone:
Whose blooming Youth in Virtue's paths hath Spent
Presages wonders from his Government:
As if the Glories of his Royal line,
Center'd in one shall on our Monarch Shine,
Auspicious Heav'n protect him all his days,
And crown his Brows with never fading Bays,
Let the Diadem sit easy on his Head,
His Enemies be fill'd with fear and dread! (1–12)

Collier's Protestant patriotism is ecstatic. She embraces the Hanoverian
succession and claims George III as her own private monarch. The
poem represents national concerns in ways none of her other writing
has ventured to do:[27]

If Heav'n will bless, none shall his Arms withstand,
His floating Fleets by Sea, or Troops by Land.
Let my thoughts roam beyond the British flood,
To trace the Lustre of the German Blood.
Our Annals will in future Ages Shine

With brightest splendour of the Royal Line
From whence our Liberty and safety Springs,
In the Succession of three Noble Kings,
By Heaven sent to save our Native lands,
From Popish Slavery and Tyrants Hands. (13–22)

Between the 1750s and the 1770s, Harriet Guest has argued, learned or accomplished women could for the first time be celebrated as representing the greatness of the British nation.[28] Collier's patriotic sentiments would have been welcomed as confirmation of the civilizing force of Britishness, forging Britons from a heterogeneity of English, Welsh, Scots, and even to some extent Irish, people.[29] If even a washerwoman could write so eloquently about the new king's imperial mission, then Britain must be the finest nation in the world. So far as we know, Collier's patriotism went unremunerated. But she had caught the temper of the times well enough to make a bid for herself as a national laureate.

'And who so frolick as the Muse and I?' Mary Leapor

In spite of her tragically early death at 24, Mary Leapor achieved greater fame than Mary Collier during the eighteenth century. Her poems were published posthumously in two volumes in 1748 and 1751.[30] As late as 1791, in seeking to praise the poet Elizabeth Bentley, a journeyman shoemaker's daughter from Norwich, William Cowper singled out Leapor as a lowborn poet of exceptional genius:

> In the present instance . . . (the poems of a certain Mrs. Leapor excepted, who published some 40 years ago) I discern, I think, more marks of a true poetical talent than I remember to have observed in the verses of any, whether male or female, so disadvantageously circumstanced.[31]

Leapor's reputation among modern scholars similarly appears set fair for her to arrive at permanent inclusion in the eighteenth-century canon.

That Leapor was perceived as something of a national treasure, in the way that learned and accomplished women had come to be seen by 1755, is demonstrated by her inclusion in two mid-century tributes to women poets. In 1755 George Colman and Bonnell Thornton brought out *Poems by Eminent Ladies. Particularly, Mrs. Barber, Mrs. Behn,*

Miss Carter, Lady Chudleigh, . . . Cntss. of Winchilsea, 118 pages of which are devoted to Leapor, more pages than are occupied by any other poet, including Aphra Behn and Anne Finch, Countess of Winchilsea.[32] Thornton also produced a remarkable essay in his periodical *The Connoisseur* the same year, advertizing the book. One by one the women must mount Pegasus, the horse of poetry, and ride him to the best of their abilities. After her show, the Duchess of Newcastle is helped to dismount by Shakespeare and Milton, Aphra Behn, who rides astride, is embraced by Lord Rochester, and Swift holds the stirrup for Mrs Barber to mount, but Leapor performs unassisted:

> Among the rest I could not but wonder at the astonishing dexterity, with which the admired Mrs. LEAPOR of *Brackley* guided the horse, though she had not the least direction or assistance from any body.[33]

As Harriet Guest remarks regarding this essay, 'Writing poetry seems indistinguishable from dressage, or from dressing elegantly; it is an appropriate feminine accomplishment.'[34] And appropriate even for a kitchen maid, it would seem, since Leapor had been in domestic service while writing most of her verse.

Mary Leapor was born on 26 February 1722 at Marston St Lawrence in Northamptonshire while her father, Philip Leapor, was gardener to Sir John Blencowe (1642–1726), former Member of Parliament for Brackley, Baron of the Exchequer and Justice of the King's Bench. After Blencowe's death, Philip Leapor moved to nearby Brackley with his wife and only daughter and started a nursery business. Leapor went into service as an adolescent, first at Weston Hall in the household of Susanna Jennens, Blencowe's daugher. The library at Weston Hall contains three sets of Leapor's poems, including one copy of the first volume inscribed 'Once Kitchen maid at Weston'.[35] Latterly she was employed at Edgcote House by the Chauncy family, an experience that inspired her most important poem, *Crumble-Hall*. She appears to have been dismissed from their employ in 1745, at least in part for writing when she should have been performing more menial tasks, at which point she returned to keep house for her widowed father (her mother had died in 1741). During this time she struck up a friendship with Bridget Freemantle, daughter of the rector of nearby Hinton, who became her patron and reported most of what is known about Leapor's life in a letter prefixed to the second volume of poems in 1751.[36]

Although Freemantle seems to have been at pains to minimize the extent of Leapor's education, Greene and other critics have found deep resonances in her work of many English poets from the Restoration onwards.[37] She had undoubtedly read a great deal more than was acknowledged by Freemantle's assertion that 'Mrs. LEAPOR's whole Library consisted of about sixteen or seventeen single Volumes, among which were part of Mr. *Pope's* Works, *Dryden's* Fables, some volumes of Plays, &c.'[38] As Greene comments, 'That an intelligent labouring person should be portrayed as a prodigy or a marvel is plain snobbery, yet it was a necessary part of the subscription process for the poet to face this humiliation'.[39]

Two of Leapor's ideologically boldest poems also rank among her most aesthetically successful. In the first, 'Man the Monarch', Leapor adopts a strain common in Englishwomen's verse from Margaret Cavendish onwards. 'The Hunting of the Hare' closes with an accusation that humankind, or rather, the female poet insinuates, the male of the species, behaves as if all other species were subject to his tyrannical dominion:

And that all *Creatures* for his sake alone,
Was made for him, to *Tyrannize* upon. (105–6)

This assertion of masculine tyranny is reiterated by Anne Finch, Countess of Winchilsea, in her 'A Nocturnal Reverie':

Their shortliv'd Jubilee the Creatures keep,
Which but endures, whilst Tyrant-*Man* do's sleep: . . .
In such a *Night* let Me abroad remain,
Till Morning breaks, and All's confus'd again; (37–8, 47–8)[40]

Both poets imply by the way they position themselves within their verse, by their narratorial stance, that as women they too are subjected to this human tyranny along with the rest of the creation. In 'Man the Monarch' Leapor wittily explores how such an injustice can have come about, using, like Collier, supposedly inaccessible erudition to think her way back to a prehistoric explanation for male dominance and female subordination. But unlike Collier, Leapor joins Cavendish and Finch in yoking Man's subjugation of women with his instrumental relation to Nature and other species:

Amaz'd we read of Nature's early Throes:
How the fair Heav'ns and pond'rous Earth arose:

How blooming Trees unplanted first began;
And Beasts submissive to their Tyrant, Man:
To Man, invested with despotic Sway,
While his mute Brethren tremble and obey;
Till Heav'n beheld him insolently vain,
And check'd the Limits of his haughty Reign.
Then from their Lord the rude Deserters fly,
And, grinning back, his fruitless Rage defy;
Pards, Tygers, Wolves, to gloomy Shades retire,
And Mountain-Goats in purer Gales respire . . .
Then joyful Birds ascend their native Sky:
But where! ah! where, shall helpless Woman fly? (1–12, 22–3)

The divine plan provides an escape route for all animals except human females, who are doomed to endure domestication instead of lighting out for the wild. Women, although daughters of Nature herself and thus fashioned to reign, are too weak to withstand Man's tyranny, from which all other species have fled. Leapor satirically offers a 'tattling Dame's' (l. 50) tale to explain how Man came to behave so badly. It was all the birds' fault, it seems, since the superior plumage of male birds gave Adam ideas and caused him to look enviously at Eve:

When our Grandsire nam'd the feather'd Kind,
Pond'ring their Natures in his careful Mind,
'Twas then, if on our Author we rely,
He view'd his Consort with an envious Eye;
Greedy of Pow'r, he hugg'd the tott'ring Throne;
Pleased with the Homage, and would reign alone;
And, better to secure his doubtful Rule,
Roll'd his wise Eye-balls, and pronounc'd her *Fool.*
The regal Blood to distant Ages runs:
Sires, Brothers, Husbands, and commanding Sons,
The Sceptre claim; and ev'ry Cottage brings
A long Succession of Domestic Kings. (54–65)

Patriarchal government and male governance, then, are a bluff. In the beginning there was on Adam's part a gesture of greedy self-assertion. Thus might the book of Genesis be disputed by popular tradition, the voice of a tattling Dame. The Popeian couplets ring with all the assurance of *An Essay on Man*. Laura Mandell has found Leapor's vantage point in this poem to be 'an as yet only ironic space . . . where the female body is neither idealized nor degraded.'[41] This space, Mandell argues, is a space of negativity 'pregnant with disruptive power that does not slip into yet another empirical positivity', and this is precisely the space that properly historicist feminist criticism 'needs continually to recover'.[42]

Like Collier, Leapor is a past-mistress of potentially feminist irony, and she is nothing if not fearlessly witty in her engagement with the traditions of English poetry. It should not surprise us that Leapor produced in *Crumble-Hall* a country-house poem that parodies the entire genre, an anti-country-house poem. Valerie Rumbold argues that as a dismissed servant, Leapor capitalized on her 'alienated insider' status to satirize both the conventions of country-house poetry and of the country-house guide-book, which was becoming a popular genre in the 1740s.[43] This sceptical detachment meant that Leapor spared nobody in her satire, not even her former fellow servants. Sophronia, brilliant at puddings and pastries, appears to be a snob about her rank in the service hierarchy, Colinettus dreams bovinely when not fretting about rain spoiling his hay, and Gruffo glares about him as he doles out the ale at lunchtime as if fearing an insurrection (whether more from the thirsty or the drunken is ambiguous), but Ursula has eyes only for Roger:

> O'er-stuff'd with Beef; with Cabbage much too full,
> And Dumpling too (fit Emblem of his Skull!)
> With Mouth wide open, but with closing Eyes,
> Unwieldy *Roger* on the Table lies.
> His able Lungs discharge a rattling Sound:
> *Prince* barks, Spot howls, and the tall Roofs rebound.
> Him *Urs'la* views; and, with dejected Eyes,
> 'Ah! *Roger*, Ah!' the mournful Maiden cries:
> 'Is wretched *Urs'la* then your Care no more,
> That, while I sigh, thus you can sleep and snore?
> Ingrateful *Roger*! wilt thou leave me now?
> For you these Furrows mark my fading Brow:
> For you my Pigs resign their Morning Due:
> My hungry Chickens lose their Meat for you:
> And, was it not, Ah! was it not for thee,
> No goodly Pottage would be dress'd by me.
> For thee these hands wind up the whirling Jack,
> Or place the Spit across the sloping Rack.

I baste the Mutton with a chearful heart,
Because I know my *Roger* will have part.'
Thus she – But now her Dish-kettle began
To boil and blubber with the foaming Bran. (130–51)

Even below stairs – or rather, especially below stairs, since upstairs seems remarkably empty – maids languish in unrequited love for man-servants. Ursula's single-minded passion for Roger makes her neglect even the pigs and poultry of which she is otherwise so proud, for serving him is not like work at all, but love (remember Collier's notion of marriage as 'Orientalized' slavery). The problem with satirizing liter-ary conventions – in this case pastoral laments – is that they rub off on one's own writing. Is Leapor responsible for yet another comic pastoral which is funny at the expense of vernacularly boorish labourers failing to live up to classical precedents? It is all too easy, as Mandell suggests, for 'rhetoric and parody' to 'slip into realism and misogyny'.[44] I would agree with Mandell that Leapor's manipulation of irony *just* makes it possible to rescue a moment of brilliant critique of these very matters from within the undecidable oscillation of satire.

Who but Leapor would have thought to parody, while describing the state of Roger's digestion, Sir John Denham's famous lines about the Thames?

Though deep, yet clear, though gentle, yet not dull,
Strong without rage, without ore-flowing full. (191–2)[45]

The couplet describes the river as a model of proper political govern-ance, but also of desirable aesthetic balance. Leapor transposes these qualities into her description of a replete and snoring body to splendid comic effect, no doubt pleasing her gentry readers by appealing to their prejudices, but also very possibly drawing their attention to the literariness of that very transposition. Similarly, the snores and the dogs' voices rebound against the roofs in that most familiar of Augustan tropes. Hackneyed imitation of her betters, or coin of the realm of verse? Like Collier and Duck before her, Leapor appears to have written because she could make verses, because she could not *not* write verse. Like Chatterton's or Keats's, Leapor's early death has meant that her work has been read within the poignant context of potential unfulfilled. As this essay has suggested, this principle has in fact governed the reception of all English labouring-class poets.

Notes

1. Landry, *The Muses of Resistance: Laboring-Class Women's Poetry in Britain, 1739–1796* (Cambridge and New York: Cambridge University Press, 1990), predates the criticism discussed here, as does my 'The Resignation of Mary Collier: Some Problems in Feminist Literary History', in Felicity Nussbaum and Laura Brown (eds), *The New Eighteenth Century: Theory-Politics-English Literature* (New York and London: Methuen, 1987), pp. 99–120.

2. Such is not yet the case with Jean Adams (1710–65), a Scottish shipmaster's daughter, who was orphaned at an early age, worked as a maid and governess for the Rev. Mr Turner of Greenock, and published *Miscellany Poems* at Glasgow in 1734. We must await the appearance of a study in progress by Bill Overton of Loughborough University. Three of Adams's poems are included by Roger Lonsdale in his anthology, *Eighteenth-Century Women Poets: an Oxford Anthology* (Oxford and New York: Oxford University Press, 1989), pp. 141–5.

3. Lonsdale, *Eighteenth-Century Women Poets*, and David Fairer and Christine Gerrard, *Eighteenth-Century Poetry: an Annotated Anthology* (Oxford and Malden, MA: Blackwell Publishers, 1999). Collier made a brief appearance in Sheila Rowbotham's *Hidden from History: Rediscovering Women in History from the 17th Century to the Present* (New York: Pantheon, 1974), pp. 25–6, and Moira Ferguson's *First Feminists: British Women Writers 1578–1799* (Bloomington: Indiana University Press and Old Westbury, NY: The Feminist Press, 1985), pp. 257–65. See also John Barrell, 'Sportive Labour: the Farmworker in Eighteenth-Century Poetry and Painting', in Brian Short (ed.), *The English Rural Community: Image and Analysis* (Cambridge: Cambridge University Press, 1992), pp. 105–32, and Mary Chamberlain, *Fenwomen* (London: Quartet Books for Virago, 1975). Duck's and Collier's major poems had previously been paired and edited by Moira Ferguson, *The Thresher's Labour (Stephen Duck) and The Woman's Labour (Mary Collier)*, Augustan Reprint 230 (Los Angeles: William Andrews Clark Memorial Library, 1985), and Marian Sugden and Edward P. Thompson (eds), *The Thresher's Labour by Stephen Duck and The Woman's Labour by Mary Collier: Two Eighteenth Century Poems* (London: The Merlin Press, 1989).

4. Raymond Williams, *Marxism and Literature* (Oxford: Oxford University Press, 1977), p. 124

5. Ibid., p. 124.

6. Ibid., p. 124.

7. Ibid., p. 126.

8. Sugden and Thompson, 'Editorial Note', in Thompson and Sugden, *The Thresher's Labour and The Woman's Labour*, pp. 27–30; this passage on p. 27.

9. Morag Shiach, *Discourse on Popular Culture: Class, Gender and History in Cultural Analysis, 1730 to the Present* (Stanford, CA: Stanford University Press, 1989), p. 51.

10. For Duck's life, see Rose Mary Davis, *Stephen Duck: the Thresher Poet*, University of Maine Series 2, 8 (Orono, ME: University of Maine, 1926).

11. Raymond Williams, *The Country and the City* (New York: Oxford University Press, 1973), p. 90.

12. E. P. Thompson, *The Making of the English Working Class* (1963; London: Victor Gollancz, 1980): 'I am seeking to rescue the poor stockinger, the Luddite cropper, the "obsolete" hand-loom weaver, the "utopian" artisan, and even the deluded follower of Joanna Southcott, from the enormous condescension of posterity' (p. 14).
13. John Goodridge, *Rural Life in Eighteenth-Century English Poetry* (Cambridge: Cambridge University Press, 1995), p. 21.
14. Mary Collier, 'Some Remarks of the Author's Life drawn by herself', in British Library shelfmark 11632.f.12, to which I shall refer hereafter as *Poems* (title-page missing; spine reads: Collier. *Poems*. Winchester, 1762), pp. iii–v. There are two collected editions of her poems now in the British Library, probably both published in 1762. See also British Library shelfmark 11658.de.53, *The Poems Of Mary Collier, The Washerwoman Of Petersfield; To which is prefixed her Life, Drawn By Herself. A New Edition* (Petersfield: W. Minchin, n.d.).
15. Linda Colley, *Britons: Forging the Nation 1701–1837* (New Haven and London: Yale University Press, 1992), p. 202.
16. *The Woman's Labour: an Epistle to Mr. Stephen Duck; In Answer to his late Poem, called The Thresher's Labour. To which are added, The Three Wise Sentences, taken from The First Book of Esdras, Ch. III. and IV.*, By Mary Collier, Now a Washer-woman, at Petersfield in Hampshire (London: Printed for the Author; Sold by J. Roberts, in Warwick-lane and at the Pamphlet-Shops near the Royal Exchange, 1739).
17. I take as my text the first edition of 1739, also the text chosen by Fairer and Gerrard.
18. 'Advertisement', *The Poems Of Mary Collier . . . A New Edition*, p. iii.
19. Thomas Gray, *Elegy Written in a Country Church Yard* (1751): 'Some mute inglorious Milton here may rest' (line 59).
20. I take my text from Duck's first edition of 1730, also the text chosen by Fairer and Gerrard.
21. Goodridge, *Rural Life*, p. 13.
22. Ibid., p. 19.
23. Ibid., p. 20.
24. On the minimizing or careful managing of rural labour in agricultural landscapes, both poetic and painterly, see John Barrell, *The Dark Side of the Landscape: the Rural Poor in English Painting 1730–1840* (Cambridge: Cambridge University Press, 1980).
25. What is most remarkable is how little rural women's wages seem to have changed beween 1739 and the nineteenth century, given the rise in prices. As late as 1843, in Wiltshire, Dorset, Devon and Somerset at least, the average women's wage remained 'six-pence or eight-pence' a day in winter; Ivy Pinchbeck, *Women Workers and the Industrial Revolution 1750–1850* (1930; London: Virago, 1981), p. 95.
26. 'The Hunting of the Hare', in *POEMS, and Fancies*, Written by the Right Honourable, the Lady Newcastle (London: Printed by T. R. for J. Martin and J. Allestrye, 1653; fac. rpt Menston, Yorks.: Scolar Press, 1972).
27. As Moira Ferguson observes in *Eighteenth-Century Women Poets: Nation, Class, and Gender* (Albany: State University of New York Press, 1995), p. 24.

242 Women and Poetry, 1660–1750

28. Harriet Guest, *Small Change: Women, Learning, Patriotism, 1750–1810* (Chicago and London: University of Chicago Press, 2000), pp. 49–92.
29. See Colley, *Britons*; Paul Langford, *A Polite and Commercial People: England 1727–1783* (Oxford and New York: Oxford University Press, 1992); and Gerald Newman, *The Rise of English Nationalism: a Cultural History 1740–1830* (London: Weidenfeld and Nicolson, 1987).
30. *Poems, Upon Several Occasions, By Mrs. Leapor of Brackley in Northamptonshire*, 2 vols (London: J. Roberts, 1748–51). James Roberts had published Duck's and some of Collier's work. The 'Rever. Mr. Stephen Duck' is listed as a subscriber to Leapor's first volume. In two ground-breaking articles, 'Christopher Smart, the "C. S." Poems, and Molly Leapor's Epitaph', *The Library*, sixth series, 5 (March 1983), pp. 22–31, and 'Molly Leapor: an Anxiety for Influence', in Paul J. Korshin (ed.), *The Age of Johnson: a Scholarly Annual* 4 (New York: AMS Press, 1991), pp. 313–43, Betty Rizzo established that Samuel Richardson printed the second volume, edited by Isaac Hawkins Browne, and that Leapor's chief patron was Bridget Freemantle.
31. James King and Charles Ryskamp (eds), *The Letters and Prose Writings of William Cowper*, 5 vols (Oxford: Oxford University Press, 1979–86), Vol. 3 (1982), p. 485.
32. [Colman and Thornton], *Poems by Eminent Ladies*, 2 vols (London: Printed for R. Baldwin, 1755). The collection was popular enough for a Dublin reprint in 1757 and a new revised edition in 1773, *Poems by the Most Eminent Ladies of Great Britain and Ireland* (London: Printed for T. Becket and Co. and T. Evans, 1773). Leapor's prominence has been computed by Richard Greene, *Mary Leapor: a Study in Eighteenth-Century Women's Poetry* (Oxford: Clarendon Press, 1993), p. 31, who observes that, even in the revised version, Leapor was still the most heavily represented poet.
33. *The Connoisseur, By Mr. Town, Critic, and Censor-General*, No. 69 (Thursday, 22 May 1755), 2 vols (London: Printed for R. Baldwin, 1755), Vol. 1, pp. 409–14 (413).
34. Guest, *Small Change*, p. 87.
35. Greene, *Mary Leapor*, p. 10.
36. On Edgcote House and dismissal, see Greene, *Mary Leapor*, pp. 15–17, 117–19, 153; on her mother's death, p. 188; on Freemantle, pp. 17–21.
37. Greene, *Mary Leapor*, pp. 171–85. Margaret Anne Doody makes a persuasive case for Swift's influence in 'Swift among the Women', *The Yearbook of English Studies* 18 (1988) pp. 68–92; on Leapor, pp. 79–82. For Pope's influence, see Caryn Chaden, 'Mentored from the Page: Mary Leapor's Relationship with Alexander Pope', in Donald C. Mell (ed.), *Pope, Swift, and Women Writers* (Newark, DE: University of Delaware Press; London: Associated University Presses, 1996), pp. 31–47.
38. *Poems*, Vol. 2, p. xxxii.
39. Greene, *Mary Leapor*, p. 161.
40. Text from Winchilsea's *Miscellany Poems* of 1713, in Fairer and Gerrard, *Eighteenth-Century Poetry*.
41. Laura Mandell, 'Demystifying (with) the Repugnant Female Body: Mary Leapor and Feminist Literary History,' *Criticism* 38 (Fall 1991), pp. 551–82 (575); reprinted in *Misogynous Economies: the Business of Literature in*

Eighteenth-Century Britain (Lexington, KY: University Press of Kentucky, 1999), pp. 84–106.

42. Mandell, 'Demystifying', p. 575.
43. Valerie Rumbold, 'The Alienated Insider: Mary Leapor in "Crumble Hall" ', *British Journal for Eighteenth-Century Studies* 19,1 (Spring 1996), pp. 63–76, which draws upon Carole Fabricant's 'The Literature of Domestic Tourism and the Public Consumption of Private Property', in Nussbaum and Brown (eds), *New Eighteenth Century*, pp. 254–75.
44. Mandell, 'Demystifying', p. 564
45. *Coopers Hill*, 'B' Text (1655, 1668), in Brendan O Hehir (ed.), *Expans'd Hieroglyphicks: a Critical Edition of Sir John Denham's Coopers Hill* (Berkeley and Los Angeles: University of California Press, 1969).

Bibliography

Anthologies

Fairer, David, and Christine Gerrard (eds), *Eighteenth-Century Poetry: an Annotated Anthology*, Blackwell Annotated Anthologies (Oxford: Blackwell, 1999)

Greer, Germaine, Susan Hastings, Jeslyn Medoff and Melinda Sansone (eds), *Kissing the Rod: an Anthology of Seventeenth-Century Women's Verse* (London: Virago Press, 1988)

Lonsdale, Roger (ed.), *Eighteenth-Century Women Poets* (Oxford: Oxford University Press, 1989)

Salzman, Paul (ed.), *Early Modern Women's Writing 1560–1700* (Oxford: Oxford University Press, 2000)

Stevenson, Jane, and Peter Davidson (eds), *Early Modern Women Poets: an Anthology* (Oxford: Oxford University Press, 2001)

Studies on women writers

Armstrong, Isobel, and Virginia Blain (eds), *Women's Poetry in the Enlightenment: the Making of a Canon, 1730–1820* (Basingstoke: Macmillan now Palgrave Macmillan, 1999)

Barash, Carol, *English Women's Poetry, 1649–1714: Politics, Community, and Linguistic Authority* (Oxford: Clarendon Press, 1996)

Brant, Clare, and Diane Purkiss (eds), *Women, Texts & Histories* (London: Routledge, 1992)

Ezell, Margaret J. M., *Writing Women's Literary History* (Baltimore: Johns Hopkins University Press, 1993)

Ezell, Margaret J. M., *The Patriarch's Wife: Literary Evidence and the History of the Family* (Chapel Hill: University of North Carolina Press, 1987)

Ferguson, Moira, *Eighteenth-Century Women Poets: Nation, Class, and Gender* (Albany: State University of New York Press, 1995)

Ferguson, Moira, *First Feminists: British Women Writers 1578–1799* (Bloomington: Indiana University Press, 1985)

Gallagher, Catherine, *Nobody's Story: the Vanishing Acts of Women Writers in the Marketplace, 1670–1820* (Oxford: Clarendon Press, 1994)

Gilbert, S. M., and S. Gubar (eds), *Shakespeare's Sisters: Feminist Essays on Women Poets* (Bloomington: Indiana University Press, 1979)

Greene, Richard, *Mary Leapor: a Study in Eighteenth-Century Women's Poetry* (Oxford: Clarendon Press, 1993)

Greer, Germaine, *Slip-Shod Sibyls: Recognition, Rejection and the Woman Poet* (London: Viking-Penguin, 1995)

Grundy, Isobel, and Susan Wiseman (eds), *Women, Writing, History 1640–1740* (London: Batsford, 1992)

Guest, Harriet, *Small Change: Women, Learning, Patriotism, 1750–1810* (Chicago and London: The University of Chicago Press, 2000)

Hobby, Elaine, *Virtue of Necessity: English Women's Writing, 1649–1688* (Anne Arbor: The University of Michigan Press, 1989)

Jones, Vivien (ed.), *Women and Literature in Britain, 1700–1800* (Cambridge: Cambridge University Press, 2000)

Justice, George L., and Nathan Tinker (eds), *Women's Writing and the Circulation of Ideas: Manuscript Publication in England, 1550–1800* (Cambridge: Cambridge University Press, 2002)

Landry, Donna, *The Muses of Resistance: Laboring-Class Women's Poetry in Britain, 1739–1796* (Cambridge: Cambridge University Press, 1990)

McDowell, Paula, *The Women of Grub Street: Press, Politics, and Gender in the London Literary Marketplace 1678–1730* (Oxford: Clarendon Press, 1998)

Mell, Donald C. (ed.), *Pope, Swift, and Women Writers* (London: Associated University Presses, 1996)

Messenger, Ann, *Pastoral Tradition and the Female Talent* (New York: AMS Press, INC., 2001)

Pacheco, Anita (ed.), *A Companion to Early Modern Women's Writing* (Oxford: Blackwell, 2002)

Perry, Ruth, *The Celebrated Mary Astell: an Early English Feminist* (Chicago: University of Chicago Press, 1986)

Smith Barbara, and Ursula Appelt (eds), *Write or Be Written: Early Modern Women Poets and Cultural Constraints* (Aldershot: Ashgate Press, 2001)

Thomas, Claudia N., *Alexander Pope and His Eighteenth-Century Women Readers* (Carbondale and Edwardsville: Southern Illinois University Press, 1994)

Turner, Cheryl, *Living by the Pen: Women Writers in the Eighteenth Century* (London: Routledge, 1992)

Wilcox, Helen (ed.), *Women and Literature in Britain 1500–1700* (Cambridge: Cambridge University Press, 1991)

Williamson, Marilyn L., *Raising Their Voices: British Women Writers, 1650–1750* (Detroit: Wayne State University Press, 1990)

Related studies of interest

Barry, Jonathan, and Christopher Brooks (eds), *The Middling Sort of People: Culture, Society and Politics in England, 1550–1800* (London: Macmillan now Palgrave Macmillan, 1994)

Benedict, Barbara, *Making the Modern Reader: Cultural Mediation in Early Modern Literary Anthologies* (Princeton: Princeton University Press, 1996)

Browne, Alice, *The Eighteenth-Century Feminist Mind* (Brighton: Harvester Press, 1987)

Colley, Linda, *Britons: Forging the Nation 1701–1837* (New Haven and London: Yale University Press, 1992)

Deutsch, Helen, and Felicity Nussbaum (eds), *'Defects': Engendering the Modern Body* (Ann Arbor: University of Michigan Press, 2000)

Earle, Peter, *The Making of the English Middle Class: Business, Society and Family Life in London 1660–1730* (London: Methuen, 1989)

Ezell, Margaret J. M., *Social Authorship and the Advent of Print* (Baltimore: Johns Hopkins University Press, 1999)

Goodridge, John, *Rural Life in Eighteenth-Century English Poetry* (Cambridge: Cambridge University Press, 1995)

Griffin, Dustin, *Literary Patronage in England, 1650–1800* (Cambridge: Cambridge University Press, 1996)

Lamb, Mary Ellen, *Gender and Authorship in the Sidney Circle* (Madison: University of Wisconsin Press, 1990)

Langford, Paul, *A Polite and Commercial People: England, 1727–1783*, New Oxford History of England (Oxford: Oxford University Press, 1989)

Love, Harold, *The Culture and Commerce of Texts: Scribal Publication in Seventeenth-Century England* (Amherst: University of Massachusetts, 1998: originally published as *Scribal Publication in Seventeenth-Century England*, Oxford: Clarendon Press, 1993)

Messenger, Ann, *His and Hers: Essays in Restoration and Eighteenth-Century Literature* (Lexington: University Press of Kentucky, 1986)

Nussbaum, Felicity, and Laura Brown (eds), *The New Eighteenth Century: Theory-Politics-English Literature* (New York and London: Methuen, 1987)

Reynolds, Myra, *The Learned Lady in England 1650–1760* (Boston, New York and Cambridge: Houghton Mifflin Company; Cambridge University Press, 1920)

Rumbold, Valerie, *Women's Place in Pope's World* (Cambridge: Cambridge University Press, 1989)

Salvaggio, Ruth, *Enlightened Absence: Neoclassical Configurations of the Feminine* (Urbana: University of Illinois Press, 1988)

Shiach, Morag, *Discourse on Popular Culture: Class, Gender and History in Cultural Analysis, 1730 to the Present* (Stanford: Stanford University Press, 1989)

Sitter, John (ed.), *The Cambridge Companion to Eighteenth-Century Poetry* (Cambridge: Cambridge University Press, 2001)

Smith, Hilda L., *Reason's Disciples: Seventeenth-Century English Feminists* (London: University of Illinois Press, 1982)

Vickery, Amanda, *The Gentleman's Daughter: Women's Lives in Georgian England* (London: Yale University Press, 1999)

Wall, Wendy, *The Imprint of Gender: Authorship and Publication in the English Renaissance* (Ithaca, New York and London: Cornell University Press, 1993)

Whyman, Susan E., *Sociability and Power in Late-Stuart England: the Cultural Worlds of the Verneys 1660–1720* (Oxford: Oxford University Press, 1999)

Wrightson, Keith, *English Society 1580–1680* (London: Hutchinson, 1982)

Zwicker, Steven N. (ed.), *The Cambridge Companion to English Literature 1650–1740* (Cambridge: Cambridge University Press, 1998)

Index

The manufacturer's authorised representative in the EU is Springer
Nature Customer Service Centre GmbH, Europaplatz 3, 69115 Heidelberg,
Germany. If you have any concerns regarding our products, please
contact ProductSafety@springernature.com

Printed and bound by CPI Group (UK) Ltd, Croydon, CR0 4YY
23/04/2026
02095587-0014